PRIVACY: THE DEBATE IN THE UNITED STATES SINCE 1945

HARBRACE
BOOKS
ON AMERICA

SINCE 1945

PRIVACY: THE DEBATE IN THE UNITED STATES SINCE 1945

Philippa Strum

City University of New York

Under the general editorship of
**Gerald W. Nash
and Richard W. Etulain**
University of New Mexico

Harcourt Brace College Publishers

Fort Worth   Philadelphia   San Diego   New York   Orlando   Austin   San Antonio
Toronto   Montreal   London   Sydney   Tokyo

Publisher	Earl McPeek
Acquisitions Editor	David Tatom
Project Editor	Michael E. Norris
Production Manager	Linda McMillan
Art Director	Brian Salisbury

ISBN: 0-15-501880-9

Library of Congress Catalog Card Number: 97-74702

Address for Editorial Correspondence:
Harcourt Brace College Publishers
301 Commerce Street, Suite 3700
Fort Worth, TX 76102

Address for Orders:
Harcourt Brace & Company
6277 Sea Harbor Drive
Orlando, FL 32887-6777
1-800-782-4479
Website address:
http://www.hbcollege.com

Printed in the United States of America

7 8 9 0 1 2 3 4 5   066   9 8 7 6 5 4 3 2 1

For Jill Norgren
with thanks

CONTENTS

Acknowledgments

My thanks go to the people who patiently shared their knowledge with me: Janlori Goldman, Wendy McGoodwin, Eli Noam, Shari Steele, and Nachama L. Wilker. Christopher H. Pyle graciously gave me a copy of the materials he and John H. F. Shattuck prepared for their course on privacy at the Harvard Law School.

The City University of New York's Faculty Research Award Program provided me with the travel money I used to pursue those mentioned above. They must blame me rather than the Foundation, however, for whatever inconvenience they may have been caused.

Grayson Williams and Anneka Norgren were the most patient and creative research assistants an author could have.

Many friends and colleagues have earned my gratitude for putting up with the thoroughly insane behavior of an author in the throes of a manuscript. I am particularly beholden to Melvin I. Urofsky, Don Haines, and Ralph Norgren for their careful reading of parts or all of the draft that became so much better because of their comments. They are responsible for many of the good things in it, and not at all responsible for whatever flaws may still exist.

Above all, I thank Jill Norgren, to whom this volume is dedicated. She took time from her own writing and busy life to provide encouragement, a balanced and humorous perspective, solace, and the most meticulous reading of a manuscript imaginable. She is a wonderful colleague and an extraordinary friend. I am fortunate to know her.

Philippa Strum

PRIVACY: THE DEBATE IN THE UNITED STATES SINCE 1945

Chapter One

INTRODUCTION

The human animal needs a privacy seldom mentioned, freedom from intrusion. He needs a little privacy quite as much as he wants understanding or vitamins or exercise or praise.

—Phyllis McGinley, *The Province of the Heart*

In June 1994, a carpenter named Paul Cox went on trial for murder, charged with entering a Westchester, New York, house on New Year's Eve in 1988 and stabbing its sleeping owners to death. There was no robbery; there was seemingly no motive for the attack; for years, the police had no suspects.

Cox was an alcoholic who later joined Alcoholics Anonymous. As he talked during group sessions, he recounted his slowly returning memory of having been drunk that New Year's Eve and committing the crime. Alcoholics Anonymous relies, as do other self-help groups, on a code of absolute confidentiality and privacy. Nothing was said about Cox's statements, at least to law enforcement authorities, for more than two years. A conscience-stricken group member then contacted local police. Other members of the group were subpoenaed and told first the police and later the trial court that Cox had described how, on that tragic night, he had entered the house where he had lived while he was a child. His parents had long since sold it, but in his drunken state Cox thought the sleeping couple who eventually bought it were the parents he had come to hate.

The trial set off consternation among members of self-help groups across the United States, who had assumed that their conversations were legally protected and that no governmental body could invade their privacy. Therapists are not required to violate their patient's privacy, they argued; on the contrary, many states forbid therapists from doing so—and in fact two years later the Supreme Court would uphold the therapist-patient privilege that already existed in all fifty states and extend it to social workers. Shouldn't the same right adhere to the privacy of people providing each other with therapy, particularly of a kind that many of these people considered effective? They soon discovered that not only did they have no such right; they had the same obligation as any other citizens to report information about possible crimes to law enforcement personnel.

No one other than the murderer suggested that the crime should have gone unpunished. (Cox admitted the crime but claimed temporary insanity. The first jury that tried him could not reach a unanimous decision. When he was tried for a second time, the jury rejected the insanity plea and convicted him of manslaughter.) The issue that seized the attention of the country was the demand of members of groups, including Cox's, for the privacy that they believed crucial to their recovery from alcoholism or other problems, and the equally important need of the society at large for the order and physical security that is the government's highest responsibility.

The media were suddenly filled with stories about the law of privacy. Citizens were shocked to discover how many limitations there are on what they had assumed to be the absolute privacy of communication between, for example, clergy and penitents, husbands and wives, doctors and patients. Surveys showed that Americans were more concerned than ever about invasions of their privacy by the state and by the media.

The concern was not a new one. By the 1880s new technology had provided the American media with Linotyping, fast presses, color printing, and photographs. These advances enabled the creation of mass circulation newspapers and newspaper "chains" that could spread information with banner headlines and photographs to large audiences. Media watchers began to talk about the advent of "yellow journalism" and the use of newspapers as reporters of gossip and scandal. Among their subjects was President Grover Cleveland, who was followed by the press on his 1886 honeymoon. The pursuit led Cleveland to attack the "new journalists" who "in ghoulish glee desecrate every sacred relation of private life."

In Boston, newspaper readers were titillated by accounts of the social life of the wealthy and prominent. One target of the press was attorney Samuel D. Warren, who had married Mabel Bayard, daughter of a three-term senator from Delaware. The young Warrens entertained lavishly, and newspaper reporters covered the events as best they could, some even allegedly disguising themselves as waiters and smuggling cameras into the parties. Warren reportedly became so enraged during one social event that he knocked a camera out of the hand of a *Boston Evening Gazette* reporter.

Warren turned to his former law partner, Louis D. Brandeis, to discuss what if any recourse the law might provide and how the law could be made to catch up to the new technology. The result, published in the December 1890 edition of the *Harvard Law Review,* was an article by the two men entitled "The Right to Privacy." In it, Warren and Brandeis raised for the first time a question that bothered not only proper Bostonians but many other people as well. To what extent could newspapers invade the privacy of the home, or exploit a person's name, in order to pander to the public's curiosity? At the time, it could hardly be said that a "right to privacy" existed in the United States either in legal terms (the word "privacy" does not appear in the Constitution) or in the public mind. The two men nonetheless argued that there *was* an identifiable "right to privacy" that protected individuals from unwanted public intrusion, and their article was so persuasive that courts and legislatures slowly but surely began to incorporate the right into decisions and statutes. Dean Roscoe Pound of the Harvard Law School commented some years later that the essay did nothing less than add a chapter to the law.

The years between publication of the article and the trial of Paul Cox have seen both a growing public concern about privacy and a surge in the number of laws protecting it. At the same time, there are more and more areas in which the privacy of Americans has been limited. Most Americans would be surprised to learn that the government can gain access to records of such everyday transactions as bank deposits, telephone calls, supermarket purchases, and rentals of movies from video stores. Technology has produced surveillance devices and information systems that enable public officials and private individuals or corporations to listen to conversations from great distances, tap into computers, trace "unlisted" telephone numbers, and identify the race, income, and consumption patterns of almost everyone in our society.

Today, people on campuses, in media, and at dinner tables discuss whether a constitutional right to privacy should prohibit government from controlling access to abortions or punishing gay and lesbian adults for sexual intimacy. Physicians and theologians are among those debating whether the "right to die" is an element of privacy that should be beyond government regulation. Only a few years ago, when President Ronald Reagan nominated Judge Robert H. Bork to the Supreme Court, there was a public outcry against Bork's insistence that the Constitution did *not* protect privacy. Americans saw Bork as opposed to a right to privacy—*their* right to privacy. In a poll that helped persuade a number of senators to vote against the ultimately unsuccessful appointment, nearly four out of five persons surveyed in the South—the nation's most politically conservative region—opposed the nomination because of Bork's views on privacy. A radical suggestion in an 1890 law review article had become part of an articulated public view of constitutional liberty a century later. What is privacy, and what makes it so important?

Warren and Brandeis called privacy "the right to be let alone." It also can be defined as the control human beings have over physical access to themselves and their possessions and over access to information about them. Human beings appear to share a need for periods of time and space away from each other, although the form privacy takes is very much a function of time and place, of society and class—so much so that anthropologists differ about whether all cultures include the concept of privacy. The opportunity for privacy, according to philosopher Barrington Moore, can be determined by the social and physical environment, the state of technology, the division of labor, and the system of authority. Some societies, like the one Margaret Mead studied in Samoa, seem to have a sense of privacy that has little to do with the wearing of clothing and more to do with psychological space and with who is permitted to be where during various activities. As technology and globalization of economies and cultures alike make the world a smaller place in the twenty-first century, concepts of privacy no doubt will become more universal and homogeneous.

Privacy is related to the concept of human dignity and the need to protect it. The linkage between these ideas can be found early in the Old Testament of the Bible, in which Adam and Eve, realizing they are naked, make aprons out of fig leaves with which to cover their private parts. In Europe prior to the great migrations to the New World, a desire for privacy certainly existed, but those in the lowest classes, such as serfs and urban workers, could hardly find private space in their cramped hovels. As one looked up the social ladder, one found increasing evidence that western Europeans did value the right to be let alone, to be free from their neighbors' inquisitiveness, to have time and space to enjoy solitude. Even at the highest levels of society, however, little privacy—by 1990s standards—could be found.

The particular expression of privacy needs found in the United States and many other Western societies is based on the concept of the individual. Political scientist Rhoda Howard describes societies that lack an emphasis on the individual as typified by "socially induced conformity, public living, and collective, stratified decision-making." As she points out, "Without privacy, one cannot develop a sense of the human individual as an intrinsically valuable being, abstracted from his or her social role." The converse is equally true: without a sense of the individual as an intrinsically valuable being, there can be no societal perception of a need for privacy.

There is a close relationship between privacy and democracy. Aristotle spoke of human beings as "political animals," meaning that we require a social and governmental entity—for him, the classical Greek polis, or city-state—to develop and fulfill ourselves. Human beings need both public intercourse with other people and space for ourselves, alone or in contact only with those whom we choose to be with. The concept of privacy is inextricably connected to society, for without society and the presence of others, we would feel no need for privacy. Privacy is not isolation, however, and it has to be chosen rather than imposed. This distinction becomes obvious if we consider solitary confinement: the imposition of enforced solitude, which we regard as a punishment. Voluntarily chosen privacy, on the other hand, gives individuals the physical and psychological space in which to think, examine and discuss ideas, form conclusions, and make the decisions that will inform their role as members of a democracy. The need to be able to express one's political beliefs privately can be seen most obviously in the institutions of the secret ballot and the voting booth: the government, with its great power to punish opposition or lack of conformity, has no right to be privy to our political choices.

Winston Churchill supposedly remarked, "Democracy is the worst form of government ever invented, except for all the others." The implication is that if there is any better way to make public policy than to have it decided upon by the people whom it will affect, we certainly have not found that way. Churchill's assumption was that the people ultimately know better than anyone else what is good for them. This does not mean that they will not make mistakes. As Brandeis argued, human beings are fallible and undoubtedly will choose wrongly on occasion. But both Brandeis and Churchill believed that ultimately the people were likely to act wisely and that in any event, no one else was more apt to be responsive to their real needs.

In order for the electorate to choose wisely it must have both access to ideas about possible policies and the privacy in which to consider them. Citizens of a democracy must know that they can quietly try out notions that differ radically from those already ensconced in law, and do so without fear of government or societal retribution. They need privacy not only to think and discuss ideas with others but to change their minds without fear of public embarrassment.

A society that places a premium on privacy gives up the stigma of public shame, a major mechanism of social control. If behavior is private, society cannot use exposure of that behavior as a means of enforcing socially determined norms. And the absence of exposure is particularly important for those people whose behavior, lifestyles, or ideologies diverge from the mainstream—a group that includes the very people society finds most threatening, as well as those most likely to come up with innovative and creative ideas. The "deviant" may be a criminal, an Einstein, or a Thoreau who wants only to be left alone at Walden Pond. It is to protect the Einsteins and Thoreaus, and to obtain the benefit of their thinking, that society must agree to respect the privacy of all.

Privacy, therefore, has a great deal to do with power. Society's power is limited and that of the individual is increased when he or she controls his or her person, home, furnishings, clothes, books, friends, activities, movements, conversation—some of the things protected by the Bill of Rights, which guarantees the rights of speech, of association, of freedom from unreasonable searches and seizures. Privacy also implies the power to control the way we are perceived by others, because privacy means that we determine how much society knows about us and its consequent perception of us.

Political scientist Alan Westin has defined privacy as "the voluntary and temporary withdrawal of a person from the general society through physical or psychological means." This definition complements the "right to be let alone" articulated by Warren and Brandeis. It implies that, although people have a role in public life, there is also a sphere in which the public must not intrude. But, as Westin notes, privacy also is "the claim of individuals, groups or institutions to determine for themselves when, how, and to what extent information about them is communicated to others." We are exercising this right when we choose not to permit public knowledge about our conversations, our activities, our possessions. It is not merely conversations, activities, and possessions that are protected by the right to privacy; it is the *knowledge* of them as well. As essayist Michel de Montaigne wrote in the sixteenth century, "It is a rare life that remains well ordered even in private." We choose not to have society know about those moments when we pick our noses, fight with our loved ones, or look our worst. We want the power to lead the somewhat disordered life that is universal while maintaining society's perception of us as model human beings and citizens. What we are protecting is not any asserted right to act criminally but simply to keep secret those frequently inconsequential things all human beings prefer for others not to know.

Privacy, then, is necessary for at least two reasons: for the psychological well-being of individuals and the space in which to develop and fulfill themselves, and for the proper functioning of democracy. Its existence enhances both the individual and the society of which he or she is a part. But however highly prized, privacy cannot be treated as an absolute that takes precedence over all other values. This is the lesson of the story about Paul Cox. The safety of citizens and the requirements of the law enforcement process are of equal importance. There are kinds of information the government must have if it is to enact appropriate policies, which is one reason that Congress has investigative powers and the Census

Bureau collects data about race, ethnicity, religion, and income. Such information also is extremely useful, for example, to attorneys fighting for racial equality, who may rely on Census Bureau data to demonstrate that neighborhoods are segregated or that mortgage lenders discriminate against people of certain races. Schools attempting to achieve diversity require information about the racial composition of student bodies. Although no formal body collects information about the health of candidates for public office, voters may legitimately ask whether those who run are healthy enough to serve full terms.

Yet each of these needs for knowledge, with its implicit limitation on the right to privacy, carries the possibility of misuse. At the same time, the right to privacy is not absolute and cannot automatically be assumed to take precedence over other values. Balancing private and public needs is a major concern of any democratic society. The boundaries of privacy in the United States are constantly in flux, are always a matter of contention. The categories of "public" and "private," philosopher David Hiley tells us, are "essentially contested concepts." Exactly what they mean at any moment, and how to strike a balance between them, is an ongoing dilemma.

The Western European idea of privacy gradually took on new meanings and importance when it migrated across the Atlantic to the American colonies. It arrived in the same baggage as other powerful ideas, such as the Puritan emphasis on community and the right of the larger society to impose specific values and behavior on individual members. Initially, according to historian David H. Flaherty, privacy "took second place to other values in the location of homes until Puritan communitarian ideals gradually disintegrated in the face of New World conditions." The community rapidly lost power in America, however, with its vast free lands. One could use the land to build homes with space—sometimes large amounts of space—between them. Moreover, the extended-family living arrangements so common in the Old World soon disappeared as people moved ever westward seeking land and opportunity, gaining privacy in the process.

The first recorded "invasion of privacy" in the Americas took place in New England. In 1624, only four years after the Pilgrims had settled at Plymouth, Governor William Bradford discovered a plot against his leadership when he intercepted letters sent by two newcomers to friends in England. The governor summoned the men to the assembly, accused them of conspiracy and, when they denied the charge, pulled out the letters and "caused them to be read before all the people." The men strongly protested this interference with their private letters. When Bradford asked if they thought he had "done evil" in opening the mail, however, they remained silent, knowing they had no legal grounds on which to complain. In the seventeenth century, English common law did not include any reference to privacy, nor did the Puritans find any such reference in the Bible to which they also looked for guidance in ruling their holy society.

By the time of the American Revolution, however, some fundamental notions of privacy had become commonplace. In 1754, Massachusetts enacted an excise tax law that required homeowners to tell tax collectors how much rum had been consumed in their households during the year. A flurry of pamphlets denounced the measure, including one which declared,

> It is essential to the English Constitution, that a Man should be safe in his own House; his House is commonly called his Castle, which the Law will not permit even a sheriff to enter into, but by his own Consent, unless in criminal cases.

Thomas Jefferson did not use the word *privacy* in the Declaration of Independence, but he referred to the colonists' outrage at George III's quartering of troops in private houses. That same year the people of Pennsylvania enacted a "bill of rights" declaring,

> The people have a right to hold themselves, their houses, papers and possessions free from search and seizure; and therefore warrants, without oaths or affirmations first made, affording a sufficient foundation for them, and whereby any officer or messenger may be commanded or required to search suspected places, or to seize any person or persons, his or their property not particularly described, are contrary to that right, and ought not to be granted.

The idea of privacy was part of the political philosophy of John Locke, which illuminated the thought of Thomas Jefferson and many other Founding Fathers. Locke postulated that legitimate government comes into existence at the behest of individuals, who turn over to it only those of their rights necessary to enable the government to provide physical protection for people and property. Individualism was central to Locke's thinking, and privacy was central to his view of individualism, which included rights such as religion, speech, and the ownership of property. Such rights were not absolute but were to be largely free from governmental interference. The English practices of subjecting Americans to political surveillance, intruding into their homes, seizing their property including their papers, and requiring that books and pamphlets bear the names of their authors before they could be licensed for publication, all violated privacy rights and were antithetical to democracy in the Lockean view. Fifteen years after Pennsylvania enacted its Bill of Rights the concerns expressed in it were translated into the Third and Fourth Amendments to the Constitution, prohibiting the quartering of troops in people's homes and guaranteeing the privacy of both home and possessions such as papers. At least as important, the First Amendment ensured privacy for ideas, including the right to free exercise of religion without fear of state coercion, the right to speak and publish without public censorship, the right to associate freely and privately with others, and the right *not* to speak or to share one's thoughts with the government.

But, as the word "privacy" appears in none of these amendments—or in the body of the Constitution, for that matter—do they nevertheless *imply* a right to privacy that could be drawn upon by future generations in, for instance, nullifying state laws against the use of contraceptives or asserting autonomy over one's body and one's sexual conduct? Did the Framers of the Constitution have any conception of privacy as such to justify Louis Brandeis's later comment that they understood that the greatest of all rights was the right to be left alone, or Judge Thomas Cooley's statement in *Constitutional Limitations* (1868) that "it is better sometimes that crime should go unpunished than that the citizen should be liable to have his premises invaded, his desks broken open, his private books, letters, and papers exposed to prying curiosity, and to the misconstructions of ignorant and suspicious persons"?

The answer to these questions depends on how one views the Constitution. Those who read the Constitution narrowly find no rights in it except those clearly enunciated in the document. These interpreters confine themselves to original intent; that is, what can be discerned as the intention of the men who wrote the Constitution in the eighteenth century and those who added the subsequent amendments. This interpretation leads to the conclusion articulated by Justice Hugo Black: "I like my privacy as well as the next one, but

I am nevertheless compelled to admit that government has a right to invade it unless prohibited by some specific constitutional provision." In the absence of the word *privacy,* Black could not discern a constitutional right to it.

On the other hand, there are justices and legal scholars who mirror the view of Chief Justice John Marshall in the early 1800s that the Constitution should be read as a document containing precepts meant to be interpreted according to changing societal circumstances and needs. They rely on the *spirit* of the Constitution rather than the way it applied to time-bound social conditions in 1787 or 1791. Justice Arthur Goldberg, for example, argued in 1965 that many rights not enumerated in the Bill of Rights are subsumed in the Ninth Amendment, which declares that "the enumeration in the Constitution, of certain rights, shall not be construed to deny or disparage others retained by the people." The pattern through most of this century has been to take a flexible approach to privacy, and the idea that Warren and Brandeis championed has slowly made its way into mainstream constitutional doctrine. The question of whether privacy is a constitutional right and, if so, how far it extends, nevertheless remains a hotly debated issue today.

This volume argues that privacy was built into the Constitution as originally written and into the Bill of Rights. It was, however, privacy only for people who were very much alike. Their homogeneity is best indicated by the nature of the franchise. Control over the right to vote, which means participation in the political system and access to the rights protected by the Constitution, was left to the states. Most of them restricted voting to white male landowners over the age of twenty-one—a very small part of the population of the United States. Although these men came from different religious backgrounds (almost all of them one form or another of Protestantism) and different geographical areas, and their work as farmers or merchants or professionals also differentiated them and led them to take opposing stands on policy matters such as tariffs, they were essentially a homogeneous group. The writers of the Constitution and the public assumed that the political system would not be one of "winner take all" but that the dispersion of powers among the two houses of Congress and the presidency would lead to the kinds of compromises that would ensure that all groups would be represented and protected. This is the principle James Madison stated in

Federalist Papers numbers ten and fifty-one. Liberty would be protected by the process built into the governmental system. The important caveat to remember, of course, is that "all groups" excluded slaves, most free people of color, and women of all races. Initially, the electorate excluded non-landowning white males as well, but this exclusion ended with the growth of an urban middle class and working class in the early nineteenth century. Still, the political system was one of controlled homogeneity: there were few major tensions among voters, however seriously they took those policy disagreements that occurred, until the fight over slavery exploded towards the middle of the nineteenth century. And members of the enfranchised population assumed that privacy was one of their rights.

The revolutionary idea behind the Declaration of Independence was that sovereignty—ultimate political power—did not belong to kings or even to democratically elected governments, but to each individual. Jefferson wrote in the Declaration of Independence that "governments are instituted" in order "to secure these rights"—the rights of the individual to "Life, Liberty, and the Pursuit of Happiness." The purpose of government, in Jeffersonian thought, was not enforcement of a community consensus but protection of individual rights. The democratic political process was designed in large measure not to empower government but to ensure individuals against government intrusion. The Bill of Rights took this idea one step further by specifying that the federal government could not stifle diversity—again, within the small community of voters—or attempt to interfere with privacy and personal autonomy. It protected diversity by including the rights to free speech and press, which imply the rights to hear and read all available ideas, and by prohibiting the government from intruding unreasonably into people's homes and prying into their lives. Thus it enshrined privacy and personal autonomy as basic American values, even though the words themselves do not appear in the Constitution.

The First Amendment, as mentioned above, forbids Congress from abridging speech and religion and does not mention privacy. But the voting public in the constitutional period undoubtedly would have been outraged had the federal government posted agents to monitor and record who attended which public lectures or which local church. The Fourth Amendment forbids unreasonable searches and seizures, again without using the word *privacy*. There would have been similar outrage, however, if the national government had issued search warrants to find out what books people had in their homes. The right "to be let alone" and the right to privacy of information about one's life were taken for granted. The highly divisive question of whether there was a constitutional right to privacy and who and what it protected did not arise until after World War II, when the politically active and therefore powerful public began to include groups that had been excluded earlier or had not made demands as groups: ex-slaves and their descendants, the many other people of color who had voluntarily immigrated to the United States and become an important part of the urban population, women, members of nontraditional religious groups, gays and lesbians, the elderly, and the physically disadvantaged.

Groups that had been quiescent began to demand the equal right to define privacy. Their demands could not simply be ignored, because equality is another value built into the Constitution. Once power was dispersed among a citizenry that was and defined itself as even more heterogeneous than it had been, the question arose of whether the nation could absorb diverse and conflicting demands even when they implied altering traditional definitions of both privacy and equality. As we will see, the problem then became not only governmental interference with privacy but the extent to which the government has an obligation to protect citizens from violations of their privacy by other citizens—as in the maintenance of computer data banks by private companies. Demands made by various groups also implied the question of whether the governmental *process* relied upon by Madison was sufficient to protect liberty, particularly privacy, or whether the *content* of lawmaking had to be monitored as well; that is, whether a specific right of privacy had to be defined and what it would include. To a great extent, explication of the right became the province of a newly active Supreme Court.

In addition, changed circumstances in the United States led the once-homogeneous electorate as well as other groups to a new concern for privacy.

Law reflects social needs and conditions, and when there is no perceived need for law to be made, courts and legislatures tend to avoid making it. Throughout most of the nineteenth century few developments occurred that pointed to a need for elaborating a law of privacy. The Bill of Rights, including its provisions for enjoying the safety and privacy of one's home, applied at that time solely against the federal government, which except for the Civil War period remained a government of limited powers and functions. On the state level, government similarly had little to do with regulating the behavior of its citizens. As one scholar has suggested, "Personal privacy [before about 1850] was related more to the circumstances of one's immediate environment (namely the home) than it was the result of any preconceived notion of a legal right, or even as a moral or natural right. . . . Because privacy was not seriously threatened, it was taken for granted." There were nonetheless various common law doctrines regarding aspects of privacy such as enjoyment of property and protection of one's name: doctrines against trespass, against disclosure of business confidences or use of others' trademarks, and against interference with the privacy of spousal or lawyer-client relations. In the late 1700s and early 1800s Congress passed laws forbidding either postal employees or private citizens from opening letters, and beginning in 1828, a majority of states enacted statutes privileging doctor-patient communications. But there was little public or private surveillance, there were no data banks with vast amounts of personal information, no government policies restricting individual lifestyles, and so there was not much law on the matter.

In the last decades of the nineteenth century, however, social and economic transformations led to new pressures on and threats to privacy. These new circumstances elicited the Warren-Brandeis article and gradually resulted in privacy becoming a matter of public concern.

The first such circumstance was an enormous increase in population following the Civil War. Massive immigration took place, especially from eastern Europe, in response to poor economic conditions there and to the needs of factories in the United States for new workers. Nearly all the newcomers settled in cities. Where the pre–Civil War United States had been primarily rural, by 1900 the nation was well on its way to becoming overwhelmingly urban. People crowded together in tenements had little privacy; the space that rural and even small-town residents enjoyed in their daily lives was markedly absent on city streets. Commentators such as E. L. Godkin noted that "local life is now much less isolated than it used to be," and condemned urban crowding as an increasing menace to privacy.

Technology also threatened privacy, as people acquired devices by which they could enter homes without physically going there. Alexander Graham Bell had invented the telephone in the early 1870s. By 1877, Boston had a telephone exchange, a phenomenon that over the next several decades would spread around the nation and the world. One did not have to be in people's houses in order to talk with them; one could now call and intrude upon private space and time. Other technological advances such as inexpensive portable cameras, cheap window glass, and even primitive sound recording devices all enabled people to pry into others' affairs.

Perhaps the greatest threat to privacy came from what novelist Henry James called "newspaperization." The press, according to Warren and Brandeis, "is overstepping in every direction the obvious bounds of propriety and decency. . . . To occupy the indolent, column upon column is filled with idle gossip, which can only be procured by intrusion upon the domestic circle." What concerned people like Godkin, Warren, Brandeis, and others was not just nosy reporters invading the hearth, but the damage done to personal reputation by these forays. Personal reputations had always been protected by the law, and even today there are legal textbooks whose titles include the word *privacy* but that are primarily concerned with reputational interests. The issue, however, was not just reputation. Expectations of privacy had undergone major if unarticulated changes. By trying to provide a remedy for the unwanted publication of private information, even if it was true, Warren and Brandeis hoped to protect individual privacy from prurient intrusion.

The right to privacy that they developed grew out of the common law, the great body of judge-made law that had evolved in Anglo-American jurisprudence over several centuries. According to legal scholar Sheldon W. Halpern, Warren and Brandeis not only relied on those few aspects of the common law that dealt with privacy but "ransacked every traditional area of the common law they could find—such as contracts, property, trusts, copyright, protection of trade secrets, and torts"—in order to pluck out the already existing legal principle underlying all of these various parts of the common law. This principle was the right to privacy, to be let alone, which they claimed was an essential component of the right to life itself. Although many aspects of the common law have changed since Warren and Brandeis wrote, the general areas they explored are still apposite in the modern law of privacy.

Starting in the 1920s, the Supreme Court went beyond the common law and began to articulate a theory of privacy based on the Constitution. The first cases seem somewhat removed from contemporary notions of privacy, but they are the legal forebears of current privacy jurisprudence, and it is necessary to examine them briefly in order to understand the legal framework in which the contemporary debate takes place.

The Fourth Amendment, more than any other part of the Bill of Rights, is concerned with the sanctity of one's home, the right to be free from government interference in one's private affairs. Police may not search a house without a warrant, which cannot be issued except on probable cause and which must identify the premises to be searched and the items to be sought. The Bill of Rights, as noted, originally applied only to the federal government. Since there was no national police force, there were few federal violations of the Fourth Amendment's prohibition against unreasonable searches and seizures and few cases in which the Supreme Court was called upon to interpret the reach of its protection. In those cases, however, the Court firmly upheld the necessity of a warrant for a search. Well before the 1920s, in the case of *Boyd* v. *United States* (1886), the Supreme Court held that the Fourth Amendment, in conjunction with the Fifth Amendment's guarantee of the right not to incriminate oneself, meant that customs agents could not legally seize invoices that might be used as evidence against importers.

In the twentieth century both state and federal police activities grew, and in 1914, in *Weeks* v. *United States,* the Court enunciated a strict interpretation of the Fourth Amendment. The defendant had been arrested on charges of using the mails for illegal shipment of lottery tickets. Police had gone to his rooms without a warrant and uncovered what they considered incriminating documents. They turned these over to a U.S. marshal, who then went to the rooms and, again without a warrant, searched the premises and found even more evidence. The papers that he seized helped convict Weeks, who appealed on the grounds that the material had been taken in violation of the Fourth Amendment and thus should not be admitted into testimony.

The Court agreed and fashioned the "exclusionary rule," which excludes the use of illegally seized evidence in federal trials. According to Justice William R. Day, "if letters and private documents can thus be seized and held and used in evidence against a citizen accused of an offense, the protection of the Fourth Amendment declaring his right to be secure [in his home]. . .might as well be stricken from the Constitution." The same problem arose in 1920, when federal agents seized the records of the Silverthorne Lumber Company without a warrant, made copies of them, returned the originals to the owners, subpoenaed the originals on the basis of the illegally gotten evidence, fined the company for contempt, and put Frederick W. Silverthorne in contempt for refusing to obey the subpoenas *(Silverthorne* v. *U.S.)* The tactic infuriated the Court, and an angry Justice Oliver Wendell Holmes declared that "the Government planned or at all events ratified the whole [wrongful] performance." The use of such tactics, Holmes said in quashing the subpoenas, "reduces the Fourth Amendment to a form of words."

A few years later the Court began the process known as "incorporation," by which the words of the Fourteenth Amendment's Due Process Clause, forbidding the states from depriving a person of "life, liberty, or property without due process of law," have been interpreted as meaning that the rights listed in the first eight amendments have become limitations on state governments. Those rights are now considered by the Court to have been "incorporated" into the due process that states must guarantee to their citizens. Even though the Fourth Amendment cases had dealt with a relatively straightforward idea of privacy in one's home, the early cases addressing states' powers outside the home also involved privacy concerns. Although they appeared unrelated to the exclusionary rule, the cases created precedents important in extending the rule to the states. In *Meyer* v. *Nebraska* (1923) the Court, speaking through Justice James C. McReynolds, struck down a state law that forbade the teaching of foreign languages in elementary schools. McReynolds held that the liberty protected by the Fourteenth Amendment included "not merely freedom from bodily restraint but also the right of the individual to contract, to engage in any of the common occupations of life, to acquire useful knowledge, to marry, to establish a home and bring up children, to worship God according to the dictates of his own conscience, and generally to enjoy those privileges long recognized at common law as essential to the orderly pursuit of happiness by free men." McReynolds framed his decision in terms of the substantive rights often associated with property, but the issues he mentioned are essentially private matters—marriage, child-rearing, and conscience.

Two years later McReynolds spoke for a unanimous Court in *Pierce* v. *Society of Sisters.* The Ku Klux Klan had pushed through the Oregon legislature a law requiring children to attend public schools, with the clear intent of driving Catholic schools out of existence. Although once again property rights seemed to be the heart of McReynolds's opinion, personal rights also figured prominently. "The child is not the mere creature of the State," he wrote. "Those who nurture him and direct his destiny have the right, coupled with the high duty to prepare him for additional obligations." Without using the term *privacy,* the Court seemed willing to acknowledge that certain personal decisions enjoyed protection under the Constitution.

The most straightforward and influential statement about privacy to emerge from the Court came in a dissent. In its fight against crime, the government had begun to use the kind of new technology that Warren and Brandeis had written about in 1890. The Eighteenth Amendment established Prohibition and gave the federal government the duty of enforcing the ban on recreational use of alcohol. For the first time the country had what amounted to a national police force. In one use of the new police powers, federal agents, suspecting a group of men of possessing, transporting, and selling liquor, spent almost five months listening to their home and office telephone conversations through wiretaps. Nearly 800 pages of notes taken by the agents provided the key evidence at the subsequent trial. The defendants claimed that the wiretaps, conducted without a search warrant, had violated the Fourth Amendment.

Chief Justice William Howard Taft, writing for the Court in *Olmstead* v. *United States* (1928), found the Fourth Amendment question irrelevant and sustained the men's convictions. There had been no actual entry but only the use of an enhanced sense of hearing, he claimed, and to pay too much attention to "nice ethical conduct by government officials would make society suffer and give criminals greater immunity than has been known heretofore."

Louis Brandeis, by then a member of the Court, considered both the acts of the government and the decision of the Court incredible in their bland disregard of privacy. Dissenting from Taft's cavalier view of government ethics, he declared that he considered it "less evil that some criminals should escape than that the government should play an ignoble part. . . . If government becomes a law-breaker, it breeds contempt for law." The most noted and influential part of Brandeis's dissent dealt with the question of privacy. It deserves further attention because it became the basis for later decisions establishing a constitutional right to privacy.

Wiretapping did far more than merely enhance the sense of hearing, Brandeis wrote. "Whenever a telephone line is tapped," he charged, "the privacy of the persons at both ends of the line is invaded, and all conversations between them upon any subject, and although proper, confidential, and privileged, may be overheard." Moreover, the tapping of one person's telephone line involves the tapping of the telephone of every other person whom she or he may call, or who may call her or him. Can it be, he asked, "that the Constitution affords no protection against such invasions of individual security?" Recalling the Fourth Amendment's writers' concern about writs of assistance (warrants that allowed general searches), Brandeis claimed that in comparison with wiretaps, writs were "but puny instruments of tyranny and oppression."

Worse still, greater invasions were undoubtedly on the way. In his *Olmstead* opinion, as earlier in his article with Warren, Brandeis looked at the new and effective tools modern science was providing to penetrate the sanctity of one's home or office, and called upon the law to protect what he considered the most treasured of all rights, privacy. "Discovery and invention have made it possible for the Government, by means far more effective than stretching upon the rack, to obtain disclosure in court of what is whispered in the closet," he warned. "The progress of science in furnishing the Government with means of espionage is not likely to stop with wire tapping. Ways may some day be developed by which the Government, without removing papers from secret drawers, can reproduce them in court, and by which it will be enabled to expose to a jury the most intimate occurrences of the home."

Brandeis considered it irrelevant that the writers of the Fourth Amendment had not specifically mentioned wiretapping. Of course no such thing existed when they wrote, but if a proper approach was taken to constitutional interpretation, he believed, it was clear that the spirit rather than the words of the Fourth Amendment banned wiretapping. Brandeis read the Fourth Amendment as including an intention to ensure privacy: "The makers of our Constitution undertook. . .to protect Americans in their beliefs, their thoughts, their emotions, and their sensations. They conferred, as against the Government, the right to be let alone—the most comprehensive of rights and the right most valued by civilized men."

This passage contains the philosophical core of modern constitutional privacy jurisprudence. Brandeis believed that the Framers wanted government to leave the people alone and that, therefore, the protections they had created should be interpreted broadly and inclusively. The actual means of intrusion did not much matter; the fact of intrusion did.

In addition, the passage reflects the connection Brandeis made between privacy and democracy and between privacy and individual needs. The protection that was given to "beliefs, thoughts, emotions, and sensations" and their expression was necessary not only to the free flow of ideas but, as well, to the growth of the individual, which could not occur if government had a right to invade privacy. The "right to be let alone" had to be guarded as closely as possible. "To protect that right," Brandeis wrote, "every unjustifiable intrusion by the Government upon the privacy of the individual, whatever the means employed, must be deemed a violation of the Fourth Amendment." The argument that government had violated the right in the name of the greater good ensured by law enforcement was relevant, but for a reason quite different from that accepted by the majority of the Court: "Experience should teach us to be most on our guard to protect liberty when the Government's purposes are beneficent. . . .The greatest dangers to liberty lurk in insidious encroachment by men of zeal, well-meaning but without understanding."

Over the years Brandeis's dissent gradually gained adherents on the Court, and, as we shall see, his call for a constitutionally protected right to privacy won over a majority of the Court in the landmark case of *Griswold* v. *Connecticut* (1965). According to various public opinion polls, a large percentage of the American people today also believes that privacy is protected by the Constitution.

The emphasis on privacy that has surfaced in the United States since 1945 is not surprising. The country is in many ways a different one, with different political issues, than it was when Warren and Brandeis published "The Right to Privacy" in 1890 and when Brandeis wrote his *Olmstead* dissent in 1928. Increased urbanization; the leaps in technology that gave us television, computers, and governmental ability to monitor citizens' lives; concerns about national security as the United States entered the Cold War with its rival superpower, the Soviet Union—all combined to push questions about privacy to the top of the public agenda after 1945.

Chapter Two

—

PRIVACY IN THE AGE
OF GENETIC INFORMATION

The personal life of every individual is based on secrecy, and perhaps it is partly for that reason that civilized man is so nervously anxious that personal privacy should be respected.

—Anton Chekhov, *The Lady with the Dog*

As a young personal injury lawyer with clients who faced substantial medical bills, Theresa Morelli became aware of how important it is to have disability insurance. In 1990 she decided to buy a policy. She called an agent, filled out an application, had a medical exam, signed a release for her medical records, and paid her first premium. When her money was returned about a month later and she asked for an explanation, she was told that the company would not insure her because her father had Huntington's disease.

Huntington's disease, a debilitating neurological illness, is inherited. Because she is the child of a parent with Huntington's, Morelli has a fifty percent chance of developing the disease. A genetic test can disclose *how probable* it is but not whether someone has in fact inherited the Huntington's gene.

Bewildered at how the insurance company could have gotten her father's health history from her medical records, Morelli discovered that the general physician who treated both father and daughter had, without telling her, made a note about the father's illness on the daughter's folder. The note was photocopied for the insurance company along with all her other records—a violation of Mr. Morelli's privacy as well as that of his daughter, who had never given the doctor permission to disclose information that she was unaware was part of her file.

The result is that Morelli cannot find a company that will issue her a health, life, or disability insurance policy. The only way she can get coverage would be to give up her private practice and go to work for a large employer that can afford to cover all its employees, whatever their health risks. But no large employer is likely to hire Morelli now. Once the record went to the insurer, it undoubtedly was passed along to the database of the Massachusetts-based Medical Information Bureau (MIB) subscribed to by all the United States' and Canada's roughly 750 insurance companies. Employers checking the data bank for anyone with a serious medical condition that might affect longevity are likely to avoid the potential complications with their insurance companies caused by someone who might develop Huntington's.

And "might" is the relevant word here, because doctors have since realized that Morelli's father probably was misdiagnosed and does not have Huntington's at all. But no law requires the Medical Information Bureau to alter its records, and Morelli has speculated that if she asks the MIB to make a correction, the request alone would raise questions and undoubtedly would be added to her file.

Although she knew of her father's diagnosis, Morelli had never been tested. She preferred the uncertainty of not knowing about her future health to the certainty that if she tested positive the information would go into her medical files, making her uninsurable and possibly unemployable. As Huntington's manifests itself only in middle age, Morelli, like some other potential victims of the disease, preferred not to suffer years of anxiety about her future if she did test positive. The right not to know can be a cherished aspect of privacy.

Morelli is far from being the only person to suffer because of the assumption that he or she is at risk of developing Huntington's. The Center for Responsible Genetics has collected numerous cases, including that of a woman, one of whose parents actually did have the disease. She and her husband decided to adopt rather than bear children in order to avoid the possibility of passing on the gene. Adoption agencies considered them to be fine prospects until they found out about the Huntington's, at which point they turned the couple down. The negative decisions were made in spite of the fact that the woman, like Morelli, is only at *risk* of developing the disease. One agency admitted that she would not be likely to get the disease, if at all, until she was around 50 and by then any child she adopted would have grown into a young adult requiring little care, but vetoed an adoption anyway.

The two stories show that there are problems implicit in the development of medical science, particularly the technology for collecting genetic information, and that privacy violations may occur without real benefits to society.

The Medical Information Bureau mentioned earlier was begun as a paper-driven system in 1902. Now its sophisticated computers are programmed with about 210 codes that physicians use to report patients' conditions. An additional five codes contain nonmedical information about related matters such as reckless driving, hazardous sports, and aviation activity. The records are as subject to human error, whether by physicians or data entry workers, as any others. MIB president Neil Day told a *Consumer Reports* researcher in 1994 that three to four percent of its database of 15,000,000 files was erroneous, a figure the Massachusetts Public Interest Research Group questioned as too low. The purpose of the data bank lies in its availability to companies that sell insurance policies covering such things as life, health, automobiles, and mortgages.

IBM has part ownership of the Physician Computer Network, which as of 1994 had access to the patient records of 41,000 doctors in the United States, roughly one out of every ten, and planned to have access to a third of all private physicians' files by 1996. The Network provides cooperating doctors with low cost hardware and software enabling them to do computerized billing and connect electronically with hospitals, laboratories, and insurance companies. The physicians in turn agree to view drug manufacturers' advertisements and to allow the Network to copy patient information directly from their computers to those of the Network.

There thus appears to be good reason for the National Academy of Sciences' Institute of Medicine to warn in 1994 that threats to medical privacy are "real and not numerically trivial." A 1993 Harris poll, commissioned by the Equifax credit bureau, found that while 85 percent of those surveyed said confidentiality of medical records was very important in health care reform, more than a quarter of the total number also reported that their medical information had been improperly disclosed.

Medical privacy has since become even more problematic. Doctors and hospitals today routinely reveal patients' records to insurance companies, government service payers such as Medicare and Medicaid, welfare agencies, researchers, employers, state occupational licensing agencies, and public health and law enforcement agencies. As the country moves toward universal managed care and the overwhelming majority of its citizens are enrolled in health maintenance organizations, an increasing number of nonmedical personnel will have access to medical records.

Errors in health records can have major consequences. The Privacy Clearinghouse discovered that a man attempting to get medical insurance was turned down because his doctor had placed erroneous information on his record, stating that he was a major health risk. Blue Cross finally agreed to insure the man if he underwent expensive medical tests that proved the information to be wrong. But because he had no medical insurance, he could not afford the tests. And most Americans are unaware that their automobile insurance policies include a clause requiring them to provide all medical records—not all "relevant" records, but all records—in case of an automobile accident. This means not only information about doctors' visits; it means access to all medical information—the kind doctors forward to the equally fallible Medical Information Bureau.

In 1995, concerned about a pending bill to ensure confidentiality of medical records, the Association of American Physicians and Surgeons (AAPS) told the Senate Labor and Human Resources Committee that it could find no good reason for the privacy abuses that inevitably accompany computerized records. "One must query why computerized information is needed in the first place," the AAPS statement said. "Computerized information is not needed for optimal clinical treatment of a patient. The key to correct diagnosis and successful treatment is the interview and examination of the patient. This can be accomplished only by face-to-face, hands-on contact by the physician responsible for the patient." The statement went on:

As part of the clinical examination, review of previous records can be helpful if not in some cases essential. However, these data do not need to be on a central computer. It may be inconvenient to request information from other physicians or institutions, but usually the treating physician can obtain needed information by telephone with minimal delay. . . . The most useful information from the standpoint of patient care is obtained from old radiographs and pathologic examinations (not just the reports), neither of which will be found in the proposed computerized record.

The doctors then turned to the problem of emergency situations and asserted that "the most important history is what happened in the last few hours, or the last five minutes. This information must be obtained directly from the patient, or if the patient cannot communicate, from a family member or other witness, and supplemented by direct observation (including physical examination, imaging, and laboratory procedures)." What about patients who have a serious problem that may not be obvious on a quick examination but that could affect proper emergency treatment? They should "wear a bracelet, even if information is on a central computer," the doctors said, as the computer might be down or identification unavailable. Other medical personnel may disagree, but the AAPS statement does recast assumptions about the necessity for computerized medical records.

There will be more such records in the future. The health care reform plan Senators Edward Kennedy and Nancy Landon Kassebaum sponsored and Congress enacted in 1996 as the Health Insurance Portability and Accountability Act calls for medical records to be computerized in vast databases and organized by the health identifier number assigned to each individual by the government. A *Time*-CNN poll published in May 1996, just months before passage of the law, found that 87 percent of Americans believed that "patients should be asked for permission every time any information about them is used." Such requests are not now mandated by federal law. Given sporadic attempts to provide all Americans with health insurance and the growth of health maintenance organizations, the collection and use of medical records surely will be one of the largest privacy issues of the late 1990s.

A major aspect of this issue is genetic information. Before the privacy issue can be examined, however, we need to take a look at genetic information, the tests used to obtain it, and the methods used to store it.

DNA Analysis
and Other Genetic Tests

Scientists have known since 1952 that deoxyribonucleic acid, usually referred to as DNA, is the molecule in each person's 100 trillion cells that determines heredity. The nucleus of each cell contains forty-six chromosomes arranged in pairs, with one chromosome in each pair inherited from each parent. Genes are the segments of DNA that control the production of proteins, the building blocks of life. Thousands of scientists have worked since 1952 to locate specific genes and discover which genes control which traits, including predispositions for diseases.

By the mid-1990s there were DNA tests for almost two dozen diseases, and new tests were being developed with increasing rapidity. Tests such as computer electroencephalograms (CEEG), magnetic resonance imaging (MRI), and position emission tomography (PET) were already creating detailed images of brains in order to detect abnormalities that might one day be able to predict neurological or behavioral diseases. PET was in fact being used to diagnose Huntington's. In even more instances, scientists had "mapped," or found, the gene related to various diseases—meaning they had identified the location of the gene on a chromosome but had not yet isolated the specific defect in the DNA. New genes were being discovered at the rate of more than one a day. The process was immeasurably speeded up by the creation of the Human Genome Project (the genome is the complete set of genes in a cell), a government-sponsored project designed to produce a detailed diagram of every bit of DNA in the human body by the year 2005. In 1995 the project announced that it was obtaining results more rapidly than expected. It had reached the halfway point in identifying genetic markers and thought its task might well be 99 percent completed by 2002 or 2003, at 70 percent of the original estimated cost of $3 billion.

The prospect of early discovery and treatment of disease is, of course, enormously exciting. Experiments with gene therapy already have begun, including the replacement of genes that predispose to various diseases with other genes and the injection of tumor-fighting genes into cancer patients. The possibility of being able to "cure" a serious or even fatal disease by eliminating or neutralizing the gene responsible for it holds the promise of great good for humanity. At the same time, however, the likelihood of misuse of genetic information is so substantial that Jeremy Rifkin, a leading opponent of some forms of genetic engineering, has commented, "Genetic privacy will be the major constitutional issue of the next generation."

Not all genetic information comes from DNA testing. Genetic predispositions for diseases such as multiple sclerosis, diabetes, and breast cancer can be extrapolated from family histories. There are traditional biochemical tests for diseases like sickle-cell anemia, in which red blood cells plug arterioles and capillaries. The Medical Information Bureau contains data about approximately 15 million Americans, much of it garnered from forms that people have filled out in order to obtain a job or insurance coverage. This database creates a privacy problem. The data include, among other things, information about drug and alcohol dependency and the results of psychological and HIV tests. Technically, the creation of a file in a data bank such as MIB's requires the individual's consent, but companies frequently will not hire or provide coverage without completion of medical history forms and most people do not realize that one of the items they have checked off on various forms gives the company the right to turn all information over to MIB, where it will be accessible to over 700 insurance companies and other interested parties. As privacy scholar Paul R. Billings has commented:

> The insurance industry routinely stores and shares health information, including genetic data, which can violate medical confidentiality. In addition, agents and underwriters sell access to much of what our society considers to be necessities of life— driving (auto insurance), medical care (health insurance), home ownership (mortgage insurance), financial safety (disability and life insurance)—and even freedom of choice and movement ("job lock" resulting from fear of losing benefits or coverages if an individual moves or changes jobs).

Medical information comes from many sources. Among them is the Guthrie blood spot routinely taken from the heels of newborns. It is a crucial tool in diagnosing phenylketonuria (PKU), an inborn metabolism problem that frequently results in mental retardation but that can be completely controlled through early diagnosis, diet, and, in some cases, continuing drug treatment. Many hospitals, however, keep the blood spot for years, on the theory that someday tests will be developed that can be used to diagnose additional diseases and that the individuals whose blood samples test positive for the diseases can be informed. Blood taken from a newborn for the Guthrie test can yield enough DNA for hundreds or thousands of genetic tests, including some that may have nothing to do with disease. With minor methodological advances, most of these tests soon will be available to technicians. Most parents have no idea that their children's blood is being kept or that cells extracted during amniocentesis and chorionic villus sampling (used to test fetuses for Down's Syndrome, a form of mental retardation, and other genetic abnormalities) are routinely retained by hospitals and laboratories and may be deposited in information data banks. So are cells extracted from children and adults alike in the course of surgical operations or biopsies. Patients' privacy is invaded when information about them is gathered or used without their consent, and the possibility of privacy invasion lasts as long as samples taken and preserved in hospitals are usable—usually for a lifetime. This length of time leaves even someone as committed to genetic mapping and testing as Francis Collins, the head of the Genome Project, worried about the accessibility of private genetic information to insurance companies and employers.

The real question is how to strike a balance between the individual's right of privacy and society's need for statistical data about diseases. State public-health agencies and the national Centers for Disease Control in Atlanta, Georgia, for example, rely on such information to further scientific research and to help minimize dangers to the public. An answer may lie in the separation of potentially identifying information from other data.

One might also ask whether an important societal purpose is served by the general availability of individually identifiable genetic and other medical information. If an individual carries a gene that will result in a disease or that indicates a predisposition to develop a disease, why shouldn't employers and insurance companies be able to minimize their risks by avoiding such people? Employers and insurers are in business for profit, after all, and having to pay for employees' treatment will raise employers' premiums and cost insurers enough to make insurance more expensive for the rest of us.

Why shouldn't law schools and medical schools, for example, be able to exclude potential students who, within one or two decades of having completed an expensive course of study, are likely to develop a disease that would make it impossible for them to practice? The public-policy implications of this question become clear when we consider that most post-graduate schools receive government grants of taxpayers' money. And why shouldn't banks be able to access the same information about people to whom they might otherwise issue long-term loans? Yes, forcing individuals to disclose such information may invade their privacy, but the risk to employers and insurers, as well as banks, institutions of higher learning, and public revenues, is substantial.

Although people may differ about whether privacy or some other value is of greater importance in any situation, a decision to elevate the profit motive or the long-range use of an education above the right to privacy is at least one that deserves a hearing. But what if the bases for the assertion of risk are mistaken and privacy is being invaded in the name of a nonexistent benefit?

SCIENCE OR ART?

Scientists disagree about the accuracy of tests that link genetic material with particular individuals and diseases. This was inadvertently demonstrated when the front page of the *New York Times,* summarizing the findings of a near-final draft of a National Academy of Science (NAS) report in April 1992, reported the NAS's conclusion that DNA identification had not been perfected sufficiently to be relied upon in criminal cases. Another *Times* article the following day described a news conference at which the chairperson of the NAS panel, a respected geneticist, said that the panel *had* found DNA reliable enough for courtroom use. Two days later the *Times,* referring to the earlier contradictory stories, acknowledged the differing views of different scientists and the difficulties inherent in transposing biological methods from the laboratory to the courtroom.

A more dramatic example of scientists at first being certain of the link between a gene and a specific disease, and finding later that they were wrong, lies in the research on cystic fibrosis (CF). Molecular geneticists were understandably elated in 1989 when they isolated the gene responsible for cystic fibrosis and the eventual lung failure CF causes. By 1993, however, biologists had found that there were more than 350 points along the gene that could be mutated (changed) and that these mutations affected the possibility of developing CF. Scientists then declared that many people who inherit mutated versions of the cystic fibrosis gene from both parents— once considered an absolute predictor—do not ever develop CF. One reason is that there are so many possible mutations—with new mutations being found every month—that the potential combinations in any person are endless. A second reason, as scientists now know, is that other genes may alter the way these mutations are expressed. A pair of mutations inherited by one person might lead to the disease, but precisely the same mutations inherited by another might not.

Cystic fibrosis is not the only example of the complex effects of genes. Complications have been discovered in predicting genetically related illnesses such as Tay-Sachs, a progressive disease that usually proves fatal in early childhood. Such complications are not new to medical research. It is now known, for example, that people whose electroencephalograms show massive brain abnormalities may have only minimal behavioral disorders—or none at all. A 1981 study of an Amish family found a genetic locus for the illness and discovered that all members of the family who manifested symptoms of manic depression had the same markers. That was not surprising, as doctors who diagnosed manic depression in numerous family members had long suspected a genetic basis. What did surprise the scientists, however, was their finding that only 60 to 70 percent of the family members identified as carrying the gene actually became ill.

The point, which is that genetic conditions are variable in their effects, is worth reiterating at a time when many individuals and institutions view genetic inheritance as predictors of health and happiness. "Genes are suddenly thought to be responsible for everything from poverty to privilege, from misdemeanors to murder," wrote *New York Times Magazine* author Charles Siebert, who had discovered that he might carry a genetic disorder that frequently results in early death. "It's as though we're witnessing the biomolecular deconstruction of humanity, the abdication of all responsibility and will to our evolutionarily pre-programmed computer chips." Dr. Lameh Fananapazir of the Clinical Center of the National Institutes of Health, a specialist in the form of hypertropic cardiomyopathy (HCM) that the *Times* author thought he might have, used stronger language: "I saw a cover of a magazine last summer: 'Infidelity: It May Be in Your Genes.' It drove me nuts. It's absurd. . . . DNA. . .may explain some predispositions to certain types of behavior, but they will be modest compared to the effect of things like education and environment." The same gene can both predispose to illness and have no effect within the same family, so that the violation of privacy inherent in unwanted testing may result in useless information.

This misleading result is as true of the tests, likely to be developed in the near future, for predispositions to various cancers, cardiovascular diseases, alcoholism, personality traits, and mental disorders, as it is of existing tests. As medical geneticist Barbara Handelin has observed, "There are exceptions to almost every rule," and attempts to associate particular combinations of mutations with specific outcomes in the general population "have been almost totally unsuccessful." She said that "the onus is on us not to sell this research in an oversimplified way." Scientists now can diagnose a predilection to alcoholism before a person has ever had a drink—but for all anyone knows, the person may have principled objections to drinking and never even have one. It is possible to test for predilections that may be exacerbated by exposure to certain chemicals in the workplace—but it is equally possible to clean up the workplace for everybody rather than to invade privacy and discriminate. And where insurance companies are concerned, according to Paul Billings, a leading medical geneticist engaged in basic and clinical genetics research, even the profit motive cannot excuse genetic discrimination, because "broad community-based actuarial data have already taken genetic conditions into account"—meaning that insurance rates have long been based on the assumption that a percentage of the population will be stricken by genetic-related illnesses.

One might respond that as science progresses, testing will become more certain. But the lesson of the "definite" diagnosis of cystic fibrosis is that science is, in a sense, an art: a frequently uncertain endeavor rather than the absolute reflection of truth that we might prefer to believe in. A classic, much publicized example is the case of the paroled prisoner who was accused of using heroin after he was given a drug test. He had in fact not used heroin but he had eaten a poppy-seed bagel just before the test was administered. The explosion of the *Challenger* missile and the radioactive contamination that resulted from a disastrous malfunction at the Chernobyl power plant are reminders that science is fallible. So, as

Brandeis repeatedly warned, are human beings. It was not the knowledge that was at fault in these instances but its application. The history of medical science is one of misdiagnoses as well as progress. When X rays and electrocardiograms were still relatively new inventions, for example, they were misinterpreted at appallingly high rates.

Should privacy invasions be permitted for possibly imperfect tests the interpretation of which may be further affected by fallible human beings? Human fallibility notwithstanding, clinical diagnoses of individuals are more accurate than screening programs for large populations, but people denied employment or insurance are not likely to know why they were turned down and therefore are in no position to demand a more personalized rediagnosis. Tests also pose the question of people's right not to know. Young adults with a genetic predisposition to develop a fatal disease in middle age might well prefer to avoid the anxiety of the intervening years, as Theresa Morelli did. Widely reported stories of the devastating effect on patients who have been told incorrectly that they tested positive for AIDS suggest the severity of the problem.

And what if the scientists compound the problems through carelessness? This question was raised by three doctors who studied the research habits of 4,000 graduate students and faculty members in four scientific fields including microbiology and chemistry. The conclusion of their study, funded by the National Science Foundation and published in *American Scientist,* was that scientists "were under enormous pressure to churn out results and the result was sloppy science." The pressure to discover and publish can be counterproductive and affect scientific methodology. In April 1994, researchers announced discovery of p16, a gene that, when mutated, clearly indicated the presence of cancer. The news was greeted as one of the most important discoveries in the molecular biology of cancer and the announcement set off additional research. Three months later new studies indicated that mutated p16 genes are found most often, not in tumors excised from human beings, but in laboratory experiments, in which cells are grown in plastic vessels containing fetal calf serum and may react quite differently than they do in human beings. "If you are going to make a statement about human tumors," commented Dr. Webster Cavenee, director of the Ludwig Institution at University of California, San Diego, "I think you should look at tumors. It only makes sense." During the

1980s, headlines blared the news that scientists had linked specific genes with reading disability, schizophrenia, psychosis, and manic depression. In 1990 great publicity was given to "discovery" of a gene responsible for alcoholism. All these findings are now held in disrepute by scientists. Articles in the January 1996 issue of *Nature Genetics* reported that two different scientific teams had identified a distinctive variant of a gene they held responsible for the personality trait called novelty-seeking: impulsiveness, fickleness, excitability, and a thirst for new sensations. In November of that year researchers from the United States National Institute on Alcohol Abuse and Alcoholism and from the University of Helsinki in Finland said their attempts to replicate the findings had failed and that they considered the link between a gene and novelty-seeking highly questionable.

To err is human, and to make mistakes is forgivable. To base decisions crucial to people's lives on "facts" that one knows may well be erroneous is not, and what is being suggested here is that the multiplicity of instances in which genetic "facts" were discovered to be wrong renders suspect the widespread use of genetic information as the basis of discriminatory decisions. Scientists corrected their errors within a few months or years, but the invidious use of their earlier findings was not easily undone. An answer to such discrimination may lie in the statutes of the eleven states that passed laws between 1991 and 1996 prohibiting health insurance companies from discriminating against people who are genetically prone to certain diseases by denying them policies or charging higher rates. Skepticism about the accuracy of genetic testing was a major factor in the laws' enactment.

The decades since 1945 have seen science elevated to a position of immutable truth. One of the lessons of the same decades, however, is that many scientific "truths" are arguable even when research is meticulous. The story of two research scientists working in the same area makes this quite clear.

Bruce N. Ames is a biochemist and molecular biologist who directs the National Institute of Environmental Health Sciences Center at the University of California, Berkeley. The inventor of the leading laboratory test to screen chemicals for their ability to damage genes, Ames has won numerous scholarly awards and produced hundreds of technical publications and is one of the world's two dozen most often cited scientists. He believes that most cancers are built into human beings and develop in large part with age, beginning at around thirty. He also believes, however, that the most important causes of cancer can be controlled through diet, which actually can suppress the cancer process.

Fellow scientists consider Dr. Ames's work both brilliant and controversial. If the award-winning scientist is correct, however, and if potential employers or insurers ought to be permitted to minimize their costs, logically they would refuse to employ or insure anyone over thirty and would insist on monitoring and regulating the diet of all employees or policyholders. Logically, too, Congress and the courts should be asked to undo the laws that make age discrimination illegal in the United States. Dr. Ames agrees with mothers who enjoin their children to "eat your vegetables." Should employers be permitted to fire anyone who is increasing her chances of developing cancer by not eating what Dr. Ames insists is the absolutely necessary five servings of fruit and vegetables a day? More pertinently, should they be allowed to invade their employees' privacy by demanding information about their diets?

Susan M. Love would say no. She is the director of the University of California, Los Angeles, Breast Center, one of about a dozen clinics in the United States that research and treat breast cancer. A cofounder of the National Breast Cancer Coalition, a federation of almost 200 support and advocacy groups that has secured greater funding for breast cancer research and prevention, she is also the author of a guide to breast cancer that the *New York Times* has called "the bible of women with breast cancer." She is convinced that even though, as has now been proved, breast cancer is affected by a gene, some women are born with it and others develop it later in life. She speculates that pesticides or pollution or food additives may be responsible for such genetic changes.

Logically, if she is right, and if employer and insurer risk is sufficient reason for invading privacy, employers and insurers should be able to insist that employees and policyholders have regular examinations for genetic change and be subject to possible firing or the cancellation of insurance coverage. Dr. Ames, however, maintains that pesticides, pollution, and food additives are irrelevant to the development of cancer, that the guilty gene is in a woman's body at the time she is born, and that smoking is as responsible as poor diet for the development of cancer. His theory has been bolstered by the discovery of a defective gene that appears to be responsible for the major form of breast cancer. So, if *he* is to be believed, it is logical that once a woman has been found free of the "bad" gene she should not have to undergo subsequent genetic testing but, to minimize employer risk, she should be tested regularly to find out if she is smoking at home. And this is only the tip of the iceberg of scientific disagreement about the causes of breast cancer and other diseases. Yet women found at risk for breast cancer may well be denied a job or health or life insurance for that reason.

THE MISUSE OF SCIENCE

An additional problem in balancing privacy concerns with the possible uses of genetic data lies in laypeople's lack of knowledge about and misinterpretation of genetic information. Linguistic confusion may exacerbate the problem. When scientists utilize terms such as "predisposed" and "at risk," they are referring to vulnerability to a disease that may or may not develop in the future, but most people take the words to mean that the disease probably will manifest itself. What scientists are discussing, however, are possibilities rather than certainties. More than 130 mutations have been found in the gene that scientists now think may be linked to breast cancer, for example, and research about which mutations are meaningless and which are deadly is still incomplete. Also, most research indicates that each of us has between eight and ten genetic "defects," meaning that we all have DNA sequences that might in some sense be considered to make us "unfit." Tests for many of them do not yet exist—but they soon will. The National Institutes of Health's Dr. Fananapazir predicted in 1995 that by the early twenty-first century there will be routine medical tests, possibly usable at home, by which people will be able to discover their genetic makeup. Similarly, the Institute of Medicine's Committee on Assessing Genetic Risks has predicted that "multiplex genetic testing based upon a single blood or tissue sample" soon will become standard medical practice, suggesting that patients will emerge from their doctors' offices with their own personal genetic report cards. May employers, once such tests are perfected, demand privacy-violative genetic testing and then use the results to pick and choose who among us shall be employed? May they utilize genetic information as a pretext for refusing to hire on what are actually grounds of gender or race or ethnic background?

Pretexts are readily at hand. Women are by far the majority of breast cancer patients. It is rare for anyone other than African Americans to develop sickle-cell anemia and equally infrequent for people who are not Jews from European backgrounds to develop Gaucher's disease, a chronic enzyme deficiency.

Today we live with the myth of genetic perfection, on which employment and insurance decisions are based. Privacy is breached, as two scholars have written, because of the assumption "that there is an ideal of biological normality or perfection against which individuals can be measured, that complex human behavior can be reduced to biological or genetic explanations, and that behavioral problems can be attributed to biological determinants with minimal reference to social or environmental influence." The privacy invasions based on this myth often result in genetic discrimination.

"Discrimination" in this context means negative action against an individual or family member because of real or perceived differences from what is assumed to be the "normal" genome of that individual. Recorded instances include an individual denied a job because the applicant's mother was schizophrenic and the employer assumed that the condition was inherited, and the denial of health insurance to a whole family because two of its four children have fragile-X syndrome, a genetic form of mental retardation that in fact frequently carries no physical disabilities or medical risks. Another individual came from a family with heredity hemochromatosis, which is excessive storage of iron in the body. It had been detected early and treated appropriately with continuing drug therapy, but the individual, who had no symptoms whatsoever, could not obtain health coverage. Doctors' letters were ignored by insurance companies. "I run 10 Km races, etc.," the individual wrote in despair. "I am not a basket case, and will not be one, ever, because of iron overload." The brother of someone with Gaucher's disease was screened and found to have unaffected carrier status, meaning that he carried the gene but would not himself develop the disease. He was nonetheless turned down for a government job. In 1996 *Science* published the results of a Georgetown University survey of 332 people who had one or more relatives with genetic disorders. Twenty-five percent believed that their family history had led to their being denied life insurance, twenty-two percent said it was the reason for their having been denied health insurance, and thirteen percent were certain it had led to their being denied or fired from a job.

There was an ironic example of both correct use and misuse of genetic information after a fourteen-day-old baby was diagnosed as having PKU and was immediately put on continuing and successful drug therapy. When she was eight years old, as her doctors attested, her mental development was completely normal except in those instances where she tested higher than the average for her age. Here was an instance of genetic testing working as it should: for the benefit of people who otherwise would be ill. But because of her PKU the youngster was refused coverage under her father's health insurance policy. In most cases PKU can be completely controlled by a proper diet. In others, as in this one, patients must receive constant and expensive drug therapy. Without health insurance the family may be unable to pay for the necessary treatment, risking developmental delays and permanent impairment.

The child's case is not unique. A man who had a perfect driving record during the twenty years he had been driving was denied automobile insurance when it was discovered that he had Charcot-Marie-Tooth disease, which can result in mild impairment of judgment or some weakness of the muscles in the extremities, but clearly had not done so in his case. In all these instances, requiring people to provide genetic information not only invaded their privacy but resulted in clear discrimination. The *Times* writer who may have carried the HCM genetic mutation had to change the name of the hometown of one large multigenerational family susceptible to the mutation because its members had already discovered that even belonging to a family some of whose members were genetically different prevented them from getting health insurance.

Two additional major privacy concerns are raised by genetic information. One is governmental intrusion; the other is the use of such data to decide who should and should not be born.

GOVERNMENT, EUGENICS, AND GENETIC PRIVACY

Issues of DNA testing by the criminal justice system are discussed in Chapter Six. It should be noted here, however, that the federal government currently has two large data banks that include genetic and other medical information. The FBI, as well as more than eighteen states, has expanded its identification data bank system, which held computer records of physical characteristics such as height, weight, hair and eye color, skin marks, dental variations, and fingerprint patterns, to include genetic information. In April 1992, the Department of Defense began to collect biological samples from all armed services personnel for the purpose of identifying "unknown soldiers." As a result the department will have samples, taken from roughly 2 million people, that could later be used to extract health-related and whatever other information scientific tests make possible, including potential personality traits. The data bank formally is closed to other federal agencies.

The question is whether such genetic information can be kept confidential. President Richard Nixon ordered aides to get supposedly unavailable information from the Internal Revenue Service about political opponents. The Clinton White House asked for and received FBI background reports on more than 300 people, some of them Republicans who had never worked in the White House or who no longer worked for the government. As the Office of Technology Assessment (OTA) established by Congress noted in 1988, "genetic information has often been used for political purposes in the past; information arising in genome projects could be similarly misused." In 1996, fears about how the information might be used led two marines to refuse to comply with the military's program of mandatory genetic testing. They were court-martialled. Americans who have long prided themselves on living in a country with no national registration might well be concerned about governmental accumulation of such massive amounts of information.

There is no guarantee that the government will use the results of such tests any more intelligently than private industry. Sickle-cell anemia is so highly debilitating, with symptoms including blood loss, painful joints, and frequent infections, that it is unlikely that someone who has the disease would not know it by the time he or she begins a permanent job. One out of ten or twelve African Americans carries the trait without suffering any illness from it and can go through life without any symptoms except in the extreme case of a major loss in blood oxygen. In fact, the only known certainty for those with the carrier trait is an apparent higher resistance to malaria.

The Office of Technology Assessment has nonetheless documented instances of people being denied jobs because they are carriers. In 1969, four army recruits with the trait died while training at high altitudes. The Department of the Navy, concerned about personnel safety, immediately ordered all recruits to be tested. Studies showed that people with only one copy of the carrier trait, rather than two, were not at any greater risk than others, but in 1979 the Air Force Academy expelled several African American men with one copy on the grounds that their health *might* be endangered by a tough training program. No apparent thought was given to the less drastic solutions of monitoring them or, in an era with numerous and widely differing job descriptions and responsibilities in all the armed services, adapting the training program. Privacy had been breached, but it was uncertain at best that the results warranted the intrusion. There is a side note: in the 1980s it was discovered that the medical directors of corporations testing for sickle-cell anemia did not know how the test results were being used and that the corporations had no coherent policies for maintaining confidentiality about the tests, the results of which were being passed on to the armed forces— which is of course a branch of the government.

The second privacy concern is typified by the story, in a 1993 report by the National Academy of Sciences, about a California health maintenance organization's discovery that the fetus being carried by a client had the gene for cystic fibrosis. The health maintenance organization (HMO) informed her that it would pay for an abortion, but that if she chose to have the child, it would not pay for any treatments. She chose to have the child and, in this instance, the threat of a lawsuit forced the HMO to back down. But in the absence of universal health coverage and as more and more Americans rely on HMOs, these organizations will likely exert increased pressure on parents not to bring to term children who will be a drain on their resources, even if the same scientific sophistication that produced the tests may yield a cure for the disease. This pressure may make sense for profit-oriented HMOs. The question of whether it makes as much sense for privacy and individual autonomy is at the heart of the debate over public policy in this area.

Parents also may be discouraged from bearing children with genes that supposedly indicate a tendency to violence. In the early 1990s, Frederick Goodwin, director of the Alcohol, Drug Abuse, and Mental Health Administration of the Department of Health and Human Services, spoke about the Department's Violence Initiative research, designed to discover biological markers by which violence-prone children could be distinguished as early as age five. Comparing inner-city youths to murderous oversexed monkeys, he said, "Maybe it isn't just the careless use of the word when people call certain areas of certain cities jungles." Although the ensuing outcry caused the National Institutes of Health to cancel financial support for a planned conference on the biology of violence, the conference later was approved by the National Academy of Sciences, and Goodwin subsequently became the head of the National Institute of Mental Health.

Most scientists acknowledge that there is no scientific merit to research for genes associated with criminal behavior, but behavioral genetics seems on the surface to be such a quick and easy source of crime control that scientists as well as ethicists and attorneys are concerned that data banks may well be misused for such "research." The connection between genetics and behavior has become so taken for granted that legal scholars Rochelle Cooper Dreyfuss and Dorothy Nelkin refer to "genetic essentialism," which "posits that personal traits are predictable and permanent, determined at conception, 'hard-wired' into the human constitution," "negates assumptions about free will," and "challenges the principle that equivalent opportunities should be extended to all." If we believe that character traits can be ascertained biologically and behavior predicted, it becomes logical to attempt to protect society at large or the school or workplace by insisting that people be tested genetically no matter how opposed they may be to that invasion of their privacy. Professor Nelkin points to a doctor who wrote to the *Journal of the American Medical Association,* "We cannot let such matters of conscience and preservation of personal freedoms stand in the way of public safety" and to a writer in an airline magazine who suggested taking "pre-emptive action" against those genetically predisposed to crime.

Prenatal tests that permit prospective parents to decide not to have children who might suffer from horrendous diseases clearly are desirable. Lesch-Nyhan syndrome, for example, is caused by a mutated gene that builds up uric acid within the body, sending children into agonizing fits of self-mutilation and ultimately resulting in retardation and death. Potential parents of children whose probable genetic makeup would mean they would be born with hypertrophic cardiomyopathy or cystic fibrosis might well choose not to produce human beings doomed to such suffering or to face the effect on themselves and other family members of attempting to cope with these debilitating and frequently fatal diseases. But if privacy means anything, it surely means that such decisions are up to individuals, not to the state.

The danger in leaving such decisions to governments can be seen in the history of "eugenics." The word was coined by the English scientist Francis Dalton, who in the late 1880s described it as the science of improving the hereditary qualities of the human race. In the ensuing years this vision has taken the form of public policies designed to encourage reproduction by the rich and successful rather than the poor, limiting immigration to the United States from countries whose "gene pools" were considered inferior, and, of course, outside this country, Nazi Germany's genocide of Jews, gypsies, and homosexuals. When, in 1924, Virginia passed an involuntary sterilization bill that included the statement that "heredity plays an important part in the transmission of insanity, idiocy, imbecility, epilepsy, and crime" and attempted to sterilize the eighteen-year-old pregnant daughter of an allegedly "feeble-minded" woman under the law, the U.S. Supreme Court of 1927 declared the statute constitutional *(Buck v. Bell)*. Justice Oliver Wendell Holmes wrote that "three generations of imbeciles is enough." Although the sterilization in fact was not performed and the young woman produced a normal daughter, California took the Court's decision as its cue to sterilize over 11,000 Californians between 1930 and 1944. The Court seemed to redeem itself somewhat in 1942 by holding in *Skinner* v. *Oklahoma* that the sterilization of a man because he was a three-time criminal offender would violate the Constitution's equal protection clause. Its rationale, however, was that although Skinner, who had been convicted of stealing chickens and of armed robbery, properly fell under the Oklahoma act, the state had not demonstrated a sufficient justification for specifically omitting from the bill various "white collar" crimes such as bootlegging, tax evasion, or embezzlement.

How tempting to insist upon genetic testing in order to predict what undesirable traits will be carried by fetuses and pressure their parents to abort them—and yet how troubling a concept, both ethically as well as legally in terms of privacy. African Americans have been found particularly susceptible to hypertension, which could suggest that we should permit fewer people with genes for dark pigmentation to be born—or it could suggest that discrimination and the resulting low socioeconomic status of a disproportionate number of African Americans result in hypertension. The correlation can be used to validate invading privacy through genetic testing for pigmentation. So, as suggested earlier, could tests for propensity for sickle-cell anemia, Tay-Sachs, Gaucher's disease, or breast cancer—which would cut down rather neatly and quite "scientifically" on the country's African American, Jewish, and female populations.

Science magazine noted in mid-1994 that the Archives of General Psychiatry were "filled with claims that heredity plays a role in everything from gregariousness and general cognitive ability to alcoholism and manic depression." The article also pointed out, however, that "the same data that show the effects of genes also point to the enormous influence of non-genetic factors." Professor Nelkin added that an emphasis on biological predisposition could lead society to ignore "the real source of crime: the social conditions," such as racism, "that are so strongly associated with violence."

The Office of Technology Assessment's 1983 publication, *The Role of Genetic Testing in the Prevention of Occupational Disease,* concluded that, as is still true more than a decade later, genetic diagnostics was "a science truly in its infancy" and that tests "do not meet established scientific criteria for routine use in an occupational setting." The correlation between genetic tests and risk of particular diseases is not sufficiently extensive for the drawing of predictive conclusions, the report stated. It added, however, that in 1982 OTA had surveyed the Fortune 400 corporations. Of the 366 corporations responding to the OTA questionnaire, seventeen had used genetic screening and fifty-nine intended to do so. The negative publicity that accompanied the study made corporations cautious about admitting to the use of genetic tests, but the *New York Times* reported in 1986 that the number of corporations interested in doing so was on the rise.

There is more information than ever available for misuse. The American Medical Association now publishes over 150 articles on advances in molecular genetics in eleven different medical journals a year. But, as Dr. Jeffrey Sklar, professor of pathology at the Harvard Medical School and director of molecular oncology at the Brigham and Women's Hospital in Boston, has warned, the tests that are reported "raise all sort of issues," including privacy.

Other doctors and scientists are worried about privacy of genetic information. When the New York Birth Defects Institute requested in 1981 that all registered laboratories undertaking diagnosis turn over to the state the names, addresses, and other identifying data about all individuals with chromosomal "abnormalities," promising that permission would be sought from the individuals involved before the information was turned over to laboratories providing genetic services, a group of genetic laboratories was so skeptical about real confidentiality that it refused to disclose the information and the state dropped the request. It was resurrected in 1987, however, this time with a requirement that social security numbers also be included. Once again the refusal of several laboratories to comply led to suspension of the requirement, but of course that need not and probably will not always be the outcome. Even the enthusiastic head of the Genome Project is worried that private genetic information will be too readily available for possible misuse by insurance companies and employers.

The field is so new and so puzzling that there have been almost no statements from the courts about genetic privacy. In November 1996 two former employees of a Boston high-tech company sued in Suffolk Superior Court because they were fired for refusing to provide 180 strands of hair for "medical research" and drug testing. They were concerned that the hair samples could be used to conduct genetic testing and might keep them from getting insurance coverage. The case will no doubt be heard by a number of courts before the issue is resolved.

Perhaps the best argument against privacy violations in the name of using genetic information as a predictor was made by Gregory Carey, a behavioral geneticist at the University of Colorado. "We already have a true genetic marker, detectable before birth, that predicts violence," Professor Carey noted. Individuals with this genotype are nine times as likely to get arrested and convicted for a violent act as people without the genes. The high-risk marker he was talking about is the gene carried by every human being who is male.

Chapter Three

——

THE INSECURITY
OF SOCIAL SECURITY NUMBERS

What we do belongs to what we are; and what we are is what becomes of us.

—Henry Van Dyke, *Ships and Havens*

Dan Quayle was vice president of the United States when George Bush was president. Quayle thought that his spending more money at Sears than he did at Brooks Brothers was private information. He was proved wrong by *Business Week* reporter and privacy expert Jeffrey Rothfeder, who wondered how much personal information he could learn about a person by using techniques available to anyone. Rothfeder later testified before Congress that he wanted to demonstrate the demise of privacy in the United States. He began by calling up an information company that charged him fifty dollars for Quayle's social security number (SSN). Plugging the SSN into his computer enabled Rothfeder to get Quayle's credit report and to find out, among other items, Quayle's unlisted address and telephone number as well as his spending habits. He used another data seller to buy television announcer Dan Rather's credit report for a month in 1992. As a bonus, the seller threw in the home telephone number of television celebrity Vanna White. Rothfeder next went to the Nexis database of real estate and learned that television talk show host Arsenio Hall had bought his house for $795,000, relying in part on a $499,950 mortgage.

A less benign example of the ease with which third parties can access someone's credit files is the man who identified himself as the owner of a small wallpaper company and asked for credit information about three landowners. He then used the information to pose as each of the landowners and took out loans amounting to $613,000 in their names.

How was it possible for these people to get what most of us would consider personal information about others? Why do the records of our lives exist in a compact form at all? When did this phenomenon begin, and how? Is the government doing anything about the problem? These questions will be explored in Chapters Three and Four.

THE HISTORY OF SSNs

Perhaps the place to start the exploration is with something most Americans simply take as a given: our social security numbers. The history of their use demonstrates how new technologies can both facilitate the flow of important information and become a threat to privacy.

SSNs were created under the 1935 Social Security Act to enable the Social Security Administration (SSA) to keep records of contributions that each worker made to the social security fund and to ensure that retired workers received the monthly stipend to which they were entitled. Workers participating in the fund still are required to give their SSNs to employers, who use the SSNs when reporting information to the Internal Revenue Service (IRS) about wages paid and taxes withheld. Originally only the SSA and the IRS had the information to use for limited purposes, and from the 1930s through the 1960s Social Security cards included the phrase, "Not to be used for identification."

Since the first SSNs were issued in 1936, however, the SSN has evolved from a single-use identifier to the identification number of choice for the public and private sector—a near-substitute for the national identity papers that residents of many other countries must carry—and, as such, a major threat to privacy. In 1937 the government decided to identify accounts in state unemployment-insurance systems by SSNs. President Franklin Delano Roosevelt inadvertently broadened the SSN's use as an identifier by issuing a 1943 Executive Order encouraging other federal agencies to use it as an efficient means of record keeping. In 1961 the Civil Service Commission began relying on the number as a way of identifying all federal employees. In 1962 the IRS mandated that every taxpayer put an SSN on individual tax returns. SSNs were required shortly thereafter to identify Treasury bond holders, old age assistance benefits accounts, and the records of state and federal civil service employees, Veterans' Administration hospital patients, Indian Health Service patients, armed forces personnel, customers' bank and securities transactions, and public assistance beneficiaries.

Two phenomena of the mid-1960s resulted in the massive spread of SSN use. One was the development of computers for nonmilitary use and a substantial drop in the cost of acquiring one; the other, the burgeoning public assistance programs that were a hallmark of President Lyndon Johnson's "Great Society." Asking government assistance recipients to identify themselves by SSNs seemed a logical way to keep records and combat fraud. The use that would be made of the information, however, was unforeseen.

Computer data entry clerks can enter information connected to a single identifier such as an SSN into massive databases. Once there, the information instantly can be exchanged, compared, verified, and linked with information in other databases, often without the knowledge and consent of the person divulging the information. This wealth of information, inevitably made accessible to federal agencies, state governments, and private-sector interests, presents a very real potential for abuse. But the demand for a simple way to identify people took on a life of its own.

During the 1970s, use of SSNs by federal, state, and local governments and the private sector expanded dramatically. Many students routinely fill in the space that asks for their SSN when they are applying to college, and all their records are filed under that number by the institution they attend. They identify themselves by it when applying for government and other loans. The number also is required for a wide variety of commercial transactions, including applications for credit, employment, service by utilities (gas, electricity, telephones), bank accounts, brokerage accounts, and insurance; as identification on a check; and when filling out papers in a doctor's office and on health plan reimbursement forms. Most people simply provide their social security number when it is requested, equally unaware of their right in most circumstances to deny it to nongovernmental entities and of the way SSNs have become the primary means of linking databases.

By 1971 the practice of using SSNs as a key to data bank information had became sufficiently ubiquitous to concern the Social Security Administration, which warned in a Task Force report of "potential dangers to society," particularly the right of privacy. Two years later the Department of Health, Education, and Welfare (HEW) issued a report strongly opposing use of a universal identifier such as the SSN, asserting that such use would enable "an individual [easily] to be traced, and his behavior monitored and controlled, through the records maintained about him by a wide range of different institutions." A national dossier system that could contain the records of one's life, the report continued, would "create an incentive for institutions to pool or link their records." The resultant "uncontrolled linkage of records about people, particularly between government or government-supported automated personal data systems," easily could result in privacy invasions.

The American people, although not fully aware of the extent to which records of their lives were being made available to almost anyone who chose to purchase them, began getting uncomfortable about the amount of information they vaguely realized was "out there." The disquiet manifested itself first, not surprisingly, among groups most likely to be suspicious of the government. As legal scholar Alan Westin commented in 1971:

> Proposals for a national identification card have often appeared a tempting "quick fix" to pressing national problems of keeping track of people, but the fact that no such card exists today is probably best explained by the visceral distrust with which most Americans react to the idea. For many, the prospect of being required to carry a national ID card conjures up the specter of "Big Brother," of the government and the private sector collecting and maintaining an enormous amount of personal information and tracking our transactions and movements.

Westin added that "many dissenting and minority groups in [American] society. . .view the establishment of such an identifier. . .as a giant step toward tightening government control over the citizen for repressive purposes," and that the problem was especially troubling for political activists.

Americans may have had a well-founded "visceral distrust" of a national identifier but they were largely unaware that it was close to reality in the SSN. Congress was more knowledgeable. Reacting in 1973 to the use of SSNs and information collected by government agencies such as the IRS and the Census Bureau, Congress began to hold hearings on the subject, mindful of HEW's recent recommendation "against the adoption of any nationwide, standard, personal identification format, with or without the SSN, that would enhance the likelihood of arbitrary or uncontrolled linkage of records about people, particularly between government or government-supported automated personal data systems."

The congressional hearings and the HEW report culminated in passage of the Privacy Act of 1974. The act in effect endorsed the Supreme Court's privacy doctrine by stating that the Constitution protected a personal and fundamental right to privacy. It added that this right was "directly affected by the collection, maintenance, use and dissemination of personal information by federal agencies" and that increasing reliance on computers and other sophisticated information technology "greatly magnified the harm to individual privacy that can occur from any collection, maintenance, use or dissemination of personal information." Congress was particularly concerned that if the "use of the SSN as an identifier continues to expand, the incentives to link records and broaden access are likely to increase." The report of the Senate committee that had considered the act described the growing use of the SSN as "one of the most serious manifestations of privacy concerns in the nation," adding that it could "become a means of violating civil liberties by easing the way for intelligence and surveillance uses of the number for indexing or locating the person."

The act established the Privacy Protection Study Commission to study the way SSNs were employed. The commission reported in 1977 that there was "a clear danger" that the SSN would become "a de facto central population register." (The federal Office of Technology Assessment would go further in 1986, stating that the SSN already operated as a de facto national identifier.) The commission recommended that Congress limit use of the SSN "until laws and policies regarding the use of records about individuals are developed and shown to be effective." Section 7 of the act makes it unlawful for any government agency "to deny anyone any right, benefit or privilege provided by law because of such individual's refusal to disclose his Social Security account number," but the act does not apply to federal statutes or regulations adopted before 1975 or to private organizations. The Section also states that a governmental agency that does request an SSN, presumably under the time exemption, must indicate whether disclosure of the number is mandatory or voluntary and what uses will be made of it. The act includes no enforcement provision, however: agencies that request disclosure without informing the individual whether compliance is mandatory or voluntary or how the SSN would be used can continue to do so with impunity.

Congress may have done the electorate and its privacy a disservice by not establishing tighter controls over SSNs. The Privacy Protection Study Commission noted that there was widespread opposition by the American people to the use of a national identifier such as SSN. It found that people resented being identified by a number, that they feared that several organizations possessing an individual's SSN could exchange information about the individual too easily, and that the number could be used to create dossiers about individuals that would follow them throughout their lives.

SSNs AND THE PRIVACY ACT

In spite of such popular concerns about SSNs, Congress quickly began making exceptions to the Privacy Act. The Tax Reform Act of 1976 gave states the power to use SSNs for motor vehicle registration, driver's licenses, tax forms, administration of welfare programs, and implementation of the Parent Locator Service, designed to find fathers who were not making child support payments. The rationale for the last was that the information might help State Child Support Enforcement units track down fathers who were failing to make child support payments—a rationale that would reappear in the mid-1990s—and would facilitate the matching of information on federal and state tax returns. The Deficit Reduction Act of 1984 required bank depositors to provide their SSNs so they could be matched by IRS computers in order to make certain that taxpayers were reporting all interest received to the IRS. The 1996 federal welfare reform legislation known as the Personal Responsibility and

Work Opportunity Reconciliation Act included a provision requiring state Departments of Motor Vehicles to keep licensed drivers' SSNs on file as well as to get the SSNs of people applying for marriage licenses, divorces, and any professional or other license issued by a state. States must create databases of "new hires" for uploading to a federal registry controlled by the Department of Health and Human Services.

States have a decidedly mixed history when it comes to SSNs and privacy. Some require SSNs for driver's licenses. Many others, such as Arkansas, Virginia, and Massachusetts, have been sufficiently concerned about misuse of SSNs either to present motorists with or to give them the option of requesting a randomly selected number rather than their SSN to appear on their driver's licenses. Only New Jersey and California restrict access to the use of information gathered from SSNs by motor vehicle offices, and a 1994 Ohio Supreme Court decision cited a constitutional right to privacy when prohibiting governmental disclosure of SSNs (*Ohio ex rel. Beacon Journal* v. *Akron*). Many other states regularly sell motor vehicle database information to entities as diverse as insurance companies and newspapers, as federal law permits them to do. An Arizona resident reported in 1996 that Phoenix police dispatchers routinely broadcast SSNs over the airwaves whenever they found a car through spotchecking that either was from out of state or was being driven by anyone not carrying a license. The resident picked up the information with a recently bought scanner available to anyone, and subsequently commented to the *Computer Privacy Digest* Moderator on the Internet, the SSN is "a number that is not to be used to identify a person [outside the SSA, but] it certainly seems that the Phoenix Police Department [has] a different opinion of what that means."

The greatest implication for SSN privacy may lie in the Tax Reform Act of 1988, which, seeking to ensure against fraud, requires that children claimed as dependents on tax returns must have an SSN. The result is that Americans now have an SSN virtually from the time they are born. The potential for misuse of the numbers is great.

Perhaps President Bill Clinton had become aware of the potential for fraud when, in 1994, he erased his and his family members' SSNs from the tax returns he made available to the media and to the public. The returns he released in 1993 had included SSNs. His concern was unhappily vindicated in 1995, when federal prosecutors charged several employees of the Social Security Administration with passing information about more than 11,000 people to a credit-card fraud ring. The information, which included not only SSNs but mothers' maiden names, enabled the ring to foil a system that is used by most banks and credit card issuers to prevent fraud. The system prevents new cards sent in the mail from being activated until customers receiving them call a special telephone number and provide precisely such information. "The human link is the weakest link in any information security program," commented Ira Winkler, technical director for the National Computer Security Association. "If you are a clerk making $12,000 or $18,000 a year, and someone offers you a few hundred to a few thousand dollars every so often to look up some specific information, it's a tempting offer." The result was a massive invasion of privacy as well as fraud.

The potential for misuse of SSNs would come as no news to Demetrios Papademetrious, who was the Labor Department's director of immigration policy from 1988 to 1992. During that time he had top-secret security clearance. In 1993, a friend of his was scheduled to accept President Clinton's nomination to head the immigration service, and Papademetrious was one of the people invited to attend the ceremony at the White House. He missed it, however, because when he arrived at the White House, he was arrested by the Secret Service, handcuffed, fingerprinted, held for several hours, and told that he was wanted for possession of stolen property. Eventually, it was discovered that the arrest warrant in question had been issued for a man with a similar name who had gotten the immigration official's SSN some years before and was using it regularly. Mr. Papademetrious frequently had to go to the trouble of clearing his name in credit checks and IRS documents. "It tells you something about the reliability of documents," he commented to the press.

SSNS AND OTHER DATA BANKS

Once computers became commonplace, the private sector realized that a great deal of information could be obtained about potential customers by using their SSNs to search through computerized data banks. Huge credit bureaus such as Equifax Credit Information Services Incorporated, TRW Credit Data (which recently changed its name to Experian), and TransUnion sprung up, their sole purpose being to collect and collate data on daily credit card transactions and to sell the resultant information to virtually anyone willing to pay for it. SSNs seemed a quick and easy way of aiding accuracy by keeping people with similar names from being confused with each other in ever-growing massive databases. Equifax, for example, has some 15,000 employees maintaining files on over 160 million Americans—more than sixty percent of the population. Experian, which claims to be the nation's largest provider of consumer credit information, boasts that it has data about nearly 170 million American consumers. But the credit bureaus act only as information "exchanges"—they decline to verify the information they receive or sell. Experian admits that it will store whatever information its subscribers send about a person: whether it is right, wrong, misspelled, or inaccurate is not Experian's concern. This is equally true of Equifax and TransUnion as well as numerous similar but smaller and more regionally based concerns, with consequences to be discussed below.

The danger to privacy lies in the use of this information for purposes never intended by the individual and about which she or he does not know, as demonstrated by the story about Vice President Quayle. By 1993 companies such as American Telephone & Telegraph, Exxon, and Philip Morris were allowing telephonic access to a stockholder's ownership, dividends, and recent trading activity. To get the information all that a curious person needed was the shareholder's Social Security number. A *Wall Street Journal* reporter got the SSN of Robert E. Allen, the chairman and chief executive of AT&T, simply by looking at his 1993 filing with the Securities and Exchange Commission. She then dialed AT&T's toll-free number and, by punching in the "menu" numbers offered by an automated program, was told the amount of Allen's last dividend check and the date on which it was cashed. She could have done the same thing for many politicians whose SSNs are included on the tax returns they routinely make public, or for anyone else whose SSN she learned. Newspapers around the country have reported instances of people learning an individual's SSN and using it to get the individual's social security benefits or other government payments, to order new personal checks at a new address on the individual's checking account, receive credit cards in the individual's name, and even obtain the individual's paycheck.

Technology marches on. One can get almost anyone's SSN while sitting at a computer terminal in the comfort of one's home or office. In 1993 reporters from *Macworld* magazine, using only commercial and government databases available on the Internet, collected information about eighteen people. Among them was William R. Hearst III, publisher of the *San Francisco Examiner.* The reporters easily "accessed" his home address, date of birth, SSN, neighbors' addresses and phone numbers, driving and marriage records, voter registration, tax liens, and outstanding debts.

Even computer neophytes can emulate the *Macworld* feat. In 1996, an Internet site called alt.private.investigator carried a posting by a Texas firm that offered to find SSNs for $75 or less. For an additional fee the company would use any SSN to find all of a person's current and former addresses, neighbors' names and addresses, any professional licenses held, and credit and banking information. A subsequent posting by a man who claimed to have been a police officer called the service overpriced. He described how, while working as a private investigator, he had opened computer-linked accounts with Equifax, TRW (Experian), and TransUnion, the country's largest credit bureaus, and had gotten SSNs of people with credit ratings by typing in their addresses. A private investigator could get anyone the same information for a mere $50 plus expenses, he added.

In mid-1996 the Lexis Internet service that reproduces court opinions began advertising a new database that contained names, current addresses, prior addresses, SSNs, and mother's maiden names of 300 million people. Lexis set up a toll-free number for people who wanted to be removed from the database, but obviously many among the 300 million were unaware of the service or the get-out option. Widespread publicity given to the Lexis database over the Internet led the company to change its database so that it is no longer possible for a user to plug in someone's name and get that person's SSN, although information such as a person's unlisted telephone number does remain available. There are other data services that still permit computerized searches for SSNs. People who acquire such information may or may not be engaged in criminal activities, such as using the SSNs to establish credit or even to collect other people's benefits; they are, however, invaders of privacy—as are the services providing the data.

Even before most Americans knew of the Internet, they reacted strongly to the discovery that private business had such extensive access to the information in the Social Security Administration's files. The reaction led the Bush Administration to announce in 1989 that the agency would not be allowed to process a batch of magnetic tapes containing 140 million names and SSNs given to it by TRW (Experian) for verification. But the disclosure of SSNs to the private sector continued, as was demonstrated dramatically by a TRW advertising brochure circulated in 1990. It stated:

> In pursuit of those who have disappeared—former customers, college alumni or missing shareholders—TRW brings you Social Search: A State-of-the-art locating tool that puts our expansive databases to work for you. . . . All you need are the Social Security numbers of those you're attempting to locate and you can reach those hard-to-find individuals who may have moved or changed their names.

At a Senate hearing in 1990, Senator David Pryor expressed outrage at the Social Security Administration's privacy violations and the fact that it was not until a year earlier that the administration had decided to halt sale of SSN verifications to the private sector:

> Unfortunately. . .this action comes too late to protect some 150,000 people whose files were violated during a test run for TRW and for more than three million people on whom verifications were conducted for Citibank and other firms in past years.

Once again, however, in spite of the ire of some members of Congress, the easy use of the SSN as a way of identifying people for purposes that seemed valid proved to be an overwhelming temptation.

NATIONAL IDENTITY CARDS AND PRIVACY

The Immigration Reform and Control Act which Congress enacted in 1986 requires employers to verify that prospective employees are not illegal immigrants. Employers who do not comply with the verification requirement are liable to sanctions. The documents that employers are permitted to rely upon, according to the act, are passports, birth certificates, driver's licenses, voter registration cards, and Social Security cards. The act states that it is not designed to authorize establishment of a national identification card, but mandates reports from various federal agencies about possible alterations in the verification system, including the use of the SSN or another identification system. As Congress soon learned from its General Accounting Office and the United States Civil Rights Commission, employers' fears of sanctions and the knowledge of the ease with which faked social security cards could be obtained were leading them to discriminate against members of racial and ethnic minorities such as Latino and Asian Americans, as there were and are substantial numbers of illegal immigrants as well as citizens and resident aliens from those groups. In many reported cases employers simply turned away foreign-sounding or foreign-looking job seekers without bothering to request documentation.

Congress's reaction was to consider a number of bills to establish a government-issued ID card that could not be faked. The proposal that came closest to enactment would have established an ID card/driver's license pilot program based on the SSN and biometric identification such as fingerprints. Only strenuous opposition from civil rights and immigrants' rights groups prevented the proposal from becoming part of the Immigration Act of 1990. Once again, a useless "quick fix" almost became the law of the land. Any system based on SSNs or driver's licenses will not accomplish its goal because of the ease with which both of the cards can be forged and the impossibility of ascertaining that a person presenting a social security card actually is the person named on it. The very real problem employers have in making certain they are obeying the law by identifying and refusing to hire illegal immigrants remains to be solved.

When the Social Security system was begun, no evidence of identity, age, or citizenship was required. That has changed. New and replacement cards now are issued on paper that is resistant to counterfeiting and tampering. Of the over 210 million SSNs in use today, however, about 75 percent were issued before the new regulations were enacted. Only 76 million tamper-resistant cards have been issued, and in 1987 the Department of Health and Human Services and the Social Security Administration sent Congress a report saying that it would be prohibitively expensive to replace all the earlier cards with tamper-proof cards containing photographs and signatures. The U.S. comptroller general has estimated the cost at between $850 million and $2 billion, not including costs for labor and purging of old records. But it is precisely the masses of these older cards that are easiest to alter or forge. Anyone walking up New

York City's 42nd Street will see stores offering faked cards for sale. And it is highly questionable whether modern technology, accessible to laypeople as well as government, makes a truly tamper-resistant card possible. Because computerized records require data entry, human error is an additional problem. The SSA acknowledges the problem by recommending that Americans and foreign workers with SSNs request a copy of their file every few years to make certain that their record is correct. Privacy expert Philip L. Bereano estimates the SSA's error rate to be ten percent. The rate of errors made by the Immigration and Naturalization Service (INS), likely to be charged with identifying legal immigrant workers under various pending bills establishing national data banks to minimize illegal immigration, is seventeen percent.

Numerous agencies and commissions, including the Department of Health, Education and Welfare, the United States Privacy Protection Study Commission, the United States Commission on Civil Rights, and the Select Commission on Immigration and Refugee Policy, have concluded that the only way to create a secure identification document, whether to establish employment eligibility or for any other purpose, would be to maintain a national population registry. The list would create a lifelong dossier for every American, and Congress has resisted the idea.

Some individuals also have fought against the use of SSNs as universal identifiers. Marc A. Greidinger, an attorney, moved to the small Virginia town of Falmouth in 1991 and began working on the staff of the U.S. Court of Appeals in Richmond. He soon discovered that it was virtually impossible to get a state driver's license, open utility accounts, or rent a video without being asked for his SSN. When Virginia officials told him he could not register to vote without providing his SSN, he said, "I had had it." He arranged a test in which he gave a friend his SSN and discovered the friend could use it to get Greidinger's university transcripts and access information about Greidinger's bank loans by telephone. He then discovered that Virginia sells its database of voter information and permits public access to registration applications, so that anyone could get a voter's SSN.

Suing Virginia in *Greidinger* v. *Davis* to have the voter requirement overturned, Greidinger argued that the voter registration application violated the section of the 1974 Privacy Act that requires government agencies to disclose their authority to ask for the SSN, inform individuals whether the request is mandatory, and specify how the SSN will be used. The Fourth Circuit Court of Appeals agreed. In 1993, it held that other data such as voter registration numbers or addresses would provide the state with enough information to distinguish voters with the same name and, citing the common criminal use of SSNs, ordered the state either to stop requiring the numbers as a condition of voting or find a way to keep them confidential. "Armed with one's SSN, an unscrupulous individual could obtain a person's welfare benefits or Social Security benefits, order new checks at a new address on that person's checking account, obtain credit cards, or even obtain the person's paycheck," the court warned. "Succinctly stated, the harm that can be inflicted from the disclosure of an SSN to an unscrupulous individual is alarming and potentially financially ruinous."

President Bill Clinton, however, was thinking along quite different lines. During the same year as the *Greidinger* decision, the president proposed that all Americans be given yet another number—one that could just as easily be misused as a national identifier. His proposed national health care plan included creation of a National Health Board that would establish "national, unique identifier numbers" for all Americans. The identity card would guarantee that an individual who moved or changed jobs would have no difficulty receiving health care, for its number would be "captured, retained, and transmitted" each time its user saw a doctor, got a prescription, or went to the hospital. The computer system would be governed by "national standards," but considering the fate of the SSN, it is worrisome to contemplate the existence of an additional data bank that would reveal if an individual ever tested positive for drugs or HIV, had an abortion, contracted a venereal disease, became addicted to a medication, or had any other medical problem that one might well want to keep private. The sample card President Clinton displayed to the press in 1993 was a "smart card": one that contains computer chips capable of holding the equivalent of thirty pages of personal information as well as fingerprints, a picture of the bearer's face, and even a recording of his or her voice. (This contrasts with the magnetic strip used on most credit cards, which holds about half a page of data.) The other option available to Clinton would be an optical card, which can hold up to 2,000 pages of data. As usual, the argument was that the card would prevent fraud, although administration officials were unable to explain either how fraudulent use of the cards would be prevented or how the system would ensure the privacy of patients.

At about the same time that Clinton displayed his model smart card, the Pentagon disclosed that it was considering replacing the traditional dog tags worn by soldiers with its own smart cards that could include medical information as well as family and service data. But a spokesperson for the secretary of defense said the Pentagon was worried about security: "To send something like that with a pilot who may have to bail out over Baghdad would be a mistake." To make a patient carry a health care card that could tell a dental assistant that a patient had AIDS, leading the assistant to refuse to help perform needed oral surgery, or that would disclose a woman's history of abortions to the admissions clerk of a Catholic hospital, might also be a mistake. Again, the conundrum arises about how to control personal information, guarantee its accuracy, and ensure that it is used only for the purposes for which is was collected. Prevention of Medicaid fraud was the justification for passage of a law, effective as of January 1996, requiring all workers to give to their employers the SSNs for everyone in their households.

We have discussed the Immigration Reform and Control Act of 1986. The desire to control immigration became a major item on the political agenda in the 1990s, and in his 1993 State of the Union address President Clinton endorsed a recommendation by the Commission on Immigration Reform for a national registry of all citizens and resident aliens. A database of all employees would be created, based on SSNs, that employers would be required to check before hiring so as not to hire illegal immigrants. Senator Alan Simpson promptly introduced a bill to implement the registry. Senator Barbara Boxer told *USA Today* that such a system might be the only way to provide accurate citizenship information. Representative Ken Calvert proposed a Social Security Account Number Anti-Fraud Act that would require the secretary of Health and Human Services to set up a system by which employers could verify their workers' social security information, and that would require employers to use the system. Representative Anthony Beilenson suggested a law for issuance of new social security cards, containing fingerprints and a photograph, that employers would have to see before hiring a worker. The proposed 1995 immigration bill would have required employers to call a toll-free number to verify the validity of an SSN presented by any job applicant. If only one percent of the information in the SSN database was wrong, the result would be disqualification of 650,000 people for jobs they might otherwise obtain. In May 1996 President Clinton announced expansion of a pilot program that requires employers to verify the legal status of job seekers by referring to a computerized data bank. The program, already in use for close to a year in two Southern California counties, had been adopted under an agreement between the INS and the nation's four largest meatpacking companies. The companies employed 80 percent of the industry's 70,000 employees and were introducing the system at 41 plants in 12 western and midwestern states.

Because the nation will undoubtedly hear future proposals for similar national identifiers, it is worth recounting the objections of civil libertarians and privacy experts. Scott Hodge of the Heritage Foundation reported that when Attorney General William French Smith proposed an identity card to an enthusiastic meeting of the Reagan cabinet in 1981, Martin Anderson, assistant to the president for policy development, spoke up. Anderson said sardonically that he had a better suggestion. "It's a lot cheaper. It can't be counterfeited. It's very lightweight, and impossible to lose. . . . All we have to do is tattoo an identification number on the inside of everybody's arm." The identity card idea was dropped.

The Commission on Immigration Reform's 1995 proposal was for a database and identification registry based on the records of the INS and the SSA, two seemingly obvious sources of correct, comprehensive information. But Lucas Guttentag, director of the American Civil Liberties Union (ACLU) Immigrants' Rights Project, reported that in Los Angeles:

> The INS routinely denies employment authorization to eligible asylum applicants because their names are missing from the INS computer file. A high-ranking INS official recently admitted that over 60,000 files had been "lost out in space" and never entered into the system. . . .In 1991 we obtained copies of INS computer discs created to identify and track 50,000 people covered by the settlement of a lawsuit. Our computer expert explained in a sworn statement that the data were virtually useless because of rampant errors that rendered a search by name or "alien number" impossible.

The ACLU learned in 1994 "that in the course of entering data on 89,000 cases in its Green Card Replacement Program, the Service had failed to distinguish between people who paid the $70 fee and those who did not."

The specter of reliance on erroneous files is particularly frightening when people's jobs and ability to leave and return to the United States are at stake. What's more, as ACLU Executive Director

Ira Glasser stated, "It is impossible to design a central database that is both easily accessible and, at the same time, limited to authorized persons and purposes. No computer system is fail-safe." This presumably is true of the system to be used under the 1996 welfare law, which, in an attempt to collect child support, requires employers to report all new hires and wage information to federal and state databases. Information meant only for government would soon get into private hands, as was seen above and as will be explored further in the next chapter.

NATIONAL IDENTITY CARDS IN OTHER COUNTRIES

The argument sometimes is heard that other countries have the equivalent of SSNs or another kind of national identification card. The fact that "other countries do it" is scarcely an answer to the question of what effect such a card would have on the privacy of Americans, who are rightly proud that they enjoy liberties and rights to a degree unmatched by most other countries. But the argument is not entirely valid in any event, because it is based on incomplete information. Most democratic societies with an ID system limit their use and maintain only decentralized number systems and decentralized data banks. This is the case in France and Germany, for example, which have resisted proposals for centralization of their systems, stating that centralization would constitute a danger to the liberty and autonomy of individuals. Germany administers its ID cards at the local rather than the national level and does not require citizens to carry them. Cards may not include fingerprints or coded serial numbers based on any personal information about the holder. Similarly, French ID cards can be obtained at 40,000 different locations unconnected by a national database. The one national database that does exist in France, for reporting stolen or lost cards, is accessible only to local authorities and police, and only when they are issuing new cards. Countries such as Denmark, Greece, Luxembourg, Norway, Spain, and Sweden, all of which use a national identifier for public and private purposes, also have a data protection agency or protective legislation or both.

Even so, concerns about the potential misuse of such information have been expressed in these countries. Canada is one such example. Since 1964, Canada has had a social insurance number

(SIN) system intended to register Canadians for the unemployment insurance program. Use of the SIN for other purposes grew so quickly by the 1980s that the Canadian privacy commissioner stated it had become a national identifier, adding that "You cannot do anything in Canada without it. You cannot cash a check without being asked the number." In 1986, tax records of 16 million Canadians, complete with SINs, were stolen from the Toronto taxation office. Because of this incident, which the privacy commissioner called "a Chernobyl for data protection," and similar events, Canada began limiting use of the SIN. In 1988 the government restricted its own use of SIN and implemented procedures for reviewing existing uses of it by the federal government. "This measure marks the first step by the government towards its commitment to cap unnecessary collection and use of SIN," commented the president of the Canadian Treasury Board. "Many Canadians feel threatened by the use of the social insurance number as a universal identifier." In other words, countries with a national identifier have localized or are attempting to minimize its use because of privacy concerns. And some, like Canada, have a state privacy commissioner whose office is charged with eliminating unjustifiable violations of privacy—an important example for the United States.

SSNs: The Debate Today

The lesson contained in the United States' own history, specifically that of the Social Security number, is that large-scale information systems may be created for a limited purpose, but they inevitably take on a life of their own that goes beyond the original objective. Few users seem able to resist the temptation to apply a cohesive body of information to additional purposes. And yet the mid-1990s may have seen the beginning of a trend toward court protection of SSNs. The *Greidinger* decision was discussed earlier. The Ohio Supreme Court case also mentioned, decided in October 1994, denied the Akron *Beacon Journal's* request for access to all of the city of Akron's 1990 and 1991 computerized employee files (*State ex rel. Beacon Journal Publishing Co.* v. *Akron*). The information in the files included not only the approximately 2,500 employees' names, addresses, telephone numbers, birth dates, education, employment statuses and positions, pay rates, service ratings, annual and sick leave information, overtime hours and pay, and year-to-date employee earnings, but their SSNs as well. The city provided the records to the newspaper, but deleted the SSNs on privacy grounds. The growing number and role of public advocacy groups in the privacy area were indicated by the submission to the court of a friend-of-the-court brief written by the Public Citizen Litigation Group and the Electronic Privacy Information Center (EPIC) on behalf of Computer Professionals for Social Responsibility, highlighting the privacy implications of SSN disclosures. EPIC had submitted a similar brief in the *Greidinger* case.

The court decided that SSNs were not the kind of "public records" referred to in the Ohio Public Records Act. The statute defined "public records" to exclude those "the release of which is prohibited by state or federal law," and the court held that disclosure of SSNs would violate the federal constitutional right to privacy. The judges relied on *Nixon* v. *Administrator of General Services,* in which former President Richard Nixon sought to prevent the General Services Administration from taking custody of an estimated 42 million pages of documents and 880 tape recordings generated during his presidency. The U.S. Supreme Court found in that case that all individuals, including government officials, have a "legitimate expectation of privacy in [their] personal communications," which the Ohio court rephrased as "a federal right to privacy which protects against governmental disclosure of the private details of one's life." As the individual's right to privacy was not absolute, it had to be balanced against the government's interest in disclosure.

Section 7 of the Privacy Act of 1974, the section that requires any government agency requesting an SSN to inform the individual of the use that would be made of the information, was passed, said the court, to "codify. . .the societal perception that SSNs should not be available to all" and it creates an "expectation of privacy" among city employees concerning their SSNs. The court stated:

> The city's refusal to release its employees' SSNs does not significantly interfere with the public's right to monitor governmental conduct. The numbers by themselves reveal little information about the city's employees. . .[but] the release of the numbers could allow an inquirer to discover the intimate, personal details of each city employee's life, which are completely irrelevant to the operations of government. As the *Greidinger* court warned, a person's SSN is a device which can quickly be used by the unscrupulous to acquire a tremendous amount of information about a person.

The court quoted its own horror story about misuse of an SSN, the tale of an Akron city employee named James E. Young whose SSN had been released once before and who had protested its possible release to the *Beacon Journal.*

> Young testified that, in 1989, he and a friend were attempting to purchase a rental property. Young was informed that he would be denied credit partly because of delinquent accounts with retail credit institutions.

Young found out why this happened when he was contacted by the ex-wife of another James E. Young, whom the court referred to as "Young 2." Young 2, the woman reported, obtained Young's SSN when Young 2 requested his own transcript from the University of Akron. The university had mistakenly sent Young 2 the transcript of Young, complete with Young's SSN. Young 2 used Young's SSN to open accounts with Firestone, Texaco, Associate Finance, and a department store in Richmond, Virginia. Young 2 had used the accounts and then not paid the bills. It cost Young almost $800 in attorney fees to clear his credit record. The court considered "the ability of a pretender using an SSN to assume another's identity" to be "perhaps the ultimate invasion of one's privacy."

"Thanks to the abundance of data bases in the private sector that include the SSNs of persons listed in their files," the court continued, "an intruder using an SSN can quietly discover the intimate details of a victim's personal life without the victim ever knowing of the intrusion." The court therefore found that "the high potential for fraud and victimization caused by the unchecked release of city employee SSNs outweighs the minimal information about governmental processes gained through the release of the SSNs."

The American public appears to agree. Its concern about privacy has been growing steadily since pollster Lou Harris began doing annual privacy surveys in 1970. A third of the Americans surveyed in that year were worried about invasions of their privacy. By 1979, those saying they were either "very concerned" or "concerned" about privacy had almost doubled, to 64 percent. The Harris survey taken in 1983 concluded that "the pervasiveness of support for tough new ground rules governing computers and other information technology" was "particularly striking." "Americans are not willing to endure abuse or misuse of information," the report continued, "and they overwhelmingly support action to do something about it.

This support permeates all subgroups in society and represents a mandate for initiatives in public policy." The survey showed that 48 percent of the public described itself as *"very* concerned" about the threats to personal privacy implicit in technology, double the number reporting such feelings in 1978. A majority of the respondents agreed that the release of personal information by government agencies to other agencies seriously invades personal privacy, and 60 percent believed the use of computers should be severely limited to safeguard privacy. The 1990 poll found that if the Declaration of Independence were to be rewritten, 79 percent of the American people would add "privacy" to "life, liberty, and the pursuit of happiness" as a fundamental right. In 1992, 78 percent of those polled expressed privacy concerns; by 1993, the number had gone to 83 percent: 53 percent said they were "very concerned" and 30 percent described themselves as "concerned." The five percentage point increase in that one year was the highest ever recorded in the history of the poll; two years later, 84 percent expressed concern. The Equifax-Harris Mid-Decade Consumer Privacy Survey published in late 1995 reported that 80 percent of Americans believed they already had lost all control over personal information.

The legitimacy of the fear that information collected by the government might be used for purposes other than that for which it initially was intended has been demonstrated repeatedly. One of the more glaring examples occurred during World War II, when Japanese American citizens were summarily removed from their West Coast homes and imprisoned in "relocation centers" because the Army feared that they might become a "fifth column" for Japan— although no evidence of such activity was ever found, nor were Japanese Americans given individual hearings. They were rounded up through the use of Census Bureau information, which supposedly was confidential and to be utilized only by the bureau. Similarly, during the Vietnam War, the FBI operated a "Stop Index" to track and monitor the activities of people opposed to the United States' involvement in the war, even though there was no indication that most of the individuals monitored in this way were engaged in any illegal activities. The index was based on the FBI's computerized National Crime Information Center, which again contains information that supposedly is held in confidence and used only for law enforcement purposes. The FBI in fact currently shares its criminal history records system with many non–law enforcement agencies, including many private sector employers. So do other governmental agencies. Congress discovered that in the late 1960s and early 1970s President Richard Nixon had used Internal Revenue Service documents and other supposedly confidential government records to compile information about political opponents.

It is not only the government that may misuse information it gathers through such devices as SSNs. As we will see, private use of SSNs and of the information with which they can be linked is even more pervasive, and a major threat to the privacy of most Americans.

Chapter Four

———

THE RECORDS OF ONE'S LIFE

My name in the London telephone directory or the electoral roll is perfectly harmless, but my name in a list of potential subversives or bad credit risks is capable of doing me harm . . . . It is what data you string together and what you do with them . . . which may or may not do harm.

—Paul Sieghart, "Information Privacy and the Data Protection Bill"

C. L. Smith moved to Spokane, Washington, in 1987. As someone who had always paid his bills on time, Smith expected to have no problem when he applied for a loan two years later. But he received no loan and, sending for his credit report, discovered that it contained multiple accounts with delinquent balances all over the United States. Also in his files were inquiries from 40 different companies. All dated from 1988 and 1989, when someone using a post office box in Texas and Smith's social security number had run up debts. Smith immediately contacted the state's attorney general, whose office was of no help. The office of the Federal Trade Commission in Seattle replied to his plea by sending him brochures. Credit Bureau, Inc., and TRW told him that he had been victimized by what they called a "credit doctor," but they did nothing about it. An attorney eventually advised Smith, "If I was you, I'd go to court and change my name and Social Security number and start from scratch." "This," Smith said, "is a nightmare."

The decades since World War II have witnessed an explosive growth in electronic technology, including the ability to create massive data banks, as well as the conversion of the United States into a credit card society. Scholar Colin J. Bennett has noted that information is "the currency of the postindustrial society": a resource in the same way steel and fossil fuels were a resource in industrial societies. Computers enable more and more transactions to be recorded and make it possible for information to be kept longer, to be given to more people and institutions, to be highly accessible, and combined and analyzed so as to yield data not contained in any one piece of information. The processing of information occupies approximately half of today's workforce.

Private companies quite logically want to use the wealth of easily accessible information in order to make their operations more efficient. Individuals are delighted at innovations like credit cards, bank machines that provide cash twenty-four hours a day, and telephones that can do such things as enable people in different cities or even countries to conduct conference calls. Everyone seems to benefit. But as privacy scholar Arthur Miller told Congress in 1971:

> Whenever an American travels on a commercial airline, reserves a room at one of the national hotel chains, rents a car, he is likely to leave distinctive electronic tracks in the memory of a computer that can tell a great deal about his activities, movements, habits and associations. Unfortunately, few people seem to appreciate the fact that modern technology is capable of monitoring, centralizing, and evaluating these electronic entries, no matter how numerous they may be, making credible the fear that many Americans have of a womb-to-tomb dossier on each of us.

"A womb-to-tomb dossier": that is the problem. Personal papers once stored in our homes are held today in easily accessible computerized form by people with whom we do business. Video rental stores and cable television companies keep information about the movies and programs we see. Libraries have files indicating which books we read. Banks retain records of the people, stores, service companies, and organizations to which we send checks.

This is the age of information, based on our turning over an enormous amount and variety of personal information in exchange for doing business with others. Companies make electronic disclosures to people and agencies such as mortgage brokers, car dealers, and employers so routinely today, the *Wall Street Journal* has reported, that many employers regularly use the companies' records to check the credit reports of prospective employees. As always, a plausible reason is given for the invasion of privacy. Employers are only attempting to protect themselves on the theory that someone with a bad credit rating may steal, sell company secrets, or behave irresponsibly at work.

One might ask why people who have done nothing wrong would be worried about the accumulation and availability of information about them. Leaving aside for the moment the question of the accuracy of the employers' assumptions and of the data they get from credit agencies, the answer goes back to the notion of personal autonomy and control. Retention of the power to decide what information to divulge, to whom, and for what purposes is crucial to an individual's sense of self. The books we choose, the movies we watch at home, and the organizations we support reveal a great deal about our personalities and politics. It seems reasonable for us to want to control the amount of information about these highly personal and sensitive aspects of ourselves that is available to the public. A few months of counseling by a psychiatrist, an arrest record for a crime we did not commit or one that we did commit when young, a less-than-honorable military discharge, previous negative decisions by insurance companies—all may be incidents of our lives that have no implications for anything we are or are not doing now but that, aware of society's attitudes, we may well want to keep private.

THE NOT-SO-PRIVATE USE OF PRIVATE FINANCIAL INFORMATION

A Lou Harris poll taken in June 1990 reported that three out of four Americans thought that consumers in the computer age had lost control over information about themselves and were more worried about its use by private businesses than by the police, the FBI, or the IRS. The convenience of credit cards clearly poses a trade-off. The requirement that credit card companies list individual purchases on consumers' bills protects the consumers but also makes more centralized information available. More than a decade earlier, as the government's 1977 report *Personal Privacy in an Information Society* stated, there was an "overwhelming imbalance in the record-keeping relationship between an individual and an organization."

The imbalance has increased since. Individuals do not know what information is being kept about them, whether the information is accurate, and to what purposes it is being put.

This was not always the case.

THE HISTORY OF CREDIT CARDS IN THE UNITED STATES

The concept of credit dates back at least to the code of Hammurabi, around 1750 B.C., and the extension of credit has a long history in societies dependent upon monetary exchange rather than barter. But credit cards did not exist in the early United States any more than the plastic upon which they are printed. There was some use of cards after the Civil War, as continuing expansion of the frontier and industrialization led Americans to become even more likely than before to change their dwelling place and to rely upon credit provided by merchants and banks. After World War I, credit cards came into usage for newly available large household items such as washing machines and vacuum cleaners and for automobiles. Card use declined during the Depression, when consumers lacked money, but began growing once again after World War II.

The post–World War I cards were issued by a relatively small number of hotels, oil companies, and department stores. Some retailers had given cards as early as 1914 to their wealthier customers. By 1928 retailers were issuing "charga-plates"; twenty years later, a group of New York City department stores would form a cooperative charga-plate system. Before World War II, however, growth in credit cards took place mainly in the gas and oil industries, which the airline companies soon emulated. In 1936 American Airlines issued a coupon book that it later converted into a credit card. Other airlines followed suit. So did the Universal Air Travel Plan, which in the late 1930s offered a card that could be used on airlines such as American, United, TWA, and Eastern.

The phenomenon of the nontransportation credit card leaped forward in 1949, when the Diners Club created a multipurpose card used primarily by salesmen for on-the-road expenses or for charging meals with clients. The club charged the merchants for whom its card provided customers and the customers to whom it extended credit. Simultaneously, computers, which had been developed with great secrecy during World War II to break enemy codes, were becoming more available and cheaper. Computers would prove crucial to the continued growth of credit cards and credit reporting companies.

The Hilton Hotel Corporation entered the field in 1958 with Carte Blanche, which had been its private credit card. So did American Express as well as the Bank of America and Chase Manhattan, the country's two largest banks. Bank of America went further in 1966 by licensing its new BankAmericard and by joining several other large banks in creating a national card system called InterbankCard Association. By the 1960s BankAmericard and Interbank were enrolling millions of Americans and soon began signing up additional banks as well. Eleven thousand banks quickly joined one or both of the networks. In 1978, the 52 million Americans who held at least two bank credit cards charged $44 million. The automatic teller machine (ATM), able to dispense cash and make deposits and transfers between accounts, was invented in 1965. A number of airlines decided to promote their own cards in the 1960s, with United pushing hard for college students and TWA turning its airline card into one that could be used for travel and entertainment.

The Federal Trade Commission, becoming concerned about the large number of lost or stolen cards and by billing errors made by the relatively primitive record-keeping systems, banned mailings of unsolicited credit cards in 1970. Congress enacted the 1970 Fair Credit Reporting Act (FCRA) which, in the words of the act, was designed to ensure that credit reporting companies would "exercise their grave responsibilities with fairness, impartiality, and a respect for the consumer's right to privacy." The act prohibits credit and investigation reporting agencies that collect, store, and sell information on consumers' credit-worthiness from disclosing records to anyone other than authorized customers. It also gives individuals the right to ascertain the "nature and substance" of the information that consumer reporting agencies hold about them. Each company is permitted to charge a fee for fulfilling an individual's request unless it is made within thirty days of the person's receiving an adverse credit decision based on the company's report. The company is under no obligation to give individuals any medical information in their files.

Arthur Miller, the privacy scholar who helped draft the act, later stated that although the preamble of the early Senate version called it a law "to enable consumers to protect themselves against arbitrary, erroneous, and malicious credit information," the act as passed might more accurately be labeled "an act to protect credit bureaus against citizens who have been abused by erroneous credit and investigative information." The purposes of consumer reports are defined so broadly that the reports are open to "market researchers, detective agencies, lawyers, and various investigative groups." The House Armed Service Subcommittee on Investigations reported in 1988 that "hostile intelligence agencies" were using private credit bureaus to find out which individuals with access to government secrets might be having financial problems, and warned that the ineffectiveness of credit privacy safeguards was jeopardizing national security.

Companies need adopt only "reasonable procedures" to assure the accuracy of their information. There is no requirement for them periodically to audit and purge their records, to separate arrest records resulting in acquittal from those resulting in conviction or to differentiate between those for minor offenses and those for serious crimes, to verify the accuracy of records before they are disclosed to third parties, or to change their records if an individual does find out that his or her files contain errors. Someone who discovers inaccuracies is permitted to give an explanatory note to the company, but all the company must do is add the note to the individual's file and tell subscribers that such a note exists. There is no obligation for the company to disclose the contents of the note, with the individual's version of the information, unless the subscriber specifically requests it. The act effectively immunizes credit bureaus from prosecution for negligently passing on erroneous information in their files.

The files are of course arranged according to social security numbers. And when the contents are disclosed, as will be seen below, they may contain rather substantial and unpleasant surprises.

The credit card business continued to grow in the years after passage of the act. BankAmericard formally changed its name to Visa in 1976 and Master Charge became MasterCard in 1980. In 1981, 12,504 banks issued MasterCards and 12,518 handed out Visa cards. And the American Express credit card system had more than twelve times as many customers as the two bank systems combined.

American Express would soon grow larger. Retail stores issued even more cards in the 1980s than did the banks, with Sears alone distributing more cards in 1981 than MasterCard and Visa combined. American Express gambled on customers' preferring to use one card only and entered into agreements with so many of the nation's department stores that by the end of the 1980s the American Express card could be used in 75 percent of them.

Other kinds of cards proliferated. In the 1970s and 1980s banks formed nationwide networks of ATMs, which gained rapid customer approval. There were 2,500 ATMs in 1974; 6,000 in 1977; six nationwide ATM networks in 1982; 81,681 ATMs in 1988. In 1986 more than 55 percent of all families in the United States had a bank card from one of the 90 percent of all banks participating in such plans, primarily Visa or MasterCard. Three years later Visa made its card usable for telephone calls.

Massive use of cards led to massive numbers of mistakes, particularly by the huge credit card bureaus that came into existence to keep track of individuals' credit ratings. Lists include information such as age, income, marital status, and place of residence. They are compiled and sold without the consent of the individuals involved—in fact, the individuals do not know that the procedure has taken place. The former chairperson of the Privacy Protection Study Commission has stated that one-third of those consumers who do examine their files find mistakes. *Time* magazine reported that a study by a New Jersey credit bureau in 1990 discovered that the three largest credit reporting companies had one or more errors concerning forty percent of the 150 million people in their files. One person's credit information all too frequently is intermixed with that of another person with a similar name, a phenomenon that sometimes results in the first person having an undeserved bad credit report. Numerous newspaper stories have described people who have been denied jobs, insurance, credit, or housing and not known why, discovering only too late that they were the victims of inaccurate records. TRW admitted in 1991 that glitches in its system had led to residents of four New England states being misbranded as "deadbeats." The clear implication is that other people who are being mislabeled never find out that such credit inaccuracies were the source of their problem. Most people have no idea that they have a right to their credit dossiers, assuming that they know such files exist. Even if they learn of errors in their files, they usually do so because of an adverse decision by a credit agency or prospective employer, and by then the damage has been done.

It was problems such as these that led Senate subcommittees to hold hearings in 1973, 1975, 1980, and 1991, and conclude, as did the Federal Trade Commission, that the act needed to be amended and strengthened. The revisions have not been made because of vigorous opposition from the credit reporting industry.

In some cases, states have successfully filled the legal gap. After TRW and other credit data collection agencies promised New York State to send each consumer one free credit report a year but failed to resolve inaccuracies in such reports promptly, the attorney general of the state sued the company. A settlement with TRW was reached in 1991 and with Equifax and TransUnion the following year; eventually, seventeen or eighteen other state task forces wrested similar agreements from the credit data collection companies, and in February 1995 a consent decree was signed by Equifax and the Federal Trade Commission. The FTC had alleged that Equifax violated the Fair Credit Reporting Act by failing to ensure "the maximum possible accuracy" of the consumer information it compiled and sold to employers and creditors around the country. The "failure" consisted of not checking into the facts of the case when subjects disagreed with their credit records and of not applying adequate controls over the release of information.

The FCRA permits credit reporting companies to give information about a consumer to anyone who the company "has reason to believe" intends to use the information for a "permissible purpose." Permissible purposes include extending credit, hiring, and issuing a license. In addition, information can be given to anyone with a "legitimate business need for the information in connection with a business transaction involving the consumer," normally meaning credit grantors, loan granting institutions, employers, and landlords.

"Legitimate" is a word that can be interpreted many ways, and it is unclear that credit rating agencies are providing adequate training to their employees. In 1995 the Privacy Clearinghouse reported the story of a young California woman who was surprised to discover how much her fiance's family knew about her finances. Much of the information could have come only from her credit report. She ordered a copy of her report and discovered that an inquiry about her had been made by a small credit bureau in the home state of her fiance's parents. When she contacted the credit bureau to ask who had made the inquiry, she was told there was no record of the transaction. Enacting privacy protection legislation is only part of the solution; implementation and monitoring are equally important.

Some legislation has been relatively successful in controlling private use of the records of one's life; some has not. The Family

Educational Rights and Privacy Act of 1974 (popularly known as the Buckley Amendment), for example, limits disclosure of educational records to third parties and requires schools and colleges to grant students access to their records. Many high school and college students know about the Buckley Amendment because of its requirement that students be told they do not have to waive their right of access to letters of recommendation.

This act appears to have worked well. Widespread computerization of student records since it was passed, however, raises the question whether tougher laws are needed to protect student privacy today. Washington State, for example, has a system that electronically tracks high school graduates from 36 school districts into college, the military, and the workplace, using the ubiquitous SSNs as identifiers. No individual consent is required, and no law specifies to whom the information might be given. At one point the system was drawn upon by the Kennewick, Washington, school district to forward behavioral information about 4,000 children to a psychiatric care center. The center had contracted with the district to screen for "at-risk" students it might be able to help. The students' parents had no knowledge that the information was being distributed. Washington also maintains a database of four-year-olds who are "at risk," an assessment which may or may not be correct but which can follow students for the rest of their lives. The U.S. Department of Education's National Center for Education Statistics has created a model student-record database with questions covering matters from the date of a student's last dental exam, through the telephone number of the student's E-mail provider, to post–high school employment and voter registration information. A national system called SPEEDE/ExPRESS will enable this information to be transferred electronically as students move from one district or state to another.

The Washington situation demonstrates that a successful law may solve one problem, but that related issues will develop and require constant monitoring. The Right to Financial Privacy Act enacted four years after the Buckley Amendment is an example of a law that has been less successful.

The Bank Secrecy Act of 1953 requires banks to maintain microfilm copies of checks for between two and six years. In 1970 Congress added the Currency and Foreign Transactions Reporting Act. Under it, banks must retain account statements and microfilms of checks of $100 or over for five years and give authorities virtually unlimited access to them. The stated reasons were a concern over use of secret foreign bank accounts to evade American laws and an attempt to help law enforcement and regulatory and tax-administration authorities track and punish money laundering. The process of selecting out checks over $99 proved so expensive, however, that most banks eventually decided to microfilm all checks.

Banks did challenge the Secrecy Act through the courts but lost in 1974, when the Supreme Court held that the record-keeping requirements did not impose unduly heavy burdens on banks (*California Bankers Association v. Schultz*). The Court also found nothing unconstitutional in government agents conducting surveillance on customers. Justice William O. Douglas, dissenting, warned of what such record keeping could lead to:

> It would be highly useful to governmental espionage to have like reports from all our bookstores, all our hardware and retail stores, all our drug-stores . . . . A mandatory recording of all telephone conversations would be better than the recording of checks under the Bank Secrecy Act, if Big Brother is to have his way . . . . In a sense a person is defined by the checks he writes. By examining them the agents get to know his doctors, lawyers, creditors, political allies, social connections, religious affiliation, educational interests, the papers and magazines he reads and so on ad infinitum. These are all tied to one's Social Security number; and now that we have the data banks, these other items will enrich that storehouse and make it possible for a bureaucrat—by pushing one button—to get in an instant the names of the 190 million Americans who are subversives or potential and likely candidates.

The Bank Secrecy Act was challenged again in the case of *United States v. Miller* (1976), involving a suspected bootlegger. A Georgia deputy sheriff had stopped a truck allegedly owned by Mr. Miller and found it to be transporting 150 five-gallon plastic jars, two 100-pound bags of wheat short, several cylinders of bottled gas, and a shotgun condenser. Less than a month later, the deputy and fire officials found a 7,500-gallon distillery and 175 gallons of untaxed whiskey while fighting a warehouse fire. The United States Treasury Department's Bureau of Alcohol, Tobacco, and Firearms, suspecting Miller of involvement in both events, presented grand jury subpoenas to the two banks where Miller maintained accounts. The banks turned over copies of his checks and bank statements to the Treasury agents without notifying Miller. In his trial for bootlegging and tax evasion,

Miller argued that the evidence obtained with the subpoenas could not be used in court because, among other reasons, the Bank Secrecy Act violated the Fourth Amendment's prohibition of unreasonable searches and seizures. On April 21, 1976, the Supreme Court held that Miller had no legitimate "expectation of privacy" in his bank records because they were the property of the bank, and that checks are an independent record of an individual's participation in the flow of commerce and cannot be considered confidential communications.

Justice William Brennan dissented, pointing out that "the totality of bank records provides a virtual current biography" and access to such records constitutes a major invasion of privacy. The 1977 Privacy Protection Study Commission report agreed, noting that electronic bank transfers "could provide a way of tracking an individual's current movements." The commission's concern was picked up by Congress which, in the Right to Financial Privacy Act of 1978, created a privacy interest in personal financial records. The act requires investigative agencies to notify individuals before releasing their records and specifies a procedure for such disclosures. But while the act forbids the federal government from going through bank account records without the consent of individuals or a warrant, it does not prohibit state agencies, local law enforcement officials, private employers, and individuals from doing so. A March 1995 article in the St. Paul, Minnesota, *Pioneer Press* disclosed that at least some banks routinely sell the names of recent depositors to investment companies.

CABLE TV RECORDS

One of the boons of cable television is that it gives viewers access to a potentially unlimited "menu" of programs. For a small fee, viewers can choose whatever programs they want, ranging from recent movies to old favorites, simply by letting their cable company know their choices. But that gives the cable companies computerized information about the viewing habits of subscribers—rather as if an outside entity could look into one's home and discover and keep track of the books and magazines one chooses to read. The privacy violation was exacerbated when cable companies began selling information about viewer habits to other companies, enabling merchants to "target" viewers for mailed or telephoned sales pitches. Responding to viewer outrage, Congress enacted the Cable Communications Policy Act of 1984, which prohibits a cable service from disclosing information about a subscriber's cable viewing habits without the individual's consent. The act requires the service to inform the subscriber of the nature and use of information collected and of any disclosures that may be made. The cable service must also provide subscribers access to whatever information is maintained about them, although it is questionable how many viewers know about or take advantage of this provision of the law.

Congress has provided further protection for people who choose to watch video programs at home. It is in fact one of the great ironies of the history of privacy in the United States that the Video Privacy Protection Act of 1988 was passed in large measure because of an invasion of privacy suffered by Judge Robert Bork. Bork's nomination to the Supreme Court sparked national debate and ultimately was turned down by the Senate because of his belief that there is no constitutional right of privacy. After Bork was nominated, a reporter from *City Paper* obtained his family's video rental list from a local store and used it in an attempt to create a profile of Bork's private character. Senator Patrick Leahy, expressing outrage, characterized the disclosure of the tapes as "an issue that goes to the deepest yearning of all Americans that we are here and we cherish our freedom and we want our freedom. We want to be left alone." A month later Representative Al McCandless proposed the Video Privacy Protection Act of 1987 to the House of Representatives, and in May 1988, Senator Leahy introduced his version of the Video and Library Privacy Protection Act of 1988 to the Senate. The 1988 Video Privacy Protection Act now prohibits video service providers from disclosing information about individuals without their consent except in limited circumstances such as the issuance of a court order, or from refusing to provide service to individuals who opt against disclosures. Customers who believe their records have been disclosed without their consent can sue for up to $4,000.

SHOPPERS' PRIVACY

In the 1990s it became fairly common for stores to offer their own credit cards entitling holders to get discounts on various merchandise.

When "swiped" through a machine, the cards not only verified the buyer's identity but also created a permanent record of the shopper's purchases. The cards, it might be argued, provide shoppers with the certainty that a store running low on a particular item will be alerted in time to restock it, and also save merchants from the time-consuming task of checking inventory manually. Nonetheless, shoppers may be surprised to learn that some of these cards contain not only their names and addresses but their ages, their SSNs, and the names of their employers, as well as information about their children, pets, and interests. The information is gleaned from the application forms originally filled out by the shoppers in order to get the cards or from the records of their purchases. Again, there seems to be an upside and a downside: the convenience of having the goods one is likely to want readily available in the store versus the danger of making supposedly private details of one's life available to strangers. Why can't the store gather the information without using customers' names? Why doesn't the store tell those solicited for cards that the information disclosed may be made available to marketers unless the customer refuses—or even better, require informed consent before it releases information about a customer to a marketer?

The same questions arise when shoppers use general credit cards and in the process produce what is known as transaction-generated information, or TGI. A credit bureau can learn from such TGI that a woman has visited a maternity shop, enrolled in parenting classes, subscribed to *American Baby,* called various 1-800 or 1-900 telephone numbers, applied for a mortgage or a loan, gone to a hospital, taken a trip, bought a car, and so on. In 1992 New York State Attorney General Robert Abrams signed an agreement with the American Express Company that required the company to inform its 26 million cardholders that such information was being compiled and sold to other companies, and to give purchasers the right to demand that their purchasing information be kept confidential. The use and sale of such information by American Express might have gone unnoticed had Abrams not been investigating TRW, and discovered that TRW was breaking down the records it obtained from American Express and selling the resultant lists to direct mailers. Eventually other states demanded similar agreements and the company entered into a consent decree with the Federal Trade Commission.

The exchange of information among huge data bank holders is relatively common. In January 1991, a Massachusetts computer consultant named Larry Seiler discovered that the Lotus Development Company was planning to join forces with Equifax in order to market "Lotus MarketPlace: Households," a CD-ROM database containing the names and purchasing habits of 120 million Americans. Seiler immediately publicized his discovery through E-mail and the two companies were inundated with over 30,000 letters of protest from around the world. The plan was dropped. Ironically, most protesters did not know that all the CD-ROM would have done was make available to small businesses information gleaned from credit card purchases that was already available to much larger companies able to afford the higher periodic fees charged by Equifax.

TRAVELING AND TELEPHONING

It appears that whenever one technological challenge to privacy is met by legislation, successfully or not, another pops up. The way that technology can be of enormous utility and yet threaten privacy became apparent once again in the early 1990s, with the creation of Intelligent Transportation Systems, or ITS.

ITS is a "smart road" system currently being organized by a private industry association known as ITS America and the United States Department of Transportation (DOT) to apply computer and communications technologies to transportation. It is also being developed in most of the world's other industrialized countries. One useful application enables roadside radio beacons at toll collection points on highways to interact with transponders attached to individual cars, deducting the cost of the toll from the driver's account without requiring her or him to stop. The savings in drivers' time and in human toll collectors' wages are obvious.

ITS already is in use by many states and, according to the *Wall Street Journal,* over sixteen of the nation's sixty-five regional toll authorities. A driver on various Florida expressways can go through the toll plazas without stopping because a radio transponder under the car's front bumper is "read" by a computer that deducts the toll from the driver's account. A similar system, using an electronic tag mounted inside the car's windshield, is in use on many New York bridges and the State Thruway. Drivers subscribing to Florida's Orlando–Orange County Expressway Authority E-Pass system get monthly detailed statements listing the time, date, and location of each toll collection. In 1997 the state of Virginia encouraged drivers on the Dulles Tollway to enroll in a transponder program that permits them to have money automatically transferred from a credit card account when their toll account begins to get low. The program provides quarterly statements at no charge, monthly statements for $2.00.

Some car rental companies have placed a chip in their cars so that drivers unable to find their destinations can use a rented cellular telephone to call the company. The company immediately activates the chip, locates the car, and gives the driver the proper instructions. The car appears on a map on the operator's computer screen, which also shows information about road rules (the speed limit, whether turns are allowed) and a "Yellow Pages" with the locations of nearby conveniences such as ATMs and 24-hour pharmacies. Planners envision cars provided with systems that would enable drivers to obtain targeted advertising. Drivers might, for example, instruct their cars to activate a digital "agent" containing a profile of their attributes and preferences along with their current or anticipated locations. A digital version of the message, "Where is a cheap family restaurant ahead on this road?" would be activated, enabling marketing organizations to respond with advertising pitches beamed directly at the drivers' onboard systems. Or, with two-way communication between car computers and the "intelligent" road, drivers could be warned about traffic congestion or told where nearby parking is available. Once again the potential danger lies in the accumulation, retention, and sale to third parties of the information received in this way. A government agency could easily use the toll mechanism or any of the other devices described to "track" a citizen's movements; a marketing organization could utilize them to compile dossiers on drivers' consumption preferences. The E-Pass reports and the Virginia quarterly statements could be used by the state or, if the information is kept insufficiently private, by marketers, private detectives, and so on.

The tension between privacy and convenience was inadvertently highlighted by an internal General Motors Newsline announcement on February 9, 1996, about the forthcoming introduction of a "new on-vehicle communications technology called OnStar—the most comprehensive and user-friendly services and communications package in the industry." Combining a cellular telephone with Global Positioning System satellite technology, OnStar would allow a driver to press the customer service button or the emergency services button on the phone. The Customer Assistance Center, locating the car's position on a digital map, would dispatch either a nearby "service provider" or "emergency services provider." Should the driver lock the keys in the car, a call to a toll-free number would elicit a command from the Customer Assistance Center instructing the car to unlock itself. No information was included in the announcement about any method of deactivating the Global Positioning System's tracking of the car.

The privacy threat, in other words, does not lie in the technology but in its application. Automatic toll systems have been offered initially on a voluntary basis. They will become mandatory as a practical matter, however, as numerous freeways and interstates are converted to automated toll roads. The cards can also be used for additional purposes. New Jersey began testing a "Smart Card" driver's license in 1996 containing a computer chip holding standard license information. The state planned to issue such cards to all New Jersey drivers in July 1997. By then, the chips would enable licensees to pay not only tolls but bus and train fares with the cards, which also would carry each person's fingerprints. In its third stage, the card would be programmed to contain arrest records, medical records, and vehicle registration, as well as to serve as a charge card at banks and stores. People must use roads not only to reach their workplaces and to visit family and friends but also, as a *New York Times* reporter noted in 1995, to participate in the full range of educational, political, social, religious, labor, charitable, and other associations that are a key component of a free society. What happens to this freedom if roads are turned into surveillance zones?

Once again, there is an alternative that provides the efficiency of automatic toll collection without invading privacy. The system in the Netherlands, for example, records only how many "units" of tolls a driver has spent, not where he or she has used them.

Another device was put into use in Southern California in the early 1990s. Faster traffic flow was given as the initial reason for experimenting with highway video cameras, which were expected to identify the causes of traffic jams. But the cameras quickly began to be used for other purposes. In 1995 it was announced that the Blue Line, a light-rail system connecting Los Angeles and Long Beach, would soon have cameras to detect impatient motorists who circumvented lowered gates at grade crossings. And the state Office of Traffic Safety stated that it was concerned about "a growing problem with commuters eating, reading, changing clothes, brushing their teeth, and generally paying less than full attention to the road," a very real safety matter. The office said it had no current plans to monitor these activities with its cameras, but the question of how much privacy drivers and passengers could expect was implicit in the state's concern. Information collected by the bulletproof cameras is transmitted to a centralized observation center in downtown Los Angeles. The draft ITS principles contained no restrictions on individually identifiable information or on the powers of access to ITS travel information that individual states could confer upon local police. It placed only very loose restrictions on secondary uses of the information by marketers—and these restrictions were merely recommendations that lack the force of law.

CALLER ID AND TELEPHONIC PRIVACY

Yet another example of new technology offering benefits and dangers surfaced in the 1990s when telephone companies began to market Caller ID as well as Automatic Number Identification (ANI) to customers. The Caller ID system works by attaching a small device to a telephone, enabling the person called to see the number of an incoming call's source as the phone is ringing. Some telephone companies initially offered Caller ID along with "blocking," which enables a caller to "block" the person being called from seeing the caller's number; others did not. A debate began to rage about whether it was too great an invasion of privacy to offer Caller ID without blocking. A Lou Harris survey, *Consumers in the Information Age,* showed that forty-eight percent of the American people believed Caller ID should be permitted only if blocking was available; twenty-three percent thought it should be available without limitations; twenty-seven percent believed Caller ID should be prohibited by law.

There are persuasive arguments for Caller ID. Businesses use it in order to gather information about people who call them. This knowledge, they say, makes them more efficient in bringing up files when a customer calls and creating and linking databases for marketing purposes. Law enforcement officials assert that Caller ID gives them the capacity to locate people in danger as well as people using the telephone for such illegal purposes as obscene or harassing calls. The possible advantage to individuals was explained by a woman during a 1995 discussion on an E-mail "bulletin board." If the device showed the number of someone who was unimportant to her right then or who had made earlier harassing calls she could ignore the phone and go on with her dinner preparations. She likened the system to her ability, when someone rang her doorbell, to "look through the window to see who's there and choose to answer or not." And users of cellular telephones, who are charged for each call they accept, can save the cost of unwanted calls.

Why, then, did New York Public Service Commissioner Eli Noam state that the marketing of unrestricted Caller ID represented a "technocratic disregard for privacy"?

Noam and others were concerned that the automatic display of one's telephone number could create life-threatening situations when, for example, a call was made to or from a battered women's shelter, or when calls were made by social workers, doctors, and others who protect their safety by keeping their telephone numbers unlisted. Technology already permitted, and in some cases telephone companies already provided, another service known as Call Trace. With it, a person who receives a harassing call can send an immediate signal to the phone company and the police. Call Trace records the telephone number of the caller and is effective even if the caller attempts to block his or her number.

Telephones account for yet another privacy problem, usually referred to by privacy experts as telephone transaction-generated information. When the calls one makes are matched with one's name, address, buying habits, and credit history, a "profile" that contains a great deal of information about a person is quickly created. The profile may include a person's organizational memberships, religion, friends, travel habits, educational background, and a plethora of other data—everything from the clothes one wears, the vitamins and medications one consumes, the magazines and books one buys, to the movies for which one reserves tickets by telephone—that constitute not only a record of one's life but a record of many of its most intimate details. Usually there is nothing shameful to be disclosed, but privacy is lost. That is one of the many reasons many telephone subscribers have unlisted numbers. As Justice Potter Stewart wrote in 1979, in *Smith* v. *Maryland,*

> The numbers dialed from a private telephone—although certainly more prosaic than the conversation itself, are not without "content." Most private telephone subscribers . . . [would not] be happy to have broadcast to the world a list of the local or long

distance numbers they have called. This is not because such a list might be incriminating, but because it easily could reveal the identities of the persons and the places called, and thus reveal the most intimate details of a person's life.

A telephone number, like a social security number, identifies people. By enabling businesses to capture phone numbers and then to match them with names, addresses, buying habits, credit history, and other information, Caller ID gives them the power to build consumer profile databases for marketing. This power is a boon to businesses but an equally great concern to the twenty-five percent of all residential telephone subscribers—the numbers go as high as forty percent in the greater Chicago area and seventy-five percent in Las Vegas—who choose not to have their numbers listed in telephone directories.

The introduction of Caller ID technology sparked an emotional debate whose resolution ultimately became the responsibility of the Federal Communications Commission. The commission's first set of rules, issued in March 1994, would have permitted telephone companies to decline to provide subscribers with an automatically activated method for blocking the display of their telephone numbers whenever they placed a telephone call. Callers could block information about their number before making a call, if, before picking up the telephone, they remembered to dial *67. Civil libertarians immediately expressed concern that callers confronted with or forgetful about the cumbersome system would lose control over when and to whom to release their telephone numbers. Rethinking its policy, the commission issued a new set of regulations in May 1995, permitting customers to select per-line blocking for both in-state and interstate calls. States that have no Caller ID or blocking regulations are required to enable per-call blocking through use of the code *67. At the same time, customers selecting per-line blocking could "lift" blockage of their number temporarily by dialing *82 before making a specific call. This option enables customers to place telephone orders with merchandisers in such a way as to allow the merchandisers to retrieve all previously gathered information about a customer, while simultaneously permitting customers to retain their privacy when they so choose.

Whether it reflected discomfort about possible privacy violations, lack of knowledge about Caller ID, or the additional cost of subscribing to the service, as of September 1995 only six to ten percent of residential customers in the United States had bought into the system. That, however, did not mean that their telephone numbers were not being accessed.

Many marketing companies have been using ANI (Automatic Number Identification), the kind of Caller ID provided to commercial subscribers with 1-800 or 1-900 numbers, for years. The blocking system for Caller ID does not apply to 1-800 or 1-900 numbers under current FTC regulations, which means that when a customer calls a toll-free 800 number to place an order or simply to make an inquiry, the caller's telephone number is "captured" by the company being called and available for its own use and for that of other marketing or credit agencies to which it sells information, as well as for cross-listing with records in large databases to increase the information available about that individual. The company is also enabled to call the customer whenever it likes or to clog her or his mailbox with junk mail. People calling toll-free numbers with inquiries frequently have no desire to establish a business relationship with the company or divulge personal information about themselves. ANI, however, is in effect an involuntary extraction of personal information, taken without the individual's knowledge.

Americans' reactions to ANI were discovered by American Express, which uses its computers to match incoming phone numbers to customer files and for a short time instructed its operators to greet callers by name. The storm of objections changed the way American Express greets its customers but not the way it, or most other large companies, uses ANI when a customer calls. And the information gained in that manner goes to credit bureaus.

As more and more services become available on computers, there will be an increase in individual use of modems, which use telephone lines, for a variety of services: to browse libraries, ask questions of medical personnel, buy products, apply for a job, send for books and magazines. The transaction-generated information left behind will add up to a fairly complete picture of a person's daily activities, habits, consumption patterns, health situation, reading interests, and so on. Its availability raises obvious privacy questions.

CONCLUSION

Technologies developed in the late twentieth century can be a boon: to merchants, to customers, to victims threatened by criminals. But as with much technology, the key question is less about the nature of the technology itself than about the use to which it is put. Large-scale information systems inevitably are touted as being created for a limited purpose. Just as invariably, they take on a life of their own, and the temptation in our information-eager society to utilize them for purposes other than those for which they were created becomes irresistible. As the Privacy Commission stated, "The real danger is the gradual erosion of individual liberties through the automation and interconnection of many small, separate records-keeping systems, each of which alone may seem innocuous, even benevolent, and wholly justifiable." Each individual today, the report went on, has a "wide array of labels in addition to his or her name—a credit-card number, bank account number, driver's license number, license plate number, health insurance number, utilities account number, employee identification number, library card number, Social Security number . . . . Information is emerging as a basic currency of social, political, and economic relationships in American society."

The computer age is one in which the price of doing business with others is loss of control over the records of one's life. It is an age in which individuals are in effect forced to relinquish control over enormous quantities and varieties of personal information. We have too little knowledge of how information about us is being used, or by whom, which leads to the threat of a watched society. And a watched society is a conformist society: one in which people are far less willing to pursue and experiment with ideas that deviate from mainstream beliefs. Externally imposed conformism and true democracy are incompatible.

The answer to the dilemma of how to maximize use of the new technologies while preserving privacy seems to lie in the founding principle of the Privacy Act of 1974: information collected for one purpose may not be used for a different purpose without the individual's consent. As we have seen, however, the achievement of that goal will require far greater public awareness and concomitant demands on elected decision makers if we are to control the records of our lives.

Chapter Five

BODILY PRIVACY AND INTEGRITY

The liberty of the individual is no gift of civilization. It was greater before there was any civilization.

—Sigmund Freud

In March 1929 a thirty-four-year-old woman in Pittsburgh died as the result of an illegal abortion. She and her journalist husband already had five children, the oldest twelve and the youngest eighteen months old. Her children later found out that one of their mother's friends helped her use a knitting needle. The family doctor treated her at home when it became clear that the needle had perforated her uterus. By the time he sent her to the hospital, it was too late; she had developed peritonitis and gangrene. Her grieving husband first sent the children off to various relatives and then brought them back to live with the first of two stepmothers, from each of whom he was subsequently divorced. One of her daughters commented more than 50 years later that she was still pained by the contrast between family photographs taken before the abortion, showing the children smiling and clearly well cared for, and those taken after the mother's death. There were fewer pictures, she said, and they were all of children who looked "generally uncared for," their clothes mismatched and their hair uncombed and wild. In 1950 the daughter asked her father why her parents hadn't used contraception. "Honey," he said, "we never talked about those things." The daughter told scholar Patricia G. Miller, "Think about that. My mother," whom she remembered as "pretty, wonderful, talented" and as a musician who was the first woman to sing on the radio in Pittsburgh, "had to die because certain things couldn't be discussed" and because abortion was illegal.

All privacy issues generate substantial emotion. The intensity of the debate about bodily privacy and the government's power to limit it, however, suggests that it differs in important ways from discussions about privacy matters such as credit cards or wiretapping. The passion that illuminates—or perhaps obscures—the discussion reflects questions about identity and the individual will that date back for centuries and may well have been thought of as soon as human beings came into existence. Attitudes toward abortion, homosexuality, and the right to die are inextricable for many Americans from deeply held religious and ethical beliefs about what constitutes a "good" life and what can and cannot be defended on moral grounds. Proponents of each asserted right speak in terms of privacy; opponents reject this formulation and call abortion, homosexual sex, and the deliberate ending of one's life immoral acts that should be criminalized by the government. Each subject is intertwined with ideas about the source of morality, the limits of individual will, the proper social role of the sexes and the relationships between them, the extent to which different people should be able to participate in the society's political and economic life, and the kind of control that the community can legitimately claim over the decisions about sexuality, lifestyle, and the quality of life.

The decisions that each of us must make about our life are directly implicated by social policies toward sexuality, reproduction, and death. "What kind of life do I want to lead and what kind of person do I want to be? Do I want to share my life with another adult? Do I want children, and if so, at what point in my life? Can the fact of life ever be less important to me than the pain or disabilities it may entail? Should anyone other than myself have legal power over my answers?" There could be no more personal or more fundamental questions. It is not surprising that Americans find them provocative, frightening, and evocative of our deepest beliefs. This becomes very clear when one looks at the history of abortion and reproductive freedom in the United States.

ABORTION AND CONTRACEPTION

Abortions were not treated as crimes during the United States's early history. In colonial America, recipes for herbal abortifacients were commonly found in cookbooks, and throughout the 1700s midwives routinely provided women with abortion-inducing substances when they wanted to terminate pregnancy. This was also the case during the first half of the nineteenth century. Advertisements of the 1840s announced the willingness of practitioners, many of them midwives, to perform abortions, and boasted of their skill. Some states prohibited abortions after "quickening," that is, after a woman first felt fetal movement, usually during the fourth month of pregnancy. Even then the act was considered no more than a minor offense rather than a crime.

Massachusetts was the first state to criminalize abortion, in 1845. It was followed by other states in the decades after the Civil War, when doctors and antiabortionists lobbied to have abortions made illegal. Many antiabortionists feared that the declining birth rate among Protestant women would lead to an increasingly large proportion of Catholics in the population; others worried that the ability of women to control their bodies and move into the paid urbanized workforce would endanger a cherished belief in the natural subordination of women. Doctors, who were just beginning to organize professionally and who wanted a monopoly over abortions, sought to discredit midwives. They emphasized the dangers of abortion and argued that consumer safety was jeopardized whenever abortions were performed by nonphysicians. The American Medical Association (AMA) issued a somewhat inconsistent manifesto declaring that although all abortions were murder, some were necessary. The only people competent to determine necessity, said the AMA, were doctors. By 1910 every state in the Union except Kentucky had declared abortion to be a felony, with most states permitting abortions only if they were necessary to save the life of the mother. The decision about whether the necessity existed usually was made by a doctor who would perform whatever abortions he chose in his home or office. It seems fair to assume that some doctors interpreted "saving the life of the mother" broadly, and that some women therefore managed to obtain abortions even when their lives were not endangered.

That situation changed after the Second World War, when the performance of minor surgical procedures moved from the home or office to hospitals. Doctors found themselves unable to make their own decisions about abortions as hospitals afraid of malpractice suits established committees and regulations to oversee and govern the procedure. During the 1950s and sixties wealthier women, who had access to doctors' networks in the United States and abortion clinics abroad and the ability to afford either, usually were able to obtain legal abortions in spite of antiabortion laws and hospital peer review. Poorer and rural women, including many women of color, went to physicians and nonphysicians alike for illegal abortions. These frequently were performed under shockingly unsanitary conditions or with no follow-up care or by people with very questionable skills. The result was that many women died or suffered permanent reproductive damage. Experts estimated that in spite of legal restrictions, one out of five pregnancies resulted in abortions during those decades (the number worldwide was one out of three), and that there were about 750,000 illegal abortions a year in the United States.

Access to birth control was limited also by such laws as the 1879 Connecticut statute that prohibited the use of any drug or device to prevent conception and penalized any person who advised about or provided contraceptive materials. Once again, most wealthy women who wished to could get birth control information and devices from their doctors. Middle-and working-class women could not.

This became an important public issue as the late 1960s and early seventies brought increased participation in the paid workforce by upper-middle-class women as well as those from the working and middle classes, almost all of them interested in limiting or spacing their pregnancies. At the same time, the women's movement began to gather political clout, and the door for discussion of sexuality and family planning was opened by the sexual revolution, the availability of birth control pills, and concern about the size of the world's population.

Attempts in the 1950s to challenge the 1879 Connecticut law were unsuccessful for various procedural reasons. In 1964, however, Estelle Griswold, executive director of the Connecticut Planned Parenthood League, joined by a doctor who had prescribed contraceptives for a married couple at the League's clinic, deliberately courted prosecution by New Haven officials. Their goal was to have the statute overturned so that birth control could be made available to poorer women. Griswold and the doctor were convicted, the

Supreme Court accepted their appeal, and Justice William O. Douglas delivered an opinion that made an indelible impact on American law and politics. In it, he not only held that married couples had a right to use contraception; he also enunciated the constitutional right of privacy.

What Douglas did, in *Griswold* v. *Connecticut* (1965), was to unite what he called the "penumbra" (shadows or emanations) inherent in specific guarantees in the Bill of Rights—the First Amendment's right of association, the Third Amendment's prohibition against the intrusive quartering of soldiers in civilians' homes during peacetime, the Fourth Amendment's search and seizure clause, the Fifth Amendment's self-incrimination clause, and the Ninth Amendment's guarantee to the people of rights not specifically mentioned in the Constitution—to fashion a legally protected right of marital privacy. It was, said Douglas, a right "older than the Bill of Rights—older than our political parties, older than our school system."

Justice Arthur Goldberg, joined by Justice William Brennan and Chief Justice Earl Warren, concurred, relying only on the rarely cited Ninth Amendment which reserves to the people all rights not specifically mentioned in the Constitution. The right to privacy, Goldberg maintained, predated the Constitution, and the Framers intended that all liberties existing at the time should enjoy constitutional protection.

Justice John Marshall Harlan also concurred, but on a different theory. For him, the notion of liberty interests embedded in the Fourteenth Amendment's Due Process Clause, which prohibits the states from denying any citizen "life, liberty or property without due process of law," made eminent sense and solved the entire problem of whether a right had been literally mentioned in the Constitution. One did not have to rely upon emanations, he thought, or look into the Ninth Amendment, the meaning of which was debatable. If the justices agreed that a certain right had great value—and privacy certainly mattered a great deal—then it could be considered a liberty interest.

Justice Hugo Black, following a literalist approach, disagreed because he could find no specific provision in the Bill of Rights for privacy. Without such a provision, he argued, there could be no constitutional protection of privacy. "I like my privacy as well as the next one," he wrote, "but I am nevertheless compelled to admit that government has a right to invade it unless prohibited by some specific constitutional provision." Black later called his dissent "the most difficult I have ever had to write. I found that law abhorrent, just viciously evil, but not unconstitutional."

Douglas's result—the creation of a constitutionally protected right to privacy—and Harlan's due process rationale established the basis for the expansion of autonomy rights in following years. *Griswold* is the forebear of the Court's decisions dealing with a woman's right to an abortion, as well as with the right to die.

The Court's declaration in *Griswold* of a constitutionally protected right to privacy is not without critics. Indeed, a bibliography of the literature on just this issue would fill a small book. But the core dispute is quite simple: does the Constitution protect only those rights that are specifically enumerated or do its various clauses also shelter nonenumerated rights? Should the Constitution be read literally, as Justice Black suggested in his *Griswold* dissent, or should it be read expansively, as Brandeis had argued in *Olmstead?* Is it reasonable and democratic for the justices to interpret the vague words of the Constitution according to new societal facts and needs, or should they adhere to the exact meaning given to the words by the people who wrote them? Is their job to enforce the spirit of the Constitution or specific, time-bound definitions? To take an example from another area, one might argue that the prohibition against Congress abridging speech means only those kinds of speech that were possible when the First Amendment was written; or one might say instead that the spirit of the amendment means that it should be applied to radio and television broadcasts, telephone calls, faxes, E-mail, and the Internet. The American public apparently endorses the second approach, if one can judge from the electorate's willingness to accept Court decisions that embody it. Indeed, the alleged harm caused by the Court's refusal to interpret the Constitution in the light of the conditions engendered by the Depression was one of the major points made in Franklin Roosevelt's reelection campaign of 1936.

Where privacy is concerned, the answer to the question about constitutional interpretation is crucial. Surely by this time no one would accept Justice Taft's argument in *Olmstead* that since wiretapping involved no physical penetration of the home, it did not violate privacy. As Justice Harlan once wrote:

> Each new claim to Constitutional protection must be considered against a background of Constitutional purposes, as they have been rationally perceived and historically developed. Though we

exercise limited and sharply restrained judgment, yet there is no "mechanical yardstick," no "mechanical answer." (*Poe* v. *Ullman,* 1961)

Griswold was decided at a time when attitudes toward abortion were changing. Fourteen states had amended their laws to permit abortions when childbirth would endanger the mother's health rather than her life, when there was likelihood of fetal abnormality, or when a pregnancy was the result of rape or incest. The states of Alaska, Hawaii, New York, and Washington permitted first-trimester abortions whatever the reason. Only Louisiana, New Hampshire, and Pennsylvania still prohibited all abortions.

By the time of the Court's 1972–1973 term *Griswold* was the law of the land, however controversial it may have been, and "Jane Roe's" attorneys thought they could use it. "Jane" was a Texas woman who had wanted an abortion in 1969 but, because of the state law that criminalized abortions performed for any reason other than to save the life of the mother, was forced to carry the pregnancy to term. She then gave up the child for adoption. Three other people challenged the law with "Roe": a doctor who said he was affected because if he performed an abortion on a woman whom he believed ought to have one for medical reasons, he could be prosecuted; and a married couple, "John and Mary Doe." "Mary" suffered from a chemical disorder that would have made it dangerous for her to become pregnant, and the couple, afraid that the Texas law would prevent her from obtaining a safe abortion should she become pregnant, joined in the suit to have the law declared unconstitutional and to have Texas enjoined from enforcing it. The name of the case was *Roe* v. *Wade,* Wade being the district attorney for Dallas County, where "Jane Roe" lived.

Justice Blackmun spoke for a majority of seven when he wrote that the constitutional right of privacy, "whether it be founded in the Fourteenth Amendment's concept of personal liberty and restrictions upon state action" or "in the Ninth Amendment's reservation of rights to the people," included "a woman's decision whether or not to terminate her pregnancy." That right nonetheless had to be weighed against the state's interest in life and health. The state had no valid interest in preventing abortions performed during the first trimester of pregnancy, because childbirth had become statistically more dangerous than early abortions. During the second trimester the state's interest in promoting the health of the mother permitted it to regulate abortion procedures "in ways that are reasonably related to maternal health," but not to outlaw abortions. The state could regulate or proscribe abortions in the third trimester, when the fetus was viable, or had "the capability of meaningful life outside the mother's womb," but it could not outlaw an abortion even then if one was necessary to preserve the mother's life or health.

Justice Blackmun thus placed the right of bodily privacy in the context of pregnancy on a trimester basis, with the privacy right decreasing as the pregnancy progressed and the public interest in health and in the life of the woman and the fetus increased. He also concluded that nothing in the Constitution suggested that the fetus was a "person" protected by the Fourteenth Amendment. To decide that it was, he wrote, would mean that the Court agreed with those who argued that life began at conception. This, Justice Blackmun declared, was a matter about which doctors, philosophers, and theologians disagreed, and "the judiciary, at this point in the development of man's knowledge, is not in a position to speculate as to the answer."

Justice William H. Rehnquist dissented, finding that the right of privacy was not at issue in the case. The Court, he argued, should have determined only whether the Texas statute had a "rational relation" to a "valid state objective" such as maternal health. The fact that a majority of the states had had abortion-restrictive laws "for at least a century" meant to him that the Texas statute was indeed "rational."

The Court did not anticipate the depth of the reaction to its decision. "When handing down *Roe* v. *Wade*," constitutional scholar David O'Brien has written, "the Court elevated the issue of abortion to the national political agenda and invited a larger political struggle within the country." Justice Blackmun told a reporter that "I suppose I'll carry *Roe* to my grave." Blackmun received thousands of letters in the years that followed the decision, many full of praise and others that were not: "Think of any name," he said, "I've been called it in these letters." Senator Orrin Hatch, referring to the pre–Civil War case in which the Court had held that black Americans were not "persons" entitled to constitutional protection, stated that the question of the rights of the unborn was "the *Dred Scott* issue of this century." And so it became, with antiabortion groups springing into life during the next years and pro-choice groups, initially inactive because they felt their battle had been won, rallying to the defense of *Roe.* The issue clearly was, and is, not only divisive but one that people approach with great passion. What are the arguments on each side?

Those who maintain that the right to abortion is a necessary part of privacy insist that nothing can be more private or a less legitimate subject for government regulation than an individual's body. Pro-choice groups do not argue that abortions are desirable, but rather that the only person who should have the power to decide how a woman uses her body is the woman herself. Should she become pregnant and choose, for whatever reason, not to have her body used to produce a baby, that decision should be honored. It is an intensely private decision, as continuation of an unwanted pregnancy can have great implications for the woman's physical and psychological health. Whichever way she decides, her life will be permanently affected. Her ability to pursue an education, to take advantage of job opportunities, to work the hours necessary to achieve promotion on the job—all will be dependent on the decision she makes. The government should not have the power to force a woman to give birth any more than it should have the power to limit the number of children a woman can have. A woman's decision to abort, whether it is based on a desire not to give birth to an abnormal child or one for whom she will be unable to care properly or on another reason entirely, is not the government's business.

Opponents of abortion view the issue as one involving not only the life of the mother but the life of the fetus. Life and personhood begin at conception, they believe, which means that abortion is nothing less than murder. Privacy is a legitimate claim as long as honoring it hurts no one else. Here, however, there is someone else to consider: the potential, if unborn, child. As the primary obligation of the state is to protect people from harm done by others, the state has no alternative but to outlaw abortion. Most antiabortionists, including many clergy, would make an exception when the pregnancy forces a choice between lives; that is, when childbirth is likely to result in the death of the mother. Some would make additional exceptions when the fetus is so damaged that childbirth will produce an infant with a very limited life expectancy or a severe handicap. Others would add to the exceptions those instances where the pregnancy is not voluntary; that is, when the woman has been raped; or where the pregnancy is the result of incest, the implication being that the woman was forcibly impregnated by a male relative.

Where the pregnancy is the result of consensual sex, however, antiabortionists argue that a woman old enough to bear a child is old enough to take the responsibility for not becoming pregnant. Once she permits herself to become pregnant, there is another life to be considered, and it is the government's duty to keep that life from being harmed.

Clearly, there are troubling questions and seeming inconsistencies on both sides of the issue. Carried to its logical conclusion, the privacy argument suggests that women should have the right to terminate a pregnancy at any time, including after the point of viability when the fetus can live on its own outside the mother's body. Many pro-choicers are disturbed by the idea of a seventh- or eighth-month abortion, although they would argue that the very few third-trimester therapeutic abortions or abortions occasioned by the discovery of fetal abnormalities should be available even then. Antiabortionists appear to undercut their insistence on the overarching importance of the fetus's life when they accept abortions that result from rape or incest. If life begins at conception, it would also appear logical for antiabortionists to oppose the use of interuterine devices and low-dose birth control pills, both of which act as post-conception abortifacients.

Congress reacted to the Court's decision in the years after *Roe* by passing over thirty laws that restricted the availability of abortions. The laws prohibited attorneys in federally funded legal aid programs from working for women seeking abortions for reasons other than health, barred the use of foreign aid funds for abortions, forbade the use of federal Medicaid funds for nontherapeutic abortions (those that were not necessary to preserve the life or health of the mother), prohibited the use of federal funds for domestic programs in which abortion was included as a method of family planning, exempted employers from paying health insurance benefits for any but therapeutic abortions, and barred the use of federal funds to enable medical personnel to get abortions at military hospitals. As the political climate heated up, a number of states enacted laws in blatant violation of *Roe*. These either criminalized all abortions unless the life of the mother was endangered, the fetus was abnormal, or the pregnancy was the result of rape or incest; or set time limits during the first and second trimesters for all nontherapeutic abortions. Expensive lawsuits had to be brought before these laws were struck down as unconstitutional.

In 1980 Ronald Reagan won the presidency and the Republican Party gained control of the Senate. Reagan ordered what Assistant Attorney General Stephen Markman called "the most thorough and comprehensive system for recruiting and screening federal judicial candidates of any administration ever." The screening included questioning potential candidates about their views on abortion, affirmative action, and criminal justice. Reagan's successor, George Bush, continued the practice.

Reagan's judicial appointments included a majority of all judges sitting on the lower federal courts and four Supreme Court justices: Sandra Day O'Connor, William Rehnquist (who was elevated to the chief justiceship from his position as associate justice), Antonin Scalia, and Anthony M. Kennedy. They replaced Potter Stewart, Warren Burger, and Lewis Powell, all of whom had voted against the Texas statute in *Roe*.

It is impossible to estimate the effect of public opinion on the members of the Supreme Court. They supposedly exist in splendid isolation, ignoring demonstrations, letters from the public about pending cases, and so on. But they read newspapers, they watch television, they mix with other people at social events, they have families who discuss current issues. Whether because of the changed personnel on the Court or because the Court was aware of the ongoing public battle about abortion or both, the Court initially defended and extended its approach to the right of bodily privacy and then gradually moved away from it. The decisions it handed down between 1973 and 1989 not only illustrate this change but also tell the story of the legislation passed in response to the antichoice movement.

The Court upheld state and federal laws withholding Medicaid funding for poor women unable to afford nontherapeutic abortions (*Maher* v. *Roe,* 1977; *Harris* v. *McRae,* 1980). Where nonmonetary issues were concerned, however, the Court tended to strike down state and municipal limitations on abortions. These included regulations requiring unmarried minors to obtain the consent of both parents before an abortion, even in cases of rape or incest, without giving the minor the option of going to a court and demonstrating she was sufficiently "mature and well informed" to make the decision herself or persuading the court to permit the abortion. Other such laws banned second-trimester abortions from being performed anywhere but in hospitals, which were more expensive than abortions performed in clinics; required doctors to tell patients that a fetus is a human life from the moment of conception and to describe fetal development at each stage of pregnancy in detail; prohibited abortion advocates from providing pregnant women with information; and mandated a twenty-four-hour waiting period after the patient had signed a consent form (*Bellotti* v. *Baird,* 1979; *Akron* v. *Akron Center for Reproductive Health,* 1983; *Planned Parenthood* v. *Ashcroft,* 1983; *Thornburgh* v. *American College of Obstetricians and Gynecologists,* 1986).

A turning point was reached in 1989, when the Court upheld Missouri's ban on the use of public facilities and employees for nontherapeutic abortions and on the use of public funds for the counseling of women to have an abortion, as well as its requirement that physicians test before performing a second-trimester abortion to determine whether the fetus is viable (*Webster* v. *Reproductive Health Services,* 1989). The opinions in *Webster* suggested that a plurality, and perhaps a majority, of the Court was ready to overturn *Roe.* Anxiety on both sides of the abortion debate therefore was riding high in 1992, when the Supreme Court heard the case of *Planned Parenthood of Southeastern Pennsylvania* v. *Casey.*

After the Court handed down its decision in *Webster,* Pennsylvania along with other states had tightened its restrictions on abortion. Its statute required that doctors counsel any woman seeking an abortion about the specifics and risks of the procedure, describe and provide materials about each state of fetal development as well as of alternatives to abortion, and obtain the woman's written consent to an abortion. The law mandated a twenty-four-hour waiting period between consent and abortion, and compelled unmarried women under 18 to obtain the written consent of at least one parent or a judicial order and to be accompanied by a parent during abortion counseling. It also required a signed statement from a married woman that she had informed her husband about the planned abortion, except where the husband was not the father or could not be located, or when the pregnancy was the result of a marital rape that was reported to the police, or if she reasonably believed that bodily injury would result from notification. In what was perhaps its most controversial clause, the law required physicians to write reports on all abortions and made the reports open to the public. A number of similar provisions in an earlier Pennsylvania statute had been struck down by the Court in 1986 by a vote of 5 to 4, but of those justices in the majority, only Justice Blackmun was still on the Court when *Casey* was heard.

The difficulty the Court had with *Casey* was reflected in its delay in handing down a decision until the last day of the Court's term, four months after oral argument. The five separate opinions in the case totaled 184 pages, and the joint opinion for the Court written by Justices Sandra Day O'Connor, Anthony Kennedy, and David Souter and read in part by each of them on the day the decision was announced was sixty pages long. The Court endorsed the right of a woman to have an abortion "before viability . . . without undue interference from the State"; confirmed the "State's power to restrict abortions after fetal viability" unless the mother's health or life was endangered; and upheld "the principle that the State has legitimate interests from the outset of the pregnancy in protecting the health of the woman and the life of the fetus that may become a child." While "the woman's right to make the ultimate decision" before viability was important, she had no right "to be insulated from all others in doing so." The balancing of the woman's desire for an abortion and the state's power to restrict access was to depend on whether or not the restriction constituted an "undue burden." No such burden resulted, the plurality said, from any of the requirements of the Pennsylvania statute, with the sole exceptions of spousal notification and the submission of a doctor's report to be made available to the public. The Court struck down those provisions because the ubiquity of spousal abuse made them an "undue burden."

Justices Blackmun and Stevens each concurred in part and dissented in part. The passions generated by the case were reflected in the conclusion of Justice Blackmun's separate opinion. Comparing the Court's approach with that reflected in the two dissents written by Justices Rehnquist and Scalia, he wrote,

> [T]he distance between the two approaches is short—the distance is but a single vote. I am 83 years old. I cannot remain on this Court forever, and when I do step down, the confirmation process for my successor may well focus on the issue before us today. That, I regret, may be exactly where the choice between the two worlds will be made.

Justice Rehnquist was no less impassioned, calling the plurality opinion "feebly supported" and the result of "an entirely new method of analysis, without any roots in constitutional law."

Both their passion and the enormous differences of opinion between Justices Blackmun and Rehnquist seemed to echo the deep feelings the abortion issue generated in the public at large. Public opinion on abortion appeared not to change significantly after *Roe,* when a little over forty percent of the public favored the decision and an equal percentage condemned it. What did take place was an increase in antiabortion lobbying and protest activities, which affected congressional and state legislative actions, and the important change in Supreme Court personnel discussed above. Antichoice forces organized a "rescue" movement that blocked access to abortion clinics, demonstrated outside both the clinics and the homes of doctors who performed abortions in them, and in some cases invaded clinics and bombed or set them on fire. The National Abortion Federation estimated in 1995 that during the preceding three years physicians had received hundreds of death threats and harassing phone calls. Five people, including doctors David Gunn and John Bayard, were murdered and fifteen others seriously wounded by antichoice protestors. Congress passed the 1994 Freedom of Access to Clinic Entrances Act making it a federal crime to interfere with doctors or patients at an abortion clinic through intimidation, force, or the destruction of property. The country appeared to be hopelessly torn on the question of whether reproductive freedom was a privacy right.

The National Opinion Research Center asked people every year after 1973 whether they favored legalizing abortions under different circumstances. As of 1991, the percentages of those polled who thought that abortions should be legally obtainable under specific circumstances were as follows:

- if the woman's health will be seriously endangered, 92 percent
- if the woman is pregnant as the result of rape, 86 percent
- if there is a strong chance of serious defect in the baby, 83 percent
- if the family's income is so low that it cannot afford more children, 48 percent
- if the woman is unmarried and does not want to marry the man, 45 percent
- if the woman is married but does not want more children, 45 percent.

Oddly enough, however, the results of public opinion surveys varied widely with the questions asked. A 1994 Cantril survey found that 82 percent of those surveyed agreed with the statement, "I don't like the idea of ending a pregnancy, but it is basically a woman's right to make such a decision on her own." At the same time, 61 percent agreed that "Abortion is the taking of a human life and is morally wrong." Strikingly, forty-five percent of the respondents agreed with both statements. In other words, the Cantril study suggests that Americans are attempting to reconcile a belief in a fundamental privacy right with a distaste for abortion. Perhaps most telling was that 77 percent believed that "a woman's right to decide for herself is so basic that it cannot be taken away no matter what the majority thinks" while 10 percent said that "a woman's ability to get an abortion should be decided by what the majority thinks," that is, by the government. (Thirteen percent responded that "it depends" or "don't know.")

Following *Casey,* a large number of states and municipalities enacted statutes requiring parental consent, waiting periods, and other elements of the Pennsylvania law that had been upheld by the Supreme Court. The attack on privacy rights was taken to one logical conclusion when the district attorney of Pennsylvania's Westmoreland County prosecuted a pregnant woman for transmitting drugs to her fetus. Michelle Kemp was charged with recklessly endangering another person, endangering the welfare of a child, and delivering a controlled substance by ingesting cocaine. In December 1992, a local judge agreed with Kemp's lawyers that the acts did not constitute a crime under state law, and the state's Superior Court upheld the ruling.

In Wisconsin, an alcoholic mother, who was drunk when she was wheeled into a Wisconsin delivery room in 1996 and whose baby had a blood alcohol level almost twice that legally required to show intoxication, was charged with attempted murder. By that time, according to the Center for Reproductive Law and Policy, at least 200 women in more than thirty states had been prosecuted for endangering their fetuses while pregnant. While the South Carolina Supreme Court ruled in 1996 that women who use illegal drugs during pregnancy can be prosecuted for child abuse, the highest courts of Florida, Kentucky, Nevada, and Ohio have interpreted their state laws to reach the opposite conclusion. In more than a dozen other cases brought primarily by medical personnel, pregnant women have been forcibly given blood transfusions or caesarean deliveries in spite of religious or other objections, all in the name of fetal rights.

The logic of these actions, and of statutes seeking to achieve the goal sought by Westmoreland County, is clear. If the state interest in fetal life is greater than the mother's privacy interest in her body, then why should states not enact laws prohibiting a pregnant woman from ingesting drugs, including alcohol; smoking cigarettes; eating unhealthfully; or engaging in sports that might present a danger to the fetus; or requiring that she deliver her child in a way considered safest for the child? Where is the line to be drawn?

While this question remains controversial, the American electorate has reached firm agreement that the right to privacy is an essential component of liberty. As noted above, when President Ronald Reagan nominated federal appellate court judge Robert H. Bork to the Supreme Court in 1987, Bork's televised mocking remarks about a right to privacy that he believed was *not* included in the Constitution led to a public outcry. Americans saw Bork as opposed to a right to privacy—*their* right to privacy. Public opinion polls showed that the electorate was against Bork: nearly four out of five persons surveyed in the South, for example, opposed the nomination because of Bork's views on privacy. The Senate bowed to public opinion and rejected the nomination.

PRIVACY RIGHTS OF GAYS AND LESBIANS

If people have a constitutionally protected right to bodily privacy, one might assume that unless the state can demonstrate a compelling interest, it has no business telling people what they may do with and to their bodies. That has not always been the view of the American public or of the Supreme Court, particularly where homosexuality was concerned. The Court's decision in *Bowers* v. *Hardwick* (1986), upholding a Georgia statute that criminalized sodomy, reflected that public distaste—even though, as we will see, the statute, and similar statutes in twenty-five other states, actually made no distinction between sodomy performed by homosexuals and that performed by heterosexuals.

Michael Hardwick, convicted of having committed sodomy in his bedroom with a consenting adult male, asked the Court to declare that the statute violated his right of privacy. The law was also challenged by "John and Mary Doe," a married couple. The Court decided that the couple had no real standing to sue because the statute was never enforced against heterosexuals, and based its decision solely on Hardwick's claim. Justice Byron White, writing for the majority of five, defined the issue not as privacy but as "whether the Federal Constitution confers a fundamental right upon homosexuals to engage in sodomy and hence invalidates the laws of the many States that still make such conduct illegal and have done so for a very long time." His question suggested the answer. Saying that there was no connection "between family, marriage, or procreation" and homosexuality, he dismissed the contraception and abortion rights cases as irrelevant. White denied that every sexual act performed by consenting adults in the privacy of their homes was constitutionally protected, citing the legitimacy of laws against adultery and incest.

Justice Blackmun, writing for himself and Justices Brennan, Thurgood Marshall, and John Paul Stevens, began his opinion:

> This case is no[t] . . . about "a fundamental right to engage in homosexual sodomy.". . . Rather, [it] is about "the most comprehensive of rights and the right most valued by civilized men," namely, "the right to be let alone."

He castigated the Court for its "almost obsessive focus on homosexual activity," pointing out that the "sex or status of the persons who engage in the act is irrelevant" under the law. Blackmun divided earlier privacy cases into those that, like *Roe* v. *Wade,* "recognized a privacy interest with reference to certain *decisions* that are properly for the individual to make," and those that "recognized a privacy interest with reference to certain *places* without regard for the particular activities in which the individuals who occupy them are engaged." *Bowers,* said Blackmun, implicated both. Quoting an earlier concurrence by Justice Stevens that stated, "the concept of privacy embodies the 'moral fact that a person belongs to himself and not others nor to society as whole,'" Blackmun accused the Court of refusing to recognize "the fundamental interest all individuals have in controlling the nature of their intimate associations with others." "No matter how uncomfortable a certain group may make the majority of this Court," he added, there is a difference "between laws that protect public sensibilities and those that enforce private morality," and the state had no legitimate interest in regulating "intimate behavior that occurs in intimate places."

When the Court chooses to interpret a challenge to a statute that prohibits private behavior by *all* couples as asserting that there is a "fundamental right" of homosexual sodomy, it is difficult to believe that Justice Blackmun was wrong in saying the Court's decision was based on its being made "uncomfortable" by the mere existence of "a certain group." This discomfort was shared by much of society, according to political scientist Kenneth Sherrill, who cited public opinion surveys when he testified in an Ohio courtroom that most Americans "do not like homosexuals." Sherrill referred to the 1992 American National Election study that measured feelings towards members of various groups, including gays and lesbians, feminists, illegal aliens, black Americans, Hispanics, Jews, Catholics, Christian fundamentalists, and people on welfare. Americans gave homosexuals the lowest possible ratings by far, exceeding by one-third the highly negative feelings about that much-maligned group, people on welfare.

The 1994 Cantril study mentioned above, however, found that 87 percent of its respondents supported the right of gays and lesbians to live wherever they could afford to; 73 percent, their right to stay in public accommodations; 55 percent, their right to teach in schools. Thirty percent thought gays and lesbians should be permitted to adopt and raise children; 29 percent supported their being licensed to marry. Eighty-three percent thought a homosexual relationship between consenting adults was a private matter and only 30 percent agreed that "homosexuality is wrong and there should be laws against it," even though 60 percent considered homosexuality to be "against God's law" and 54 percent said that "homosexuality threatens the values of the American family." Again, the wording of the questions was crucial and the answers reflected great ambivalence: over 80 percent of those who felt homosexuality was "against God's law" nonetheless agreed that homosexual relationships were a private matter, as did three-quarters of those viewing homosexuality as a threat to family values. Big business had already decided that homosexuality was a private matter. In 1991, Lotus Development Corporation became the first of more than 200 major American companies, including Coors Brewing Company and Disney, that would extend "domestic partnership" benefits such as health and life insurance and family leave to homosexual as well as heterosexual couples.

Public attitudes toward homosexuality were in a state of flux in the early nineties with federal and state officials and courts in various states demonstrating both positive and negative attitudes toward gay and lesbian rights. One of President Bill Clinton's first acts in 1993 had been to declare that homosexuality was not a bar to service in the American military. After much publicized criticism from the military and its allies in Congress, Clinton changed the policy to what became known as "Don't ask, don't tell": members of the military could not be asked about their sexual orientation by superiors and homosexuals could remain in the military as long as they did not mention their sexual orientation or engage in homosexual acts. As of 1997 federal district courts and appeals courts around the country were in conflict as to whether the policy was a violation of speech and privacy rights, virtually assuring that the issue eventually would be taken up by the U.S. Supreme Court.

In 1992, fifty-three percent of Colorado's voters approved Amendment 2, a measure prohibiting state and local governments from passing laws protecting homosexuals from discrimination. The U.S. Supreme Court in 1996 found Amendment 2 to be in violation of the Equal Protection Clause (*Romer* v. *Evans*). Speaking for the six-judge majority, Justice Kennedy held that the amendment imposed a "special," "broad and undifferentiated disability" on homosexuals, forbidding them "the safeguards that others enjoy or may seek without constraint." The amendment "identifies persons by a single trait and then denies them protection across the board," he went on, saying that the "resulting disqualification of a class of persons from the right to seek specific protection from the law" was "unprecedented in our jurisprudence . . . . It is not within our constitutional tradition to enact laws of this sort."

What was most astonishing about *Romer* was perhaps less the decision itself than the attitude toward gays and lesbians implicit in Kennedy's language. Justice White's majority opinion in *Bowers* v. *Hardwick* had expressed shock at the idea that there could be any connection "between family, marriage, or procreation" and homosexuality, and equated a law he believed to be aimed at homosexuals with those that outlawed adultery and incest. Justice Kennedy spoke in *Romer* just a decade later, quoting a 1973 case:

> "[I]f the constitutional conception of 'equal protection of the laws' means anything, it must at the very least mean that a bare . . . desire to harm a politically unpopular group cannot constitute a legitimate governmental interest." Even laws enacted for broad and ambitious purposes often can be explained by reference to legitimate public policies which justify the incidental disadvantages they impose on certain persons. Amendment 2, however, in making a general announcement that gays and lesbians shall not have any particular protections from the law, inflicts on them immediate, continuing, and real injuries that outrun and belie any legitimate justifications that may be

> claimed for it . . . . [Amendment 2] is a classification of persons
> undertaken for its own sake, something the Equal Protection
> Clause does not permit.

A majority of the Court had agreed in 1986 that homosexuality was within the sphere of government regulation and not a private matter because it constituted a threat to decency. That view was rejected by a majority of the justices in 1996, as was apparent when *Romer* was argued orally before the Court. Justice Kennedy commented that he had never before known a state to "fence out" a class of people from local antidiscrimination laws. Justice Sandra Day O'Connor asked whether the Colorado amendment meant homosexuals could be denied access to a public library. Justice Ruth Bader Ginsburg queried counsel about whether the amendment permitted denial of gays' and lesbians' access to restaurants and hospitals. Justice Stephen Breyer wanted to know what it meant for police protection against "gay-bashing."

Even Justice Scalia's scathing dissent described the 1996 gay and lesbian community as different from what it had been in 1986. He now considered it a "politically powerful minority" with access to the "elite class" in charge of interpreting the nation's laws. That was another way of saying that popular attitudes toward gays and lesbians had changed during the decade. They had, and the change had major implications for privacy, but Scalia was right: the change was greatest among the elite. While the country might therefore appear and actually be more tolerant of homosexuality, within and between the elite and the citizenry at large there was still conflict.

As of 1995, nine states (Wisconsin, Massachusetts, Connecticut, New Jersey, Hawaii, Vermont, California, Minnesota, Rhode Island) and the District of Columbia had statutes prohibiting discrimination against gays and lesbians. The sodomy laws that every state in the Union had on its books in 1960 had been repealed by the legislature or struck down by a state court as a privacy violation in twenty-six states, and over twenty states recognized a lesbian mother's right to keep her child. At the same time, other states, most of them with antisodomy laws still on the books, ruled out homosexuals as custodial parents.

American attitudes toward privacy have been challenged further by the issue of single-sex marriage.

Hawaii residents Ninia Baehr and Genora Dancel wanted to make each other beneficiaries of their life insurance policies but were informed by state officials that they could not do so because they were not married. The two women sued in 1990 for the right to wed. Hawaii's Supreme Court ruled in 1993 that the state's refusal to license the proposed Baehr-Dancel marriage illegally deprived them of financial and legal benefits (*Baehr* v. *Lewin*), and returned the case to a lower court for procedural reasons.

The case generated a much-discussed conflict involving differing ideas of privacy, marriage, and morality. The Hawaii legislature promptly passed a law defining marriage as being between a man and a woman. *Newsweek* magazine found 65 percent of Americans opposed to homosexual marriages. The Hawaii Commission on Sexual Orientation and the Law recommended in December 1995 that the state legalize same-sex marriages, deciding after extensive research and testimony that the state had no compelling interest in violating the marital privacy right. In 1996 Congress and the president responded by passing the Defense of Marriage Act. The law defines marriage as a "legal union between one man and one woman," permits states to ignore same-sex marriages performed elsewhere, and denies such couples pension, health, and other benefits available to married people. For technical reasons the Hawaii Supreme Court returned the case to a lower court which in December 1996 reaffirmed the right to same-sex marriages. Hawaii currently is appealing the ruling.

Does the Constitution include a legal right to sexual and marital privacy for gays and lesbians? For this issue, as in that of abortion, the answer appears to lie less in the words of the Constitution than it does in changing public opinion. The Constitution hadn't been altered when the Court enunciated a constitutional right to privacy in 1956, when it told the country in 1973 that the privacy right extended to most abortions, or when it decided in 1992 that the right to abortions was more limited than it had been in 1973. What had changed were social values. New values also affected the discussion about the right to die.

THE RIGHT TO DIE

Nancy Cruzan was twenty-five years old when an automobile accident left her in a persistent vegetative state. After watching their unconscious daughter lie in a fetal position for seven years, kept alive by a feeding tube inserted into her stomach, Cruzan's parents asked judicial permission to remove the tube and end what they said was no longer a real life. When the case reached the U. S. Supreme Court, the justices had to confront a new question about bodily privacy: whether a constitutional right to privacy and autonomy permits hopelessly ill but mentally competent people to refuse medical treatment, to write a binding "living will" or name a proxy in case they should become terminally ill and incompetent, or even to take more active measures to end their lives with or without assistance.

In 1990, the Supreme Court ruled in the *Cruzan* v. *Director* case that competent adults have the liberty to refuse medical treatment—the right to die—but that the right must be balanced against the state's interest in preserving life. The majority opinion written by Chief Justice William Rehnquist rejected the Cruzans' petition, saying that there was no conclusive evidence that Nancy Cruzan would have wanted her life to be ended. A blistering dissent by Justice William O. Brennan accused the Court of "rob[bing] a patient of the very qualities protected by the right to avoid unwanted medical treatment" and forcing the patient to lead a "degraded existence." Within two years every state in the nation and the District of Columbia had enacted laws legitimizing living wills and forty-eight had also recognized the right to name a health care proxy, who was empowered to make decisions on a person's behalf about such matters as ending life-sustaining measures if the person became incompetent to do so.

The Court's decision did not answer all of the related questions. One is how old a person has to be to invoke the right to assisted suicide. Under current law, minors have a right to abortion with the consent of a parent or a court. Do they also have a right to refuse treatment and thereby decide to die? Fifteen-year-old Benito Agreglo refused in 1994 to take anti-rejection drugs after two liver transplants because of the drugs' extremely painful side effects and the prognosis that his life would be short in any event. He was not asking for assisted suicide but for the right not to be medicated, which was in effect a decision to die sooner and without discomfort. Agreglo's mother respected the wishes of a son she called mature and bright. What if his mother had disagreed with him?

Given the growing acceptance of the right to bodily privacy, a person's expressed desire not to be kept in a vegetative state by artificial means was easily validated by most Americans in the 1990s.

However, whether the individual's right to bodily privacy means that a terminally ill person may be assisted by a physician or close relative in committing suicide because of great pain or incurable incapacitating illness has proved a far more troubling issue.

The issue has gotten great publicity through the actions of Dr. Jack Kevorkian, a retired pathologist who has aided over 45 terminally ill people to die since 1990. Kevorkian has done so by supplying victims of such diseases as amyotrophic lateral sclerosis (better known as Lou Gehrig's disease), multiple sclerosis, and cancer with carbon monoxide gas and injections of lethal drugs. His stated intention has been to have assisted suicide legalized. At other times, however, including his appearances before juries, he has said that "it is not the ending of life, but the ending of suffering, which is the genuine issue" and that competent adults have "a constitutionally protected right to end intolerable pain or suffering." Prosecutions of Kevorkian have failed because juries have refused to find him guilty of any crime. When the Michigan prosecutor who failed to persuade two separate juries to convict Dr. Kevorkian was defeated for reelection and the media subsequently almost ignored the death of Dr. Kevorkian's thirty-fifth assisted suicide, a *New York Times* reporter commented that physician-assisted suicide seemed in effect to have been decriminalized in Michigan.

Thirty-six states have laws against assisted suicide; there is no law in the other states permitting suicide. In May 1994, Judge Barbara Rothstein of the federal district court in Seattle, Washington, decided that the 140-year-old state law that made assisted suicide a felony and thereby prevented three terminal patients from getting the aid of doctors in committing suicide was an unconstitutional violation of the plaintiffs' liberty. "At the heart of liberty," Judge Rothstein wrote, "is the right to define one's own existence . . . and there is a Constitutionally protected realm of personal liberty which the government may not enter." Finding no difference between withdrawing treatment of a terminal patient and assisting another terminally ill patient to hasten death, she asserted that in both cases the patient had a constitutional right to bodily integrity:

> Both patients may be terminally ill, suffering pain and loss of dignity and subjected to a more extended dying process without some medical intervention, be it removal of life support systems or the prescription of medications to be self-administered.

She cited the multistep process created by Compassion in Dying, an organization that brought the terminally ill patient and doctors together to make the decision to end life. The step-by-step process was designed to allow either side to withdraw from it at any time.

In April 1996, one month after the Ninth Circuit Court of Appeals upheld Judge Rothstein's decision, the Second Circuit Court of Appeals handed down a similar decision overturning New York's anti-assisted suicide law. A Gallup poll taken that month showed that 75 percent of Americans supported the terminally ill's access to doctor-assisted suicide. Two months later the American Medical Association's House of Delegates demonstrated its disagreement by voting almost unanimously to continue the AMA's policy opposing doctor-assisted suicide.

The Supreme Court chimed in on June 26, 1997, unanimously rejecting the two decisions by the appeals courts and upholding the Washington and New York laws (*Washington* v. *Glucksberg; Vacco* v. *Quill*). Chief Justice Rehnquist wrote for the Court that the Due Process Clause does not include a right to assisted suicide. He based his opinion on the long history of Anglo-American laws against both suicide and assisted suicide and on the state's strong interest in protecting "vulnerable" people from "the real risk of subtle coercion and undue influence in end-of-life situations." Noting that "Americans are engaged in an earnest and profound debate about the morality, legality, and practicality of physician-assisted suicide," he added that the Court's decision "permits this debate to continue, as it should in a democratic society."

The unanimity of the decision was misleading. While the five justices who wrote their own opinions also focused on protection of the vulnerable, they disagreed with Rehnquist's statement that the cases were about a blanket right to suicide. Justice O'Connor, with whom Justice Ginsburg agreed "substantially," wrote a concurrence emphasizing that while there is no "generalized right" to suicide, she joined the Court only because the two states in question had no prohibition against dying people in great pain obtaining medication "from qualified physicians to alleviate that suffering, even to the point of causing unconsciousness and hastening death." Justice Stevens stated that "a more particularized challenge" to the laws where "an interest in hastening death is legitimate" might be "entitled to constitutional protection" and that he hoped there would be "further debate about the limits that the Constitution places on the power of the States" to punish assisted suicide. Justice Souter cited the "liberty interest in bodily integrity" found in the abortion rights decisions and the *Cruzan* case, saying they suggested that "a physician's assistance here" might well fall "within the accepted tradition of medical care in our society." He thought further discussion might show that the individual interest outweighed that of the state, assuming that the problem of guidelines for physicians and for protection of the vulnerable could be solved. Justice Breyer added that the issue was not a right to suicide, but "a 'right to die with dignity.'"

The majority of the justices were as troubled about the terminally ill *not* having a right to bodily integrity and to the assistance of physicians in dying as they were about the possible misuse of physicians' power. They returned the complex questions involved in assisted suicide to the states, which means that they are likely to remain on the American political agenda for some years.

These questions include the criteria by which terminal illness is to be determined, the test of willingness to die, the possible right of a potential suicide to be assisted, the possible right of physicians to provide assistance, the possible responsibility of doctors to assist, and the claims by members of the relatively new field of pain management that those who ask for assisted suicide often change their minds once their pain is brought under control.

Assisted suicide is a difficult issue because, unlike the privacy right of a woman to control her body, of a gay or lesbian to engage in consensual sexual activities, or of a terminally ill person to refuse artificial life-prolonging measures, assisted suicide involves more than the individual him- or herself. Doctors estimate that perhaps 25 percent of physicians have quietly helped people to die, but what about physicians who object to assisting suicide? What about physicians who may be too eager to assist? Is there also a right *not* to die; that is, to be given expensive treatment even when treatment is hopeless? As managed medical care becomes the norm in the United States and doctors and hospitals fall under pressure to hold down costs, will terminally ill patients be encouraged to commit suicide as a cost-cutting measure?

In November 1994, voters in Oregon passed a ballot measure allowing doctors to hasten death for a terminally ill person who has six months or less to live, who has repeatedly asked doctors to prescribe a lethal dose of drugs to end what the patient considers to be unbearable suffering, and who is able to administer the drug her- or himself. Similar proposals were defeated in Washington in 1991 and California in 1992, but those proposals permitted the doctor to administer the drug. Some people argue for adoption of the approach taken by the Netherlands. There, while euthanasia and assisted suicide are punishable by jail terms of up to 12 years, physicians can escape prosecution by demonstrating that their consciences gave them no choice but to end a patient's life. The law specifies that the patient must be suffering intolerable pain and must have asked repeatedly to die, and that the patient's relatives and another physician have been consulted. The U.S. Supreme Court was unconvinced that the Dutch system provided sufficient safeguards against arbitrary decisions by physicians—which is the major reason the debate continues.

CONCLUSION

There is no aspect of asserted privacy rights that generates greater emotion or is more hotly contested than the right to bodily privacy. Control of one's body in the context of reproductive freedom, gay and lesbian lifestyles, and assisted suicide presents all the hard questions: What, exactly, is privacy? Where does the individual's right to privacy end and society's power begin? Issues involving bodily privacy reflect in the most dramatic way possible the fact that the boundaries of privacy rights may never be completely established to the satisfaction of anyone. That is because of the primacy for all human beings of such decisions as whom we live with, which lifestyles we choose, whether and when we reproduce, when and how we die, which beliefs and faiths underlie our choices, and how far we are willing to recognize society's interest in and possible control of our decision making. Privacy is related to power. The debate about privacy ultimately is one about how we divide power between the individual and society, and inevitably there will be many people on all sides of the debate.

Although the sometimes conflicting demands of privacy and of criminal justice have not been as frequently and hotly discussed by the public, bodily privacy is also an element of that dilemma, as the following chapter will show.

Chapter Six

THE CRIMINAL JUSTICE SYSTEM AND PRIVACY

Something negative or suspicious can always be noted down against any man alive. Everyone is guilty of something or has something to conceal. All one has to do is to look hard enough to find out what it is.

—Alexander Solzhenitsyn, *Cancer Ward*

The television screen shows police wrestling a suspect to the ground while saying rapidly, "You have a right to remain silent. Anything you say may be used as evidence against you . . . ." It is almost certain that James Madison, one of the writers of the Constitution, had no idea that a few words he penned in 1789 would result in such scenes.

When Madison drafted proposed amendments for consideration by the first Congress of the United States, he did know that he had to satisfy a major objection to the original Constitution—one felt so strongly by many citizens that it had almost jeopardized the Constitution's ratification. That was the absence in it of a Bill of Rights.

Madison and the other delegates to the constitutional convention had included few specific limitations on the federal government's powers in the body of the Constitution (two exceptions were the rights against bills of attainder—bills aimed at a particular person—and *ex post facto* laws—laws that criminalize otherwise legal actions after they have been taken). This omission followed from the Framers' theory that the government created by the Constitution was one of explicit and limited powers; that is, the federal government would have only those powers detailed in the Constitution. As the Constitution nowhere mentioned speech or religion or imprisonment, the federal government had no power to act at all in those spheres. But that assumption was insufficient for Thomas Jefferson and many of the delegates to the ratifying conventions in Massachusetts, Virginia, and other states, who balked at approving the Constitution until they were promised that the first Congress would pass amendments expressly limiting the national government's power over citizens and would send those amendments to the states for ratification. Otherwise, the rights-conscious objectors feared, the government, made up of fallible human beings likely to be corrupted by the politician's omnipresent desire for power, would ride roughshod over the people's liberties.

The concerns about rights were a reflection of the abuses committed by the British king and his local minions before the Revolution, and they are worth recalling here so as to make clear the history Madison had in mind and the reasons for the ultimate inclusion of various criminal justice-related privacy guarantees in the Bill of Rights.

The Pilgrims had left England for Holland and then in 1620 for the colonies in part because of the English government's searches of their homes, searches that were aimed at ferreting out heretical writings. The phenomenon of governmental searches followed them. Although Parliament had declared in 1641 that all Englishmen, even commoners, had the right to be free from "arbitrary" searches and seizures, and while these rights supposedly applied at least in some way to the residents of the English colonies, the king's colonial representatives and the colonists disagreed throughout the seventeenth and eighteenth centuries about the meaning of *arbitrary*. Government writs of assistance, for example, empowered Boston customs agents to search for smuggled goods. Even though common law courts issued warrants good only for a single search, writs of assistance and general warrants specified no persons or places and therefore were usable against anyone or in any place. Attorney James Otis had argued powerfully but to no avail before the Superior Court of Massachusetts in 1761 that such writs permitted arbitrary searches and therefore violated the colonists' rights. Having government agents storm into their homes was understandably a major issue for the colonists, so it is not surprising that within a year after the Revolution began in 1776, the states of Virginia, Pennsylvania, Maryland, North Carolina, and Vermont adopted constitutional provisions against general warrants. Massachusetts went even further. In language that anticipated the Fourth Amendment, its 1780 Declaration of Rights included an article declaring that "Every subject has a right to be secure from all unreasonable searches and seizures of his person, his house, his papers and his possessions. All warrants, therefore are contrary to this right, if the cause or foundation of them be not previously supported by oath or affirmation."

The motivation behind the declaration was a need and a demand for privacy, for the right that had led William Pitt to proclaim dramatically to Parliament not long before that "a man's house is his castle":

> The poorest man may, in his cottage, bid defiance to all the forces of the Crown. It may be frail; its roof may shake; the wind may blow through it; the storm may enter; the rain may enter; but the King of England may not enter; all his force dares not cross the threshold of the ruined tenement.

Leading colonists were in agreement. The Rhode Island Code of 1647 declared that "a man's house is to himselfe, his family and goods as a castle," and John Adams had told a jury in 1774, "An Englishman's dwelling House is his Castle. The law has erected a Fortification round it."

Neither Pitt nor the colonists were defending a right of criminals to find asylum in their homes. Rather, they feared that government would trample the rights of the innocent. They were arguing on behalf of privacy and the right of all people to close their doors so that the government had no way of knowing what they were doing or thinking or saying. If law enforcement officials could not convince a magistrate that they had good reason to suspect that they would uncover evidence of a specified crime or discover a named criminal in a specific place, the government should not be permitted to search that place. This skepticism about the possible reasons behind governmental intrusions on privacy should be remembered as we look at the U. S. Supreme Court's later development of rules regulating searches and seizures.

The Massachusetts language quoted above, picked up by Madison and altered somewhat during the legislative process, became the Fourth Amendment to the Constitution.

The history of and reasons for the Fifth Amendment are similar. During the sixteenth century, the king's Star Chamber tortured suspects to elicit confessions. By the 1660s the right not to testify against oneself had been established in England, but the authorities had no obligation to inform a suspect of this right. Indeed, English judges routinely urged suspects to confess up until 1848, and even today the British police have no obligation to inform suspects of their right to remain silent.

Again, the concern elicited by confessions was not a desire to protect the guilty but the recognition that an unfettered government might well attack its political enemies or take a shortcut to what it sincerely believed was the truth by forcing confessions. The only way to keep that from happening was to forbid the use of compulsion. So Madison proposed an amendment that "No person . . . shall be compelled to be a witness against himself," which Congress altered to read, "No person shall . . . be compelled in any criminal case, to be a witness against himself." This statement appeared to mean that, unlike Madison's original version, the clause could not be used in civil cases or legislative hearings.

The Fourth and Fifth Amendments were ratified by the necessary three-quarters of all the states, as were the other parts of the Bill of Rights, and became part of the Constitution. But in 1833, the Supreme Court held in *Barron* v. *Baltimore* that the Bill of Rights was binding only on the federal government and not on the states. This decision left the particular formulation of the kind of privacy protections available to those suspected of criminal activity or accused in criminal proceedings up to each state. The question of whether there was a national standard arose after the ratification of the Fourteenth Amendment in 1868. Its Due Process clause forbids any *state* from abridging "life, liberty or property without due process of law." The amendment leaves unclear exactly what "liberty" it protects. The Supreme Court permitted the states great leeway in interpreting "liberty" as it was affected by the criminal justice system, with the Court holding in the 1908 case of *Twining* v. *New Jersey,* for example, that the privilege against self-incrimination was not so "fundamental" as to be protected by the Due Process Clause. The Court was not saying that states should or should not encourage self-incrimination, but simply that the federal constitution left them free to do so if they wished.

The Court did, however, issue what were in effect privacy decisions limiting the powers of the federal government. It decided in 1877 that the Fourth Amendment's search and seizure clause was violated by the opening of mail, since the postal system is a federal entity. In 1886, in *Boyd* v. *United States,* the Court struck down two federal laws that permitted government agents to enter the premises of importers of what were suspected to be undeclared goods in order to seize relevant papers and books. That, Justice Bradley declared for the Court, was precisely the kind of arbitrary power denounced decades before by James Otis. It was an unacceptable violation of privacy:

> It is not the breaking of his doors, and the rummaging of his drawers, that constitutes the essence of the offence; but it is the invasion of his indefeasible right of personal security, personal liberty and private property, where that right has never been forfeited by his conviction of some public offence.

By condemning "any forcible and compulsory extortion of a man's own testimony or of his private papers to be used as evidence to convict him of crime or to forfeit his goods," Bradley brought together the Fourth and Fifth Amendments as protective of the citizen's right of privacy.

Even though the Court recognized a right of privacy and was prepared to use it on occasion to negate action by the federal government, the circumstances under which it would do so were limited. This caution, as we saw, was evident in *Olmstead* v. *United States,* which held that wiretapping did not constitute a search. The Court extended the *Olmstead* doctrine in 1942, finding that a "detectaphone" that was placed against an office wall by federal agents and used as a means of listening to conversations did not constitute the kind of trespass forbidden by the Fourth Amendment (*Goldman* v. *U.S.*). So, as the country emerged from the Second World War, the doctrine of privacy in state criminal cases appeared to be severely circumscribed.

SEARCH AND SEIZURE AFTER WORLD WAR II

Most of the cases the Supreme Court heard from the time it came into existence through the 1940s involved matters of federalism and the nature of the United States's economic system. The constitutional assumption that the federal government would be one of limited powers and that most governmental functions would be performed by the states was brought into question by technological change. The industrial revolution that began in the United States during the early nineteenth century and proceeded with leaps and bounds after the Civil War changed the country from one based on small farms to a nation increasingly dominated by large interstate corporations and the assembly line.

By the early twentieth century Americans were as likely to be urban factory workers as they were to be owners of small farms. Large corporations were gaining more and more political influence as well as control over workers' lives, which led reformers to argue that government had to act to protect both the political system and the average American. The Progressive movement, signaling a partial veering away from the idea of limited government, insisted that it was the government's responsibility to respond to the needs of the people. This could be done to some extent by state governments, but a major role had to be played by the government in Washington. State legislatures were largely under the control of the new economic interests, and even if the legislatures had been willing to rein in the corporations, their success necessarily would be limited while corporations could simply move to friendlier states. Some states nonetheless made an attempt, enacting laws limiting workers' hours and setting minimum wages. Most of the statutes were struck down by the Supreme Court as encroachments on what the Court saw as the constitutionally protected liberty of workers and employers to make whatever contracts they chose.

The Depression that began with the stock market collapse of 1929 and that quickly led to widespread unemployment and poverty changed the thinking of many Americans and, ultimately, that of the Court. Franklin D. Roosevelt was elected in 1932 on the promise of doing something about the country's economic situation. The famous first "Hundred Days" of his administration indicated that he had every intention of keeping his word and that the Congress was with him. Together, president and Congress enacted fifteen major pieces of legislation aimed at getting the economy back on its feet. Other statutes followed in the ensuing months and years. All of them reflected a new assertion of federal power.

In 1937 the Court began to uphold New Deal legislation on the state and federal levels, and the country moved into the era of the semiwelfare state. By the mid-1940s, questions about the relationship of the state and federal governments and about the nature of the country's economic system were largely resolved: the federal government would be permitted to enact almost any regulatory economic legislation it wanted, as would the states, and the country would adopt a system of welfare capitalism under which private ownership was combined with government regulation for the benefit of workers and consumers.

The spate of federal laws and administrative rules required the creation of bureaucracies to interpret and implement them. The federal bureaucracy grew even bigger with the Second World War and the need for rapid mobilization. The Founding Fathers would not have recognized the federal government that had evolved by the late 1940s. The existence of a sprawling bureaucracy with sufficient power to participate in management of the economy and oversee a large army also meant that there was a new concentration of power, one that could easily result in such threats to individual rights as governmental electronic surveillance.

Both the Cold War and new technology contributed to a new political reality. J. Edgar Hoover, director of the Federal Bureau of Investigation, publicly defended the government's extensive use of wiretaps in the late 1940s and fifties to detect suspected Communist sympathizers, and in 1954, Attorney General Herbert Brownell told Congress that the federal government had about 200 wiretaps in place. Privacy came under additional attack as federal agencies and state law enforcement personnel began using new devices such as parabolic microphones, small hand-held transmitters, and miniature television transmitters. The states used the devices in pursuit of criminals; the federal government, in its hunt for subversives.

No longer involved in defining the economic system, the Court and public-spirited citizens began to turn their attention to individual rights and liberties. Two major questions had to be answered. One was whether the Court would interpret the Constitution as protecting citizens' rights such as privacy from violations by the states as well as the federal government. The second was how expansively the Court would read the constitutional protections.

The Court had a handful of precedents with which to work. It had declared in 1925 (*Gitlow* v. *New York*) that the free speech clause of the First Amendment was binding on the states, finding that speech was part of the "liberty" protected by the Due Process Clause of the Fourteenth Amendment. The press was brought under the First Amendment's protection in 1931 (*Near* v. *Minnesota*), and in

1947 the Court declared that the states as well as Congress had to respect the "wall of separation" between church and state that was established by the First Amendment (*Everson* v. *Board of Education*). So by the 1950s, some parts of the Bill of Rights applied to the states as well as the federal government. This did not include the portions dealing with the criminal justice system, however, and relatively few cases involving individual liberties were to be found on the Court's docket before the 1950s.

Then, however, the pace picked up dramatically. The Fourteenth Amendment's Equal Protection Clause prohibits every state from "deny[ing] any person within its jurisdiction the equal protection of the laws." In *Brown* v. *Board of Education* (1954), the Court held that "separate but equal" schools were not really equal, that they denied black students "equal protection of the laws," and that segregated public schools were in violation of the Constitution. A series of cases in the following years made it clear that the Court believed that racial discrimination in other areas of life no longer deserved legal sanction. Eventually the president and Congress came to agree, and in the 1964 case of *Katzenbach* v. *McClung* the Court upheld the federal 1964 Civil Rights Act, forbidding most discrimination based on race, national origin, or gender.

While the Court was reinterpreting the Equal Protection Clause and teaching the people of the United States that the Court had become the institution most protective of their liberties, scholars became increasingly aware of governmental access to privacy-intrusive devices and began condemning government surveillance. Congress held hearings on the subject in the 1960s and newspaper editorials started calling for legislation to limit electronic surveillance. In January 1967, President Lyndon B. Johnson noted the problem in his State of the Union address, telling the country, "We should protect what Justice Brandeis called the 'right most valued by civilized men'—the right to privacy." A few months later, the Supreme Court heard oral argument in the case of *Katz* v. *United States*, involving a conviction for bookmaking.

Under the leadership of Chief Justice Earl Warren, the Court of the 1950s and sixties had undertaken what some commentators called the "due process revolution." It "incorporated" one provision of the Bill of Rights after another into the word "liberty" of the Fourteenth Amendment's Due Process Clause, just as it had done with the rights to free speech, press, and religious practice. The

Court also read the Constitution in a manner that allowed old clauses to yield new rights. This was precisely what happened with the Fourth and Fifth Amendments and the right of privacy as it applied to the area of criminal justice, as is evident in the *Katz* case.

Charles Katz was arrested after federal authorities had recorded his telephone conversations by attaching an electronic listening device to the outside of the Los Angeles telephone booth he regularly used to place bets in Boston and Miami. Justice Stewart spoke for the Court in rejecting both Katz's contention that a phone booth was a "constitutionally protected area" and the government's argument that as long as there was no physical penetration of the booth there was no unconstitutional privacy invasion. The case, he said, had nothing to do with "areas" but with people, because "the Fourth Amendment protects people, not places." The Court's new doctrine was based on its belief that what someone "seeks to preserve as private, even in an area accessible to the public, may be constitutionally protected." Stewart noted that it would be ignoring "the vital role that the public telephone has come to play in private communication" to say that Katz's rights were negated simply because he was visible through the glass booth. If privacy inhered in the person, not in areas, then the absence of physical intrusion or the fact of visibility was irrelevant. Katz had "justifiably relied" on the privacy of the phone booth, so the government's electronic invasion of it violated his Fourth Amendment rights. Only a search warrant, obtained after the federal agents had convinced a judicial officer that they had probable cause to suspect Katz of a crime, would have validated the search of his conversations.

Here the Court reinterpreted a section of the Constitution to keep up with new social realities, something it had refused to do in *Olmstead.* The right of privacy was brought into the electronic era. Justice Hugo Black, dissenting, made the kind of argument that other justices would make when privacy rights were extended into the areas of abortion and bodily integrity. The people who wrote the Fourth Amendment clearly could not have been thinking about electronic searches, Black wrote, and the Court had no business redefining "searches and seizures" to apply to anything other than "tangible things with size, form, and weight." Conversations did not fit that description.

Even if one accepts the Court's willingness to reinterpret *privacy,* the discussion is not ended, because the question whether the right of privacy is involved in a particular situation is a matter of judgment. The most important language in *Katz,* as subsequent years would demonstrate, was to be found in Justice John Marshall Harlan's concurring opinion. The basis for decision in search and seizure cases, Harlan said, should be whether "a person has a constitutionally protected reasonable expectation of privacy." He elaborated by adding that a person's privacy is constitutionally protected when that person has "exhibited an actual . . . expectation of privacy" and "the expectation [is] one that society is prepared to recognize as 'reasonable.'" This standard would be adopted by the Court in the 1968 case of *Terry* v. *Ohio.* It was still left to the Court, however, to determine whether someone has an "expectation of privacy" that "society is prepared to recognize as reasonable." And *reasonable* has even more possible meanings than *privacy.*

That ambiguity helps explain the somewhat tortuous path the Court has taken since 1967 in deciding what acts by law enforcement officials have or have not been "reasonable" when the right of privacy has been invoked. The problem had been foreshadowed by the Court's 1950 decision in *United States* v. *Rabinowitz.* There federal agents had gotten an arrest warrant against a man who previously had been convicted of forging postal stamps, who had now sold such stamps to a government agent, and who, the agents had probable cause to believe, had thousands more such stamps in his possession. They arrested Rabinowitz in his office. While there, they spent an hour and a half searching his desk, safe, and file cabinets. Some of the stamps they found during the search subsequently were determined to have been forged and became part of the evidence used to convict Rabinowitz.

Rabinowitz argued that, as the agents had no search warrant, the search was not a "reasonable" one and anything found during the course of it ought not to be admissible in court. It was already well-established doctrine that illegally seized evidence could not be used as a basis for conviction. The underlying rationale was that denying government authorities the benefits of anything found during an illegal search was the best way of discouraging such searches and thereby safeguarding privacy.

In *Rabinowitz,* however, the Court held that it was reasonable to search a room during a valid arrest in a place of business, when the room being searched was technically under the individual's control and the fruits of the search were things it was illegal to possess.

Justice Felix Frankfurter dissented. He was unpersuaded by the fact that the agents had found contraband. "The main aim of the Fourth Amendment is against invasion of the right of privacy as to one's effects and papers," Frankfurter wrote. "The justification for intrusion into a man's privacy was to be determined by a magistrate uninfluenced by what may turn out to be a successful search for papers, the desire to search for which might be the very reason for the Fourth Amendment's prohibition." Reminding the Court of the searches for politically unacceptable material that had prompted enactment of the Fourth Amendment, Frankfurter argued that effective law enforcement does not depend upon violation of the rights of the innocent nor does a finding of "guilt" necessarily mean that a search was justified. "The knock at the door under the guise of a warrant of arrest for a venial or spurious offense was not unknown" to the Founding Fathers, he reminded his unconvinced brethren, and there have been "grim reminders in our day of their experience. Arrest under a warrant for a minor or a trumped-up charge has been familiar practice in the past, is a commonplace in the police state of today, and too well-known in this country . . . . The progress is too easy from police action unscrutinized by judicial authorization to the police state."

Frankfurter asserted that a search incident to an arrest was permissible only when it was necessary. This meant, to him, occasions when law enforcement officials had to protect themselves from a suspect's possible access to weapons, when a prisoner might otherwise be able to destroy evidence, or when the place in which a suspect was arrested was a moving vehicle that could easily disappear before police officers obtained a search warrant. That standard was adopted in 1969 in *Chimel* v. *California*. Santa Ana police, arrest warrant in hand, arrested Chimel in his home. They then searched his entire three-bedroom house, including the attic, the garage, and a workshop, in the process directing Chimel's wife to open drawers and move the contents of them so they could see everything that was there. Items discovered during the search, conducted without a search warrant, were used in the trial leading to Chimel's conviction for robbery of a coin store.

The Court, convinced by the criticism of *Rabinowitz* in the intervening years, found that this search was not warranted. It now found that in the absence of a search warrant, police could search only the area within an arrestee's immediate control. The decision specifically overruled *Rabinowitz*, in effect holding that an arrested person retains important privacy rights.

Court decisions since *Chimel* have left a confusing trail, perhaps attesting to the difficulty of deciding where people have a "reasonable" expectation of privacy. It has held that the expectation is violated by bugging devices placed in an office (*Berger* v. *New York*, 1969), seizure of obscene material in a home (*Stanley* v. *Georgia*, 1969), searches of cars for illegal aliens at traffic checkpoints (*U.S.* v. *Ortiz*, 1975), random spot-stops of automobiles to check driver's licenses and car registrations (*Delaware* v. *Prouse*, 1979), warrantless searches of luggage in a train by dogs trained to "sniff out" marijuana (*Arkansas* v. *Sanders*, 1979), and court-ordered surgery to remove an incriminating bullet from a robbery suspect over his objection (*Winston* v. *Lee*, 1985). The expectation is not violated by searches of an individual's bank records (*U.S.* v. *Miller*, 1976) or the telephone numbers he or she dials (*Smith* v. *Maryland*, 1979); high school administrators searching a student's purse for marijuana (*T.L.O* v. *New Jersey*, 1985); sniff tests of luggage in an airport by trained drug dogs (*U.S.* v. *Place*, 1983); narcotics agents searching an open field marked with "No Trespassing" signs (*Oliver* v. *U.S.*, 1984); law enforcement officers using a private plane to fly over a house at 1,000 feet, from which marijuana plants could be seen growing in the back yard (*California* v. *Ciraolo*, 1986); by a search, for evidence of narcotics use, of the garbage put out on the street by a householder for pickup (*California* v. *Greenwood*, 1988); or a helicopter search of a greenhouse from 400 feet up that enabled police to detect marijuana plants through missing roof panels (*Florida* v. *Riley*, 1989); by sobriety checkpoints used to detect drunken drivers on highways (*Michigan* v. *Sitz*, 1990); or by random drug testing of public school athletes (*Vernonia School District* v. *Acton*, 1995).

These decisions illustrate the tendency of the Court in the 1980s and 1990s to favor law enforcement when balancing the right of privacy against governmental actions aimed at the drug trade and at drunken driving. The Court has maintained its insistence on the privacy of the home but, in drug-related cases, has declined to extend the concept of "home" to property surrounding it, as indicated by the cases involving greenhouses, back yards, and adjacent fields. One legal scholar noted in 1992 that "the existence or non-existence of Fourth Amendment privacy now appears to be dependent" on whether the accusation involves drugs.

The increase in and great publicity given to drug-related crimes in the United States during the last decades of the twentieth century led to an understandable fear of illegal drug use and massive if unsuccessful attempts to curb the drug trade. Nineteen eighty-four was the first full year of operation by a nationwide network of organized crime drug enforcement task forces, combining the efforts of eleven federal agencies and offices. It was also the year in which federal intercept orders jumped by 38.9 percent.

During the next decade the FBI and Drug Enforcement Administration learned that wiretaps in drug investigations frequently led to convictions, and in 1993 alone, the number of wiretaps and instances of electronic monitoring by federal agents in narcotics investigations increased by nearly fifty percent. The Administrative Office for U.S. Courts reported 333 court-approved taps and bugs that year, up from 226 in 1992. In 1994 Congress enacted and President Clinton signed the Violent Crime Control and Law Enforcement Act, one section of which provides for post-conviction drug testing of people found guilty of federal crimes. Only intense lobbying by civil liberties groups prevented the law from permitting *pre*-trial drug testing of those accused of federal crimes—*pre-trial* of course meaning, under the American system of law, that the accused person still is presumed innocent.

Clinton circumvented this limitation in December 1995, directing Attorney General Janet Reno to have everyone who "enters" the federal criminal justice system tested for drugs. As Clinton said at a press conference, people had a right to refuse to be tested, but their refusal would become part of the information available to the judge who had to make a bail determination. He reported that in those areas where his order had been tested, eighty percent of the accused agreed "voluntarily" to be tested. The attorney general added that the meaning of the order was that "if you are going to get bail you may have to agree to testing, you may have to agree to continued testing, to supervision, to certain conduct while you're on bail."

The Communications Assistance for Law Enforcement Act of 1994, discussed at greater length in Chapter Eight, requires telecommunications carriers and manufacturers of telecommunications equipment to make it easy to wiretap the nation's communications system. It also authorizes the attorney general to pay carriers for costs incurred in modifying older equipment to enable tapping. FBI Director Louis J. Freeh told a congressional committee in March

1995 that "the drug cartels are buying sophisticated communications equipment" and law enforcement bureaus needed new powers as the nation began to convert from analog to digital communications technology. Simultaneously, the federal government increased its use of wiretaps and other forms of electronic surveillance. In 1995 the federal courts approved more wiretaps than all the state courts combined, due in large part to the stepped-up use of electronic eavesdropping against suspected narcotics traffickers. The 1995 Wiretap Report issued by the Administrative Office for U.S. Courts stated that it had been years since a federal district court judge turned down a prosecutor's application for a wiretap order. The FBI told Congress that it expected electronic surveillance to increase 54 percent by 1998 and 130 percent by 2004.

Apparently the Clinton administration considered a narrower definition of "reasonable" expectation of privacy to be appropriate in light of what it perceived as society's needs. Justice Department opinion polls, however, showed that more than 70 percent of Americans disapproved of wiretapping. This seems to indicate that a country worried about crime also is concerned with the possible misuse of power—the same problem faced by James Madison. Is there a way to reconcile the need for effective law enforcement with the right of privacy? The Court has thought that a partial answer might lie in the exclusionary rule.

THE RATIONALE FOR THE EXCLUSIONARY RULE

The exclusionary rule, which prohibits the prosecution from bringing into court any illegally seized evidence—usually evidence seized without a search warrant—has been the subject of much discussion and of attack. "Why," its opponents ask, "should admittedly relevant evidence of criminal activity be excluded from the courtroom? If the evidence proves that a person committed a crime, why should he or she go free simply because the police failed to obtain a search warrant? Do we want such people on the street?" It is a good question. So is the one asked by proponents of the rule: "How will you keep the police from violating the privacy of anyone they suspect of a crime, or of invading the home of anyone who fits the 'profile' of a criminal, or simply harassing people they suspect or dislike, if you do not prevent them from using the admittedly relevant evidence they occasionally may find?"

The same kinds of questions are asked about the Court's exclusion of self-incriminating testimony taken from a suspect in the absence of legal counsel. If a person admits guilt, is society best served by putting a criminal back on the street because the arresting officers made a procedural error? The counterquestion is, "How does one discourage misbehavior by the police when they are interrogating suspects, unless by telling them coerced confessions will result in alleged criminals going free? And how certain can one be of the validity of a confession gained under circumstances in which the constraints of the Fifth Amendment are violated?"

Answers have been provided by the Court, particularly in cases decided under the leadership of Chief Justice Earl Warren in the 1950s and sixties, when it expanded the rights against search and seizures and against self-incrimination.

In 1961, Cleveland police tried to search the house of Dollrae Mapp but she refused to let them in. They returned three hours later, still without a warrant, and broke down the door, claiming they were looking for a fugitive in a bombing case. They searched the entire house, and although there was no sign of the fugitive, they found obscene pamphlets and photographs in a trunk in Ms. Mapp's basement. She appealed her conviction for possessing "lewd and lascivious books, pictures and photographs" (*Mapp* v. *Ohio*).

The police and prosecution relied on the 1949 Court's holding in *Wolf* v. *Colorado* that the exclusionary rule was not binding on the states. When *Wolf* was decided, almost two-thirds of the states had considered and rejected the doctrine. By the time of *Mapp*, as Justice Tom Clark pointed out in his majority opinion, more than half of the states that had earlier rejected the exclusionary rule had adopted it in part or in whole "because other remedies have completely failed to secure compliance with the constitutional provisions" against illegal searches and seizures. The exclusionary rule and the rule against use of coerced confessions protected the American people, the Court ruled, against "unconscionable invasions of privacy," and the "right of privacy" was "embodied in the Fourth Amendment." Yes, Clark wrote, the exclusionary rule meant that "the criminal goes free . . . but it is the law that sets him free. Nothing can destroy a government more quickly than its failure to observe its own laws, or worse, its disregard of the charter of its own existence."

Clark added that there was no indication whatsoever that the FBI, which had operated under the exclusionary rule for almost fifty years, had in any way been rendered ineffective by it.

The country's police forces initially were shocked by the decision. Their reaction indicated how accustomed to violations of privacy through warrantless searches the police had been. A *New York Times* reporter quoted a deputy police commissioner as saying,

> Before this, nobody bothered to take out search warrants. Although the Constitution requires warrants in most cases, the Supreme Court had ruled that evidence obtained without a warrant—illegally, if you will—was admissible in state courts. So the feeling was: Why bother?

Five years later, in 1966, the nation's police were equally shocked by another decision, this one concerning the Fifth Amendment right against self-incrimination. The Court declared in the case of *Miranda* v. *Arizona* that the exclusionary rule applied to statements made to state police officers by any prisoner in "custodial interrogation" whose right against self-incrimination had not been properly protected. By "custodial interrogation," Chief Justice Warren explained, "we mean questioning initiated by law enforcement officers after a person has been taken into custody or otherwise deprived of his freedom of action in any significant way." The procedural safeguards he enunciated have become a famous part of American history:

> Prior to any questioning, the person must be warned that he has a right to remain silent, that any statement he does make may be used as evidence against him, and that he has a right to the presence of an attorney, either retained or appointed. The defendant may waive effectuation of these rights, provided the waiver is made voluntarily, knowingly and intelligently. If, however, he indicates in any manner and at any stage of the process that he wishes to consult with an attorney before speaking there can be no questioning. Likewise, if the individual is alone and indicates in any manner that he does not wish to be interrogated, the police may not question him.

Warren went on to cite cases from the 1930s through the 1950s in which the Court had been given evidence of police brutality—"beating, hanging, whipping [and] sustained and protracted questioning incommunicado in order to extort confessions." In a then-recent New York City case, "the police brutally beat, kicked and placed lighted cigarette butts on the back of a potential witness under interrogation for the purpose of securing a statement incriminating a third party." Although Warren stated hopefully that such examples had become an exception, he recognized that they were still widespread. "Unless a proper limitation upon custodial interrogation is achieved," Warren and the majority of the Court believed, "there can be no assurance that practices of this nature will be eradicated in the foreseeable future." Warren surveyed police manuals to show that their emphasis was on psychological rather than physical techniques but that the methods still invaded privacy. Referring to Ernest Miranda and three other people appealing in similar cases decided at the same time, Warren commented that each defendant had been "thrust into an unfamiliar atmosphere and run through menacing police interrogation procedures . . . . It is obvious that such an interrogation environment is created for no purpose other than to subjugate the individual to the will of his examiner. . . . To be sure, this is not physical intimidation, but it is equally destructive of human dignity."

The constitutional foundation of the right against self-incrimination, Warren declared in *Miranda,* was "the respect a government—state or federal—must accord to the dignity and integrity of its citizens." The only way a fair balance between individual rights and governmental need could be struck was by demanding that "the government seeking to punish an individual produce the evidence against him by its own independent labors, rather than by the cruel, simple expedient of compelling it from his own mouth." The Court could see no way of maintaining privacy, justice, and a fair government without excluding from trial confessions that were extracted by psychological or physical force.

A number of scholars have pointed out that the impact of *Miranda* on law enforcement has been minimal, just as Justice Clark had noted in *Mapp* that the FBI had found itself unhampered by the exclusion of improperly obtained evidence. The confession rate did not drop, and a plethora of studies found that *Miranda* warnings had little if any impact on the propensity of guilty suspects—and, occasionally, innocent ones as well—to respond to the accusatorial atmosphere of the station house with a confession. "Next to the warning label on cigarette packs," commented scholar Patrick Malone in 1986, "*Miranda* is the most widely ignored piece of official advice in our society." The reason appears to be human suggestibility. Malone cited an experiment with college students in which a group of eight students were shown a set of lines of quite obviously identical length. Seven had been coached to say that the lengths were different. Of fifty students who were put into the last place when the experiment was repeated forty-nine times, only thirteen were able to resist suggestion and insist that the lines were the same length. This human propensity, Malone implied, combined with the police station atmosphere, helped account for the continued high confession rate.

In 1965 three federal agents arrested a man, whom they suspected of narcotics violations, without a warrant. As Justice Brennan later described it, the agents "manacled petitioner in front of his wife and children" and, threatening to arrest the entire family, "searched the apartment from stem to stern" (*Bivens* v. *Six Unknown Named Agents of the Federal Bureau of Narcotics,* 1971). The Court upheld Bivens's right to bring suit for damages against the agents. Critics of the exclusionary rule point to just such suits as a more reasonable remedy for misuse of police power. The Court has held, however (*Imbler* v. *Pachtman,* 1976), that *prosecutors* enjoy absolute immunity from liability, even if they have initiated illegal searches. The Court decided in 1986 that only the officer who actually undertook the search could be sued for damages. The criterion for finding him or her liable would be whether there was a warrant and whether a "reasonably well-trained officer" would have been able to assess the legitimacy of the warrant (*Malley* v. *Briggs,* 1986). This decision makes the effectiveness of such suits highly questionable.

As the 1960s gave way to the late 1970s and 1980s and the perceived increasing danger of crime, the Supreme Court, which had a number of new justices, began chipping away at the exclusionary rule. It upheld convictions based on evidence obtained during an arrest under a statute later found to be unconstitutional (*Michigan* v. *DeFillippo,* 1979) and on evidence seized under a search warrant later found to be unsupported by probable cause (*U.S.* v. *Leon,* 1984). When Justice Byron White in *Leon* carved out a "good faith" exception, permitting admission of evidence seized by police who assumed that they had a valid warrant, Justice John Paul Stevens dissented. "The notion that a police officer's reliance on a magistrate's warrant is automatically appropriate is one the Framers of the Fourth Amendment would have vehemently rejected," he wrote. "The precise problem that the Amendment was intended to address was the unreasonable issuance of warrants . . . . The Framers of the

Fourth Amendment were deeply suspicious of warrants; in their minds the paradigm of an abusive search was the execution of a warrant not based on probable cause. The fact that colonial officers had magisterial authorization for their conduct when they engaged in general searches surely did not make their conduct 'reasonable.'" In other words, Stevens argued that the Fourth Amendment was designed to limit judges as well as police: lower court judges who issued warrants without probable cause and other judges, such as those sitting on the Supreme Court, who then heard cases challenging the illegal acts. The case of course had an impact on damage suits. If the Court upheld the legitimacy of a search based on a flawed warrant, then no successful suit could be brought against the searching officers.

The Court moved somewhat awkwardly into the computer age in 1995, when it upheld the warrantless arrest and the later conviction of Isaac Evans in Phoenix. Evans was stopped by police while driving the wrong way on a one-way street. After Evans told the officer that his license had been suspended, the officer turned to his patrol car's computer and found that there was an outstanding misdemeanor warrant for Evans's arrest. The subsequent search of his car turned up a bag of marijuana and he was charged with possession of an illegal substance. The police discovered only later that the arrest warrant had been quashed seventeen days before the incident—information that workers in the local judicial court had neglected to enter into the computer. In other words, the officer had relied on what turned out to be a computer error. Rejecting Evans's claim that evidence seized as a result of a warrantless search had to be suppressed under the exclusionary rule, Chief Justice Rehnquist held for the Court in *Arizona* v. *Evans* that the rule did not apply to computer errors made by court employees rather than *police* officers, because it was designed to deter police conduct rather than "mistakes by court employees." Justice Stevens protested in dissent that the Court "overlooks the reality that computer technology has changed the nature of threats to citizens' privacy over the past half century." He equated the "offense to the dignity of the citizen who is arrested, handcuffed, and searched on a public street simply because some bureaucrat has failed to maintain an accurate computer data base" with the "outrage" of the Bill of Rights' authors at the use of general warrants. "In this case, of course," Stevens continued, "such an error led to the fortuitous detection of respondent's unlawful possession of marijuana, and the suppression of the fruit of the error would prevent the prosecution of his crime. That cost, however, must be weighed against the interest in protecting other, wholly innocent citizens from unwarranted indignity." He concluded that "the cost is amply offset by an appropriately 'jealous regard for maintaining the integrity of individual rights.'"

Evans's case was not unique. As Justice Ruth Bader Ginsburg pointed out in dissent in *Evans,* a similar situation had arisen in 1982, when the Los Angeles police put into the FBI's National Crime Information Center (NCIC) computer an arrest warrant for a man, suspected of robbery and murder, who had been impersonating Terry Dean Rogan. The warrant erroneously named Rogan and the Los Angeles Police Department failed to include a description of the suspect's physical characteristics in its computer bank. As a result of the "incorrect and incomplete information in the computer," Ginsburg reported, "Rogan was arrested four times during the next two years, three times at gunpoint, after stops for minor traffic infractions." The chief clerk of the justice court in East Phoenix testified in *Evans* that errors of that kind occurred only "once every three or four years" but admitted that after the error concerning Evans was discovered, a check revealed that three other errors of the very same kind had occurred on the same day.

The cases led Ginsburg to agree with the Arizona Supreme Court that there was a "'potential for Orwellian mischief' in the government's increasing reliance on computer technology in law enforcement" and to add:

> Widespread reliance on computers to store and convey information generates, along with manifold benefits, new possibilities of error, due to both computer malfunctions and operator mistakes. Most germane to this case, computerization greatly amplifies an error's effect, and correspondingly intensifies the need for prompt correction; for inaccurate data can infect not only one agency, but the many agencies that share access to the data-base.

The NCIC databases, Ginsburg pointed out, contain over 23 million records available to approximately 71,000 federal, state, and local agencies.

In 1985 the FBI released a study of the nation's computerized criminal information systems showing that at least 12,000 invalid or inaccurate reports on suspects wanted for arrest were being transmitted each day to federal, state, and local law enforcement agencies. Computer data banks have grown since then, with the possibility of human error keeping pace. There is also the question of whether, even when no computer error exists, the use of mobile police computer terminals to access information about cars and drivers at random constitutes the kind of general search that led to passage of the Fourth Amendment. By mid-1995, three New Jersey cases had been brought involving the arrests of motorists who had not been observed to be violating any laws. They were stopped during random checks of moving automobiles and arrested because of information subsequently obtained through the patrol cars' computer terminals. David Banisar of the Electronic Privacy Information Center commented that the police "should not be able to go out willy-nilly to investigate everyone on a whim or a hunch . . . . The British in 1776 were saying, 'We're trying to investigate illegal smuggling and you only have to worry about it if you're guilty.' But they were investigating everyone's house," just as mobile data terminals are being employed to check cars in the absence of specific suspicion.

Today's police departments are combining the use of mobile data terminals with highly advanced gun detectors, long-range eavesdropping devices, and closed-circuit television. Police in Redwood City, a suburb of San Francisco, began in late 1995 to spread sophisticated listening devices, designed to detect gunfire, throughout a crime-ridden section of the city. At about the same time, police wired a 16-block area of Baltimore with video cameras that enabled them to monitor and record everything that happened on every street, sidewalk, and alley in the area around the clock. Redwood City acknowledged that with minor adjustments its devices could be focused on conversations inside houses; Baltimore officials admitted that their cameras could be tilted to look inside windows. To the video system, privacy expert Randall Coyne of the University of Oklahoma Law School responded, "It is just chilling to me that there is a permanent record being made of your every public action." Defenders of privacy argue that hidden cameras placed to videotape city streets or moving cars in the name of fighting the drug trade and traffic offenses will permit the government to monitor innocent people engaged in legal activities that they would prefer to keep private.

Police applaud the various new technologies as an aid to deterring or catching criminals; privacy experts, although agreeing that they can work well, fear that these, like other tools in human hands, will be misused. Faced with an ever-growing arsenal of innovative technological devices, courts are having to make decisions designed to reconcile privacy, the Fourth Amendment, and the exclusionary rule with the need of law enforcement agents to search and seize. The subject of the use of computerization and other high-tech inventions in the criminal justice system, the massive collection of information made possible by computers, and the potential for error, misuse, and invasion of privacy has only begun to be explored by the courts and the public.

PRIVACY, DNA TESTING, AND THE CRIMINAL JUSTICE SYSTEM

Much of the American viewing public watched in amazement in 1994, when television cameras provided live coverage of the short police freeway chase of former football star O. J. Simpson. Simpson was about to be charged with the murder of his ex-wife and one of her friends. What the country did not know then was that the Simpson trial would provide it with a lesson in the way DNA is used in the criminal justice system.

We have already seen that DNA is the basic hereditary material found in all living cells. It can be taken from blood, hair, saliva, semen, and other bodily substances. Today it is routinely taken from such substances found at the site of crimes or on the persons of victims or of the accused. After being broken down, exposed to radioactivity, and converted into a "fingerprint" image, it is compared with a similar fingerprint taken from a known specimen— which frequently means from a suspect. Only identical twins have precisely the same DNA "code," so properly tested fingerprinting can be employed with a high degree of accuracy. Of the two available DNA tests, the restriction fragment length polymorphisms test (RFLP) is the more definitive. It requires a relatively large blood sample ("large" in this connection means about five thousand cells, or a twentieth of a drop of blood) in good condition. The second test, polymerase chain reaction, can be performed with as few as fifty cells found in a minute speck of blood, with a sample in which the cells have become somewhat degraded. The test can be completed in about five days but has a six percent failure rate. That means that if blood samples from two people were tested, they would turn up as having been taken from different people ninety-four percent of the time, not one hundred percent of the time. RFLP testing takes from five to twenty-five weeks to perform and can be used only if at least a dime-sized drop of blood is available. Researchers look for matches at several places along the sample. If there are matches at five points, the proof of culpability is considered definitive. When both tests are used, misidentification is possible in only one out of 7 billion cases.

DNA fingerprinting was first used successfully in American courtrooms in 1987. It has since been utilized to identify otherwise elusive criminals and to free people wrongly convicted of crimes. David Vasquez, a young Arlington, Virginia, janitor of borderline intelligence, for example, was convicted of a rape and murder after he confessed to the crime during what the *New York Times* described in 1995 as "hours of intense police interrogation." A number of other eerily similar crimes were committed in that part of Virginia after Vasquez's conviction, and an Arlington police officer enlisted the help of Lifecodes, one of the first laboratories to employ DNA technology for forensic testing. With its help, he was able to track down the real murderer, who subsequently became the first person in the United States executed on the basis of DNA evidence. Mr. Vasquez was released after spending five years in prison.

Other less fortunate people have been freed through the use of DNA evidence only after serving much longer jail terms. In mid-1996 the Justice Department found that since 1989, twenty-eight men convicted of rape, some of whom had been sentenced to death, had been freed after DNA testing proved their innocence. In addition, the department said, during that period DNA testing had exonerated the primary suspect in about twenty-five percent of the sexual assault cases referred to the FBI's crime laboratory. So there is no question about the utility of scientifically obtained and properly analyzed DNA in the criminal justice process. The privacy question arises because the intrusive nature of DNA testing can be justified only if the evidence gathered is scientifically valid and therefore actually contributes to the meting out of justice.

The use of any evidence that must first be processed by a laboratory and that is dependent upon an expert's interpretation raises problems of accuracy and honesty. A non-DNA horror story demonstrates the latter. In 1994, Texas and West Virginia indicted a blood analysis expert for allegedly falsifying test results in hundreds of criminal cases over the preceding fifteen years. The "expert" was accused of having reported inconclusive results as conclusive, altering laboratory records, omitting reports of conflicting test results, and failing to consider additional testing when such conflicts were discovered. Many defendants were sentenced to long prison terms on his testimony, and suspicion about his "expertise" was raised only when some of them were subsequently exonerated for reasons such as confessions by the real culprits.

Even assuming that "experts" are attempting to do an honest job, however, problems remain. The crime commission appointed by President Lyndon B. Johnson in 1967 reported that "the great majority of police department laboratories have only minimal equipment and lack highly skilled personnel able to use the modern equipment now being developed." In 1974, a commission appointed by the Nixon administration reported similar findings: "Too many police crime laboratories have been set up on budgets that preclude the recruitment of qualified, professional personnel." The situation had not changed when the only nationwide survey of criminal laboratories ever undertaken was done in 1978. It found that 71 percent of labs reported faulty results in blood tests, 51.4 percent made errors in matching paint samples, 35.5 percent erred in soil examinations, and 28.2 percent made mistakes in firearms identifications. There have been no minimum certification requirements for personnel in the nation's crime laboratories, nor have the laboratories themselves been subject to regulation or external review.

Even though clinical laboratories that perform tests for hospitals and doctors' offices are regulated, those labs that may hold findings of guilt or innocence in their hands are not. Molecular biologist Eric Lander wrote in 1989 that the lack of regulation of forensic science has had the "paradoxical result" of requiring laboratories diagnosing strep throat to meet higher standards than those whose results could "put a defendant on death row." Between 1992 and 1995, the private American Society of Crime Laboratory Directors tested the nation's approximately sixty-five DNA laboratories but gave accreditation to only about a third of them. In May 1996, a committee of the National Academy of Sciences reported that there was no longer any reason to question the reliability of properly analyzed DNA evidence and that courts could now accept it with complete confidence. The committee was referring to "properly analyzed" evidence, however, and Dr. James F. Crow, a professor emeritus of genetics and the committee's chair, warned of "the relative ease with which DNA evidence can be mishandled or manipulated by the careless or unscrupulous."

The nation realized during the Simpson trial that accreditation of laboratories does not mean perfection. One point of contention was the procedures followed by "experts" working with the police department, who had failed to preserve the stomach contents of the victims' bodies or take the victims' body temperatures until more than ten hours after the police arrived on the scene. Stomach contents and body temperatures are crucial in estimating the time of death. The prosecution's expert statistician testified that only one in 1,400 people could have been a source of the bloodstains taken from Simpson's car and a glove found at the scene of the crime, and that the DNA markers for both were consistent with Simpson's. After being questioned by defense attorneys, however, the expert reworked his data, concluded that his mathematics had been mistaken, and admitted that the DNA markers could have been in the blood of one out of 570 people. Swatches taken from the bloodstains were placed not inside paper containers but in plastic ones, which allow DNA to degrade. The Los Angeles Police Department's lab, where the DNA was initially tested, is not accredited, and was described at the trial by a Denver molecular biologist as the worst he had ever seen. While the "expert" laboratory doing DNA testing for the prosecution had received the highest scores ever awarded by the American Society of Crime Laboratory Directors, courts had thrown out the lab's results as sloppy in four of 330 cases in which it had been involved. The percentage of successes is impressive. That it is not one hundred percent, however, raises the fear that innocent people might have been convicted in other cases, whether the tests were performed by the same laboratory or others.

The *Seattle Times* described similar sloppiness in cases handled by seriously understaffed and under-equipped Washington State crime laboratories. It reported finding that "thousands of pieces of evidence collected from crime scenes sit unanalyzed and ignored on shelves in laboratories and police stations across the state." A Justice Department investigation in 1997 of the FBI's highly regarded high-tech forensic laboratory concluded that agents mishandled evidence in such cases as the Oklahoma City bombing investigation before sending it to the laboratory, that laboratory technicians were sometimes unreliable in their processing of evidence, and that FBI agents and supervisors frequently went ahead with cases even when the laboratory told them that the evidence did not validate their suspicions about specific suspects.

The reliability of scientific evidence has become increasingly important as DNA has become accepted as a major source of evidence in trials for serious crimes. Privacy is implicated when suspects are required to give blood or hair samples. The Supreme Court has ruled that taking such samples is constitutional, holding that no self-incrimination is involved when the evidence taken from a suspect is physical rather than "testimonial," or verbal (*Schmerber* v. *California,* 1966; *Cobey* v. *Maryland,* 1989). Again, however, the privacy invasion is justifiable only if it will result in reliable evidence.

The mistakes inevitable in forensic laboratories clearly make it desirable for the defense to be able to perform its own experiments. Since the accuracy of the restriction fragment length polymorphisms test depends upon the availability of a relatively substantial blood sample, it is important for the defense to have access to one that is sufficiently large. Because of the great expense involved, however, most defense lawyers do not seek their own tests but, at most, call their own expert witnesses to attack the results of the prosecution's tests. Even the use of expert witnesses in that limited manner typically costs more than most defendants can afford to pay. The kind of countertesting done in the Simpson case costs at least $100,000. The services of the Denver molecular biologist alone reportedly cost $30,000. "DNA is a deadly weapon," defense lawyer Steven E. Feldman has said. "Where the defense is funded on a shoestring, we're being out-gunned. The biostatistician comes to court and says, 'There's a one in 10 billion likelihood that someone other than the suspect placed that specimen there.' But nobody really knows how good the labs are."

The use of DNA data banks of convicted offenders leads to another potentially disquieting invasion of privacy, particularly since, as we have seen, convictions based on DNA may be mistaken. In 1988 the FBI set up a Technical Working Group on DNA Analysis Methods to develop quality-control guidelines and establish its own computerized DNA data bank. We noted in Chapter Two that in April 1992 the Department of Defense began to collect biological samples from all armed services personnel for identification of "unknown soldiers." The samples, which are expected to number 2 million, could later be used to extract health and other information. Other federal agencies supposedly will not have access to this data bank. In 1993 the Washington Supreme Court became the first state high court to endorse forced genetic testing of people convicted of sexual offenses or crimes of violence—in spite of the Department of Justice report, issued a year earlier, stating that only three percent of convicted rapists repeat the offense once released from prison. In the two years following the passage of the federal Crime Control Act of 1994, which called for establishment of a nationwide DNA data bank, forty-two states passed laws requiring prison inmates to give blood or saliva samples that can be used for DNA analysis—*all* inmates, even though that sort of biological evidence is rarely left behind in the kinds of crimes, such as burglary, that are most likely to be committed by recidivists. Twenty-six of these states set up databases to keep the information on file along with records of physical characteristics such as height, weight, hair and eye color, skin marks, dental variations, and fingerprints. The databases eventually will be linked by the FBI with the nationwide network mentioned in the 1994 law.

As Chapter Two indicated, DNA databases differ from such techniques as fingerprinting in that the fingerprint test is simple and almost infallible and DNA tests reveal information that has nothing to do with criminality. Personal non-crime-related data, such as predisposition to various illnesses, now are available to the government through DNA databases. The data include information about people convicted of minor crimes as well as others later found not guilty. That is disturbing, given past and recent government misuse of information. Pointing to such instances, privacy expert Philip L. Bereano has commented:

> Living with conflicting values . . . is built in to the fundamentals of our system. For example, our criminal system does not have the identification of the guilty as its only goal. If it did, we would not have developed the rules of evidence that we have, such as preventing spouses from testifying against each other . . . [or] the exclusionary rule . . . . Of course, such a [DNA-based identification] system would help find guilty people, but if the system is going to compromise other important social values, perhaps we should not implement it.

Bereano's point brings us back to the basic question: how do we balance the value of privacy against other goals of the criminal justice system? Presumably there will be extensive exchanges of information among the computerized systems of the states, that of the FBI, and possibly that of the Pentagon—and, perhaps, those of non-governmental entities. At the same time, the rate of technological accuracy undoubtedly will continue to rise. Scientific accuracy will not eliminate human error, however, and therefore will not negate the concern that privacy is being violated for unacceptable purposes. And yet society can scarcely afford to give up one of its weapons against crime. Perhaps the answer lies in giving the accused the right to and the means to pay for a separate DNA analysis. That, however, raises the issue of whether society is willing to foot a rather hefty bill for the sake of privacy rights.

LEGISLATIVE AND EXECUTIVE ACTION

Congress, the president, and state legislatures also have been involved in balancing privacy and the needs of the criminal justice system. The Federal Communications Act of 1934 prohibited wiretapping and the disclosure of information gained through wiretapping. In spite of two Supreme Court decisions holding that the act was binding on federal agents, Attorney General (later Justice) Robert H. Jackson announced in 1941 that the government interpreted the act as meaning that it was legitimate for the FBI to wiretap as long as the information was kept within the executive branch. The act therefore did not discourage government wiretapping. In fact, there are numerous accounts of illegal wiretapping by the FBI from the 1930s through the 1970s.

By the late 1960s law enforcement agencies were demanding the power to use electronic searches. Simultaneously, citizens' groups were insisting upon privacy protections. Congress responded by enacting Title III of the Omnibus Crime Control and Safe Streets Act of 1968, the first congressional effort to regulate electronic surveillance by government or private agents. It provided that electronic searches should be as minimal as possible so as not to interfere with the privacy of people not suspected of crime. It also limited wiretaps to certain listed crimes, but it added that the statute was not meant to interfere with the president's power to take measures he considers necessary for the protection of the United States.

Technology continued to develop, and by 1986 faxes and electronic mail generated by and sent to computers had become a fact of life. Congress therefore passed the Electronic Communications Privacy Act of 1986, which prohibits unauthorized interception and disclosure of a variety of types of electronic communications. "Unauthorized" is defined in part as interception of communications by law enforcement officials acting without a search warrant. In February 1995 the House of Representatives passed the "Exclusionary Rule Reform Act." It would have extended the good faith exception provided by the Supreme Court to any "objectively reasonable search or seizure," meaning that the searching officers need only believe they have reasonable grounds for suspicion. The exception would have existed even in cases where the officers had no search warrant, and was premised on the theory that this latitude would enhance law enforcement efforts. The American Bar Association, represented in congressional hearings by a Wisconsin state prosecutor, argued strongly against the bill, predicting that it would increase illegal warrantless searches and decrease police professionalism. The bill's sponsors were unable to cite any case where the new law would have made a difference and so it was interpreted by opponents as an unnecessary invasion of privacy returning full circle to the days when government agents who believed they had cause to suspect citizens of criminal activity could search their premises at will. The extent to which the bill was designed to negate the privacy protections of the Fourth Amendment became evident with the defeat of a proposed amendment that would have replaced the text of the bill with the words of the Fourth Amendment itself. As Senator Warren Rudman, a New Hampshire Republican, had said on the subject in 1991 when a similar bill was proposed, "Under this proposal the police would have a powerful incentive to—to use a polite word— customize and shape their good faith after the fact."

Bills enacted by the same Congress demonstrate how difficult it can be to balance privacy rights with legitimate societal concerns. The Violent Crime Control and Law Enforcement Act of 1994 contains the Jacob Wetterling Crimes Against Children and Sexually Violent Offender Registration Act. When combined with "Megan's Law," signed by President Clinton in May 1996, the legislation requires anyone convicted of a criminal offense against a minor or of any other sexually violent offense and released from prison or placed on parole to register his or her address with a designated state law enforcement agency. States must create registries for the information or lose 10 percent of the funds they would otherwise receive under the 1994 act. They must make public any "relevant information that is necessary to protect the public" about such offenders, including addresses. Opponents of "Megan's Law" noted to no avail that most sex offenses are committed by friends and relatives of the victims rather than strangers who have been convicted in the past and that generating hysteria about a small group of people for a short period of time does not address the problem. They also asked whether releasing an offender from prison was not an admission that the required debt to society had been paid and whether continued public exposure therefore did not violate privacy rights. Proponents of the bill argued that sex offenders tended to repeat their crimes and that parents certainly should be informed when a convicted sex offender moves into their neighborhood. Neither side, obviously, wanted children to be endangered. The difficult and still unresolved question was whether the benefits of community notification about former offenders who might or might not commit another crime were outweighed by the certain effects of such information on their lives and privacy rights.

By May 1996, forty-seven states already had enacted such laws, some of them similar to the proposed federal legislation. Some went further. The Louisiana law, for example, required sex offenders on probation or parole to notify their neighbors of their criminal records, post a notice on their houses, and wear clothing that marked them as sex offenders. Twenty of the statutes required some kind of community notification. A *Wall Street Journal* editorial called such laws "clumsy and probably unconstitutional" and, remembering Nathaniel Hawthorne's novel *The Scarlet Letter,* likened them to laws making people wear a scarlet *M* for "molester."

The federal and state governments have been divided on the constitutionality of the laws. Some courts have upheld the statutes in their entirety; others have upheld provisions mandating registration with the police but have struck down the community notification requirements. On June 25, 1996, President Clinton ordered the attorney general to begin the process of developing a National Sexual Offender Registration System so that all the data collected under the federal law and its state counterparts would be pulled together in one computerized system. States have taken other measures to protect their citizens from what some consider potentially dangerous sex offenders. In 1993, the state of Washington's Supreme Court became the first state high court to find constitutional a statute requiring defendants convicted of sexual offenses or crimes of violence to submit to blood tests so that the states could establish a

DNA database of past offenders. Thirty-two other jurisdictions enacted similar statutes during the late 1980s and early 1990s. The Washington court, like the Fourth Circuit Court of Appeals that heard an attack on a similar Virginia statute, rejected a contention that postconviction testing amounted to warrantless search and seizure and an invasion of privacy without specific cause.

CONCLUSION

New problems in balancing the needs of the criminal justice system and the right to privacy are bound to emerge. Defenders of privacy are concerned that this will permit the government to monitor innocent people engaged in legal activities that they would prefer to keep private. School officials attempting to prevent drug use have become increasingly willing to search students, in some cases resorting to strip searches of minors without obtaining warrants or informing the students' parents. The Supreme Court said in one school search-and-seizure case that "although this Court may take notice of the difficulty of maintaining discipline in the public schools today, the situation is not so dire that students in the schools may claim no legitimate expectation of privacy" (*T.L.O.* v. *New Jersey,* 1985). The parameters of that expectation still need to be spelled out.

Technological advances will continue to generate additional dilemmas. On-line criminal-justice information systems that centralize information could be misused if access to them is not limited in terms of authorizing personnel to use them and preventing access by computer hackers. The FBI has a database of fingerprints, converted into mathematical formulas, of 24 million people convicted of crimes and also has the fingerprints of 38 million other Americans such as military veterans and federal employees on file. Some credit card companies are considering embedding such numerically coded fingerprints onto credit cards. Scanners hooked up to the mathematically coded and computerized fingerprints can be installed in police cars, stores, or welfare offices. Civil libertarians are concerned that law enforcement agents would undertake mass searches through such databases, accessing extraneous private information in the process. Some states have reacted by barring welfare officials from sharing prints of welfare applicants with the criminal justice system.

The problem of how society protects itself against crime while securing the privacy rights of the innocent clearly is a continuing and complicated one. It is made even more difficult by the dilemma of who will watch the watchguard: can public safety be used as an excuse for politically motivated law-enforcement and other governmental officials? This is the subject of the next chapter.

Chapter Seven

BIG BROTHER REALLY IS
WATCHING YOU

The part that frightens the hell out of me is the government deciding where technology goes.

—Senator Patrick Leahy, on the FBI's proposed Digital Telephone surveillance legislation, April 1994

Representative Robert Drinan of Massachusetts wandered away for a moment from the tour of the FBI's Washington facilities that the bureau had organized for members of the House Judiciary Committee. It was 1975, and the FBI had vehemently denied that it held dossiers on members of Congress except when a criminal investigation was in progress. Now it invited committee members to see for themselves. Drinan did. In his wanderings, he noticed that one drawer in a bank of file cabinets was labeled "DRI-." Drinan, who had never been accused of any criminal activity, pulled the drawer open out of curiosity and discovered 25 file cards containing information about himself—the kind of files the FBI had just denied existed.

Musician Leonard Bernstein also had an FBI file. His contained 666 pages that the FBI had amassed between the 1940s and the early 1970s. FBI Director J. Edgar Hoover apparently considered "left-leaning artists" to be a security risk, and Bernstein's file was part of Hoover's collection about people such as singer Josephine Baker, actress Jean Seberg, writer E. B. White, painter Georgia O'Keeffe, sculptor Alexander Calder, and cartoonist Bill Mauldin. (The FBI and the Immigration and Naturalization Service also collected more than twenty-six pounds of information about Engish-born singer John Lennon.) Bernstein's file contained hundreds of pages about his quite legal support for the civil rights and antiwar movements—as well as the notation that after Bernstein held a fund-raising event for the Black Panthers in 1970, the agency schemed to undermine his reputation through damaging news leaks to the media.

The Reverend Martin Luther King, Jr. was another object of FBI surveillance and action. There is disagreement about whether the motivation was Hoover's general fear, reflected in FBI files, of what he deemed "black hate groups" and of the possibility of King's uniting black Americans, or whether King became Hoover's target in 1962 when civil rights groups attacked the FBI for watching passively when demonstrators were beaten up in the South. Whatever the reason, the FBI leaked information to journalists about the alleged Communist Party affiliation of some King associates, recorded sexual liaisons in his hotel bedrooms, threatened him with blackmail by sending him and his wife the resultant tapes, and gave them to President Lyndon F. Johnson to play for the president's friends and to various members of Congress and journalists.

The three stories reflect the propensity of government intelligence-collecting and surveillance agencies to squirrel away information regardless of whether its collection is warranted, to misuse it, to lie about its existence, and to respond to officials' politically motivated desires for supposedly confidential information. The result is massive violations of privacy rights. Those rights can be violated just as easily by the misuse of records legitimately obtained by the government. This chapter explores the privacy problems raised by government surveillance, access to information, and record keeping.

We have seen that the New Deal and the creation of the welfare state brought a huge governmental bureaucracy with a need for large quantities of information and the resulting ability to violate the privacy of citizens. The Cold War between the Soviet Union and the United States that followed the end of World War II generated a fear of threats from both without and within the country, leading to the growth of security agencies, the surveillance of citizens and non-citizens alike, and the collection of yet more data.

The federal government had not always kept personal data in its files. According to the Privacy Protection Study Commission report of 1977, records through the mid-1880s tell little about the average American:

> Attendance at the village schoolhouse was not compulsory and only a tiny fraction pursued formal education beyond it. No national military service was required, and few programs brought individuals into contact with the federal government . . . . The most complete record was probably kept by churches, who recorded births, baptisms, marriages, and deaths . . . . Records about individuals rarely circulated beyond the place they were made.

Once government does begin collecting personal information, however, "[A]ccumulations of information about individuals tend to enhance authority by making it easier for authority to reach individuals directly." The report went on,

> [T]he voracious appetite of investigators for information causes them [authorities] to collect and retain virtually any personal data uncovered unless the collection or retention is *clearly* illegal. This attention to avoiding what is improper rather than accomplishing only what is necessary and proper, leads investigative agencies into abuses of citizens' rights.

Why should anyone be concerned about government files holding information about innocent activities? Accumulation of personal data by the government means that individuals no longer control how others use information about them. The U.S. Supreme Court commented in 1977, in the case of *Whalen* v. *Roe,* "The collection of taxes, the distribution of welfare and social security benefits, the supervision of public health, the direction of our Armed Forces, and the enforcement of the criminal laws, all require the orderly preservation of great quantities of information." The Court added, however, that there is a "threat to privacy implicit in the accumulation of vast amounts of personal information in computerized data banks or other massive government files . . . much of which is personal in character and potentially embarrassing or harmful if disclosed." When personal data are combined with surveillance, the result can be social control, unwillingness to participate in political activity, and conformity—the antithesis of the privacy necessary to individual growth and to the qualities needed by a democratic citizenry.

Surveillance of citizens and noncitizens occurred during both World War I and World War II as well as the interwar period. The chilling effect that government accumulation and misuse of information can have was demonstrated by the House Un-American Activities Committee and Senator Joseph McCarthy's investigating committee in the late 1940s and fifties. The committees held highly publicized investigations of allegedly subversive citizens and simultaneously disclosed information about people's political activities years earlier. People who had attended as little as one meeting of the Communist Party in the 1920s, when it was perfectly legal to do so, now found themselves branded in public as un-American by the committees. Some of the innocent people tarred by the negative publicity of the investigations discovered that public hysteria cost them their jobs; others were forced to seek anonymity in other states. Not a single criminal indictment resulted from these investigations. The Senate eventually censured McCarthy, but only after a substantial number of lives had been ruined and a climate of fear had permeated the country.

State governments followed suit. Mississippi is only one example. Its Sovereignty Commission, created in 1956, expired in 1977. Throughout its existence the commission used a network of informers and agents to spread propaganda and monitor people active in the civil rights movement, spying on at least 87,000 people and keeping files on 250 organizations and 10,000 individuals.

Dramatic as it was in the 1950s, government surveillance did not reach record levels until the 1960s and 1970s, when hundreds of organizations and hundreds of thousands if not millions of individuals were investigated. In the 1920s the FBI had launched its Counter-Intelligence Program (COINTELPRO) to infiltrate, gather information about, and neutralize groups it considered threatening to national security. The program ballooned in the 1960s and 1970s, concentrating particularly on groups in the civil rights and antiwar movements. A federal court found in 1986 (*Socialist Workers Party* v. *Attorney General*) that COINTELPRO was responsible for at least 204 burglaries by FBI agents, the use of 1,300 informants, the theft of 12,600 documents, 20,000 illegal wiretap days, and 12,000 bug days. At the height of FBI surveillance of the Socialist Workers Party (SWP) in the early 1960s, according to the court, ten percent of SWP members were reporting to the FBI. The surveillance lasted for more than thirty years but resulted in absolutely no finding of or arrest for any violation of federal law. During the same period the FBI operated a "Stop Index," using its computerized National Crime Information Center to track and monitor people opposed to American participation in the Vietnam War.

The CIA's counterpart to COINTELPRO and the "Stop Index" was "Operation Chaos," which infiltrated peace groups. The military had its own program, CONUS, an acronym for Continental United States. It monitored civilian political activity, keeping records in 350 centers around the country. Its files on more than 100,000 political activists included Senators Adlai E. Stevenson III, J. William Fulbright, and Eugene McCarthy, and groups such as the Southern Christian Leadership Conference, Clergy and Laymen United Against the War for Peace, the American Civil Liberties Union, Women Strike for Peace, Young Americans for Freedom, Americans for Democratic Action, and the National Association for the Advancement of Colored People. Specific surveillance efforts were given colorful code names like STEEP HILL, ROSE BUSH, PUNCH BLOCK, and LANTERN SPIKE. Freedom of association and the right of privacy of association were seriously infringed. Justice William O. Douglas dissented from a 1972 Supreme Court decision that the subjects of one such investigation had no right to sue CONUS. "The purpose and effect of the system and surveillance," he wrote, "is to harass and intimidate the respondents and to deter them from exercising their rights of political expression, protest, and dissent 'by invading their privacy, damaging their reputations, adversely affecting their employment and their opportunities for employment'" (*Laird* v. *Tatum*). Douglas described the way CONUS operated:

> The army uses undercover agents to infiltrate these civilian groups and to reach into confidential files of students and other groups. The army moves as a secret group among civilian audiences, using cameras and an electronic ear for surveillance. The data it collects are distributed to civilian officials in state, federal, and local governments . . . and these data are stored in one or more data banks.

He added, "This case is a cancer in our body politic."

Congress gradually became more and more concerned about privacy as investigations unearthed additional once-secret governmental invasions of it. There were forty-seven sets of congressional hearings and reports on privacy-related issues between 1965 and 1974. One, a series of hearings held by the Senate Subcommittee on Constitutional Rights in the late 1960s, convinced Senator Sam J. Ervin and others in Congress of a need for a regulatory privacy commission. Senator Ervin chaired the subcommittee's probes into agency record-keeping practices between 1970 and 1974 and oversaw the production of the report *Federal Data Banks and Constitutional Rights,* which recommended that data banks be regulated by law.

Nineteen seventy was an important year for privacy. Former army intelligence officer and political scientist Christopher H. Pyle published an article in the *Washington Monthly* about the Army's surveillance of civilian political activities, raising the question of why the Army was investigating civilians. The American Library Association discovered that United States Treasury agents were attempting to gain access to private circulation records, prompting thirty-eight states and the District of Columbia to pass protective statutes. President Richard M. Nixon, convinced that the intelligence community was not doing its job of ferreting out the subversives he considered to be behind the civil rights and antiwar movements, adopted a plan devised by former White House staffer Tom Huston. A Senate panel later described the Huston plan as allowing the intelligence community to "transcribe the communications of Americans using international communications facilities; eavesdrop from near or afar on anyone deemed to be a 'threat to national security'; read the mail of American citizens; break into the homes of anyone tagged as a security threat; and monitor in various ways the activities of suspicious student groups." Nixon wrote in his memoirs that it was only J. Edgar Hoover's refusal to cooperate with the plan for fear of discovery that led Nixon to drop it four days before it was due to be implemented.

Nineteen seventy also brought the Fair Credit Reporting Act, an indication that citizens and Congress alike were worried about the effect of data collection by large institutions. But at the same time, the executive branch announced that supposedly confidential information about individual taxpayers would be made available to the Department of Agriculture to aid in statistical analysis. Charges that tax returns were being used to harass Nixon's political adversaries began to be heard. The outcry about privacy led to congressional hearings on the propriety of various uses of tax information. The Senate Judiciary Subcommittee on Constitutional Rights investigated and reported on *Federal Data Banks, Computers and the Bill of Rights* in 1971.

In June 1972 the headquarters of the Democratic National Committee in Washington's Watergate complex were broken into under a plan hatched by Nixon aides, and Nixon ordered a cover-up after the FBI began investigating the crime. By the following spring the whole country knew about the administration's troubling malfeasance, exacerbating the suspicion many Americans already had about their political leaders. In July 1973 the commission created by Secretary of Health, Education and Welfare Eliot Richardson to study privacy and computers issued a report suggesting a code of fair information practices. The Family Educational Rights and Privacy Act, regulating governmental access to personal education records and ensuring the right of students to see their own records, was passed in 1974. Members of Congress were concerned about what they rightly suspected was extensive illegal activity by U.S. intelligence agencies. A Senate select committee chaired by Senator Frank Church began to accumulate copious information about the number of intelligence-gathering and surveillance operations directed at U.S. citizens who were engaged in legal political activity. It found that government intelligence-gathering and surveillance agencies had systematically violated privacy rights and other constitutional rights of citizens. On May 1, 1974, Senators Sam Ervin, Charles Percy, Edmund Muskie, and Abraham Ribicoff introduced legislation to create a Federal Privacy Board. Instead the Congress enacted the Privacy Act, which President Gerald Ford signed on December 31, 1974.

THE PRIVACY ACT OF 1974

By the election year of 1974 Congress was eager to enact major privacy legislation. President Nixon recognized that demonstrating concern for privacy was good politics and, in the midst of the Watergate controversy, created a Domestic Council Committee on the Right of Privacy chaired by Vice President Gerald Ford. The committee was charged with drafting "direct, enforceable measures" and reporting back within four months. As that was scarcely enough time for serious investigation and drafting, the committee relied heavily on a 1973 Department of Health, Education and Welfare report, "Records, Computers, and the Rights of Citizens," which proposed a "code of fair information practices."

Senators who became involved in writing the bill wanted it to include a permanent Federal Privacy Protection Commission that would issue regulatory guidelines under the new privacy law. The Senate Committee on Government Operations thought that a commission, which it envisioned as "an independent body of experts charged with protecting individual privacy as a value in government and society," was absolutely necessary to safeguard privacy:

> The Committee is convinced that effective legislation must provide standards for and limitations on the information power of government . . . . it is not enough to tell agencies to gather and keep only data which is reliable by their lights for whatever they determined is their use, and then to pit the individual against government, armed only with the power to inspect his file, and the right to challenge it in court if he has the resources and the will to do so.

There was an "urgent need" for government experts who would be available to assist the legislative and executive branches and who would be "sensitive both to the privacy interests of citizens and the informational needs of government."

No Privacy Protection Commission was created, however. Ford, who succeeded to the presidency as the result of Nixon's resignation in 1973, was adamantly opposed to a commission. The Senate nonetheless voted for one, but the House of Representatives did not. Ford's and the House's opposition, and the nearness of election day, raised the possibility that no statute would be passed in 1974. Congress, however, wanted to honor privacy-conscious Senator Ervin, who was about to resign. A compromise Privacy Act therefore was enacted, with the compromise including striking out the provision for a commission. Implementation was left to the president's Office of Management and the Budget (OMB), and further investigation and recommendation of reforms were delegated to a Privacy Protection Study Commission.

OMB initially was somewhat cooperative but largely unable to oversee enforcement of the Privacy Act because of its many other duties and of its being understaffed. Most other federal agencies in effect declined to take on the additional responsibilities mandated by the Privacy Act because no new funds were allocated for its implementation. The token gesture many agencies made was to appoint a Privacy Act officer, invariably someone relatively junior who had other time-consuming responsibilities. In 1986 the congressional General Accounting Office found that neither the Department of

Education nor the Department of Labor had anyone in charge of Privacy Act implementation; only the Departments of Defense, Energy, and the Interior had assigned crucial Privacy Act duties to a Privacy Act officer. The one piece of overall privacy legislation enacted by Congress had failed to make much of a dent in the executive branch's disinclination to protect privacy.

In spite of the poor implementation record, the principles laid down in the act are important as a statement of what should be done and as a guideline for those branches of the government that have made some effort to follow them. They were summarized in the Privacy Protection Study Commission's 1977 report, *Personal Privacy in an Information Society,* which remains the leading compendium of the flaws in U.S. privacy protection and suggested corrective measures. In addition, it carefully examines the problems of privacy in the private sector, for the act covers only federal officials and agencies.

The first principle enunciated by the report is, "There shall be no personal-data record-keeping system whose very existence is a secret and there shall be a policy of openness about . . . record-keeping policies, practices and systems." The act requires all agencies, including information-gathering agencies, to publish a description of their data collection systems in each year's *Federal Register*—a compendium that certainly is unknown to and unread by most Americans. Privacy expert Jeffrey Rothfeder discovered in 1993 that even this standard was not being met and that there was no public information about at least eleven percent of federal government data systems.

Under the act, agencies must tell individuals from whom they request information what the purposes for the collection are and the "routine uses" to which the information will be put. "Use" includes disclosure to other agencies. The interpretation of "routine use" leaves a wide hole in privacy protection. ACLU Legislative Director John Shattuck, later assistant secretary of state for human rights, commented during 1983 congressional oversight hearings about the Privacy Act that "the rule limiting disclosure of personal information without the subject's consent has been all but swallowed up by its exceptions, particularly the broad exception for undefined 'routine uses.'. . . In practice this has come to mean any use which an agency deems to be appropriate." As long as a "notice of routine use" is published in the *Federal Register* by a government agency,

Shattuck said, "just about anything goes." Should an agency want to release records to law enforcement agencies or the press, for example, it need only decide that there is a legitimate reason for doing so and publish a notice of its intentions in the little-read *Register.*

The Carter and Reagan administrations ruled, according to Christopher Pyle and John Shattuck, that "any use that an agency labels routine must be routine." In other words, an agency can label anything it wishes as "routine." The FBI interprets the statute as permitting it to share criminal files with other law enforcement agencies at the federal, state, and local levels as well as with foreign law enforcement and intelligence agencies, doing so on the basis of an informal decision made by almost any FBI agent. Congress has inadvertently worsened the situation by enacting laws permitting the systematic comparison of computer files collected for unrelated purposes in order to uncover welfare cheats, student loan defaulters, fathers not paying child support, undocumented immigrants, and to pursue a variety of other goals. Even a generous reading of "routine use" does not comport with the first principle of privacy in data collection, which is that information cannot be used for purposes other than those for which it was initially obtained.

The *kind* of information the government may collect is limited by the Privacy Act, which permits agencies to collect only information necessary to accomplish a lawful purpose. The agency itself, however, determines what a "lawful purpose" is. The act follows the principle laid down in the 1964 Freedom of Information Act (FOIA) that people should have access to at least some of the records about them held by government. Individuals have the right to ask for and challenge the contents of their records on the grounds that they are incorrect. The burden of obtaining and challenging records, however, lies with each individual. Whereas FOIA mandates a response to individuals' requests for information within ten days, the Privacy Act gives agencies no deadline, thereby virtually encouraging lack of compliance.

It should be remembered that a primary purpose of the Privacy Act was to regulate if not prevent computer matching and the development of an integrated national data bank. Given the exceptions for "routine use" and for agencies' disclosure of information that law enforcement officials consider relevant to a specific violation of law, the protection of the act in practice is minimal and dependent upon those interpreting it.

Scholar David Flaherty makes clear in *Protecting Privacy in Surveillance Societies* that the Privacy Act has done relatively little to protect the privacy of Americans from either government collection and use of information or government surveillance. Neither has subsequent legislation. The few attempts made in more recent years to create a privacy protection body have run up against what some have perceived as conflicting values, such as effective law enforcement and efficiently administered social insurance programs. Other groups have perceived conflict as well between privacy and civil liberties such as speech and press. The media, for example, is concerned that real privacy protection could limit its access to information. As most of us rely upon the media to inform us about what the government is doing, this is a serious problem.

Most Americans do not fully understand the overall problem of privacy. The 1994 Cantril report, *Live and Let Live: American Public Opinion About Privacy at Home and at Work,* indicates that although individual Americans were worried about various aspects of privacy such as the use of personal information, telephone monitoring in the workplace, abortion, drug testing, and gay and lesbian rights, they did not see connections among these issues. The result is, according to both the Privacy Protection Study Commission in 1977 and the Cantril in 1994, that there is no "privacy constituency" with a coherent view of the subject, an established set of policy goals, strong and widespread support, and effective resources.

SUBSEQUENT GOVERNMENT ACTION

Four months after the Privacy Act was enacted, Congress passed the Right to Financial Privacy Act, in angry reaction to a Supreme Court ruling.

Two decades earlier, in 1953, Congress passed the Bank Secrecy Act, requiring banks to maintain microfilm copies of checks for two years. In 1976 (*U.S.* v. *Miller*), the Court ruled that a customer has no legitimate "expectation of privacy" in his or her bank records because they are an independent record of an individual's participation in the flow of commerce and the property of the bank. The Right to Financial Privacy Act overturned much of that decision by establishing a protectible privacy interest in personal records held by banks. The 1977 Privacy Protection Study Commission's report nonetheless warned that electronic bank transfers "could provide a way of tracking an individual's current movements." "The dramatic shift in the balance of power between government and the rest of society that such a development could portend," the report added, "has persuaded the Commission of the compelling need to single it out for special public-policy attention and action."

President Jimmy Carter sent Congress a Privacy Initiative on April 2, 1979, proposing bills providing privacy protection for medical records, federally funded research records, financial records, and news media notes and materials. Hearings were held about the proposals but no legislation followed, and in January 1981 Carter was replaced as president by Ronald Reagan.

A number of actions somewhat protective of privacy took place during the eight years of the Reagan administration, largely as the result of congressional initiative. These included the Debt Collection Act of 1982, which on the one hand limits the government's release of personal information about bad debts to credit agencies but on the other permits it to give the agencies information about delinquent nontax debts. The first congressional oversight hearings on the Privacy Act were held by a subcommittee of the House Committee on Government Operations in June 1983.

Nineteen eighty-four was of course the year made famous by George Orwell's 1949 novel of the same name, which described a society without privacy. The Cable Communications Policy Act of 1984 was designed to protect the privacy of cable television subscribers by placing a heavy burden of proof on law enforcement agencies seeking court orders and allowing individuals whose rights have been violated to sue. The year 1984 saw hearings by the House Subcommittee on Courts, Civil Liberties, and the Administration of Justice on "1984 and the National Security State" and by the Senate Subcommittee on Oversight of Government Management on computer matching of taxpayer records. Nineteen eighty-four was also the year, however, in which the privacy-invasive Deficit Reduction Act was enacted. It requires states to establish information systems containing income and wage information acquired from employers and to exchange the data with other state agencies and with the Department of Health and Human Services, so as to minimize the possibility of fraud in the welfare system.

In 1984 Senator Patrick Leahy asked the Justice Department whether the Wiretap Act of 1968 (Title III of the Omnibus Crime Control and Safe Streets Act of 1968, discussed in Chapter Six) covered interceptions of E-mail or other computer communications. The reply was no, because the law limited a person's "reasonable expectation of privacy" to "aural" conversations and computer communications were then only "visual." A number of members of Congress then got involved, as did a broad coalition coordinated by the ACLU Project on Privacy and Technology and including major communications industry associations and corporations such as AT&T and IBM. The industry had a solid economic motive: it understood that users had to be guaranteed privacy if they were to buy its services. The Electronic Communications Privacy Act of 1986 updated the 1968 act by putting constraints on the government's ability to intercept and record new forms of electronic, non-aural communication such as electronic mail, cellular (but not cordless) phones, transmissions of computer data and videos, voice or display paging devices (but not tone-only paging devices); and by requiring warrants for electronic surveillance in espionage cases. (Even though the 1968 act mandated warrants for electronic surveillance in espionage cases, every president since its passage had ignored this provision with the assertion that the president has inherent power to wiretap or bug suspected foreign agents and use the information in prosecutions.) The Senate Judiciary Committee approved the 1986 act with the statement, "The law must advance with the technology to ensure the continued vitality of the fourth amendment." One section of the act states that people have a reasonable expectation of privacy in the numbers they dial and regulates governmental access to records of long distance telephone calls.

As noted, enactment of the Video Privacy Protection Act of 1988, which prohibits video service providers from disclosing information about individuals without their consent except in limited circumstances such as the issuance of a court order, followed media coverage of Supreme Court nominee Robert Bork's video rental records. The Computer Matching and Privacy Protection Act of 1988 places some limits on computer matching by government agencies, requiring them to formulate procedural agreements before exchanging databases and establish Data Integrity Boards within each participating agency.

Notably, these statutes actually place very few restrictions on governmental action other than that by law enforcement agencies. The Privacy Act does not permit individuals whose privacy has been violated to sue the offending states or private entities, nor does it give individuals recourse against federal *agencies* as opposed to individual federal *employees* who work for the agencies and who violate the law. Government records are still largely unregulated. This is a major lack when the largest 178 federal agencies maintain nearly 2,000 data banks, each with millions of files. In addition to his charge that the public has not been told about eleven percent of these systems, Jeffrey Rothfeder alleges that some government agencies "have their computers comb the country's data banks to create 'propensity profiles' on citizens. The purpose is to target people who, though they've committed no crimes, might one day cheat on their taxes or carry out a terrorist act." The question of who might carry out terrorist acts can be as difficult to answer as the question of who might some day commit a "subversive" act—or cheat on income taxes. So existing statutes do little to protect Americans from government invasions of their privacy. And such invasions are threatened or actually undertaken each time the nation is faced with a real or a perceived crisis.

One such crisis is the AIDS epidemic. FBI officials apparently thought they were acting appropriately when, as the agency has admitted, they spied on such groups in the AIDS activist movement as the Gay Men's Health Crisis, a social service agency that provides assistance to people with AIDS, Clergy and Laity Concerned, and ACT UP, a group that demonstrates against what it believes is insufficient attention and funding given to finding a cure for AIDS and helping its victims. FBI surveillance of AIDS groups was greatest in 1990 and 1991, under the Bush administration, when weekly meetings of ACT UP–New York regularly attracted 1,000 people. The organizations were completely legal, suggesting that government surveillance of citizens attending their meetings was a classic case of misuse of power and collection of unnecessary information in violation of privacy rights. It appears that although the country saw the outbreak of AIDS as a crisis, the FBI was and is at least as troubled by the existence of activist groups that are less than pleased with government policy.

DRUGS, SURVEILLANCE, AND TERRORISM

Technology is constantly improving in the field of electronic communications and law enforcement agencies quite logically expect to be permitted to use it. Whether taking advantage of specific technological innovations will aid law enforcement, however, and whether the price paid in privacy might be a greater concern, are other questions. It arises in the context of wiretaps, new telephone technology, and the Internet.

The privacy problem inherent in wiretaps is simple: the government's own estimate is that over 80 percent of the conversations overheard during a wiretap are not related to any criminal activity. Government-requested wiretaps are nonetheless on the rise.

Justice Department figures show that orders for "national security" electronic surveillance rose after the creation of the Foreign Intelligence Surveillance Court, a secret court included in the Foreign Intelligence Surveillance Act of 1977. It has never turned down a request for an electronic surveillance order. The number of wiretaps permitted by the court was 207 in 1979, 512 in 1987, and 576 in 1994. These numbers do not represent the totality of wiretaps and electronic bugs, however; the federal government taps under other statutes, and so do the states. The Administrative Office of the United States Courts reported in 1996 that 9,553 electronic surveillance applications had been filed by federal and state authorities between 1985 and 1995. Nineteen ninety-five was the first year in which federal courts approved more wiretaps than all the states combined, with the expansion driven in large part by concern about narcotics traffickers. Seventy percent of the wiretaps in existence in 1996 were for narcotics investigations; eighteen percent were for gaming and racketeering investigations; less than 0.2 percent were for arson, bombing, or firearms—a number that should be remembered when reading the section below about terrorism.

A wiretap may be of one telephone line or a "roving" wiretap that permits tapping of any telephone that might be used by a suspect. A "roving" tap might include pay phones used by the general public or telephones in the home of friends or relatives of people considered suspicious by law enforcement agencies. Americans may not know that most wiretapped conversations are unrelated to criminal activity, but wiretaps certainly make them uncomfortable: the Justice Department's own publications report that in the 1990s more than 70 percent of Americans consistently disapprove of wiretapping.

In 1994 the Clinton administration proposed what became the Communications Assistance for Law Enforcement Act (CALEA), also known as the FBI Wiretap Access Bill or the Digital Telephony Law. It required the nation's telephone carriers to build in special access for government wiretappers as they developed new digital telephone systems, enabling government agents to tap calls made on digital lines and fiber-optic cables and to do so while sitting in their offices rather than having to go out and attach equipment to targeted telephone lines. In November 1994 FBI Director Louis J. Freeh wrote to the *New York Times,* "There is no intention to expand the number of wiretaps or the extent of wiretapping." Only four months later the FBI gave Congress a statistical projection of future wiretapping needs for the next 10 years, showing that electronic surveillance would increase 54 percent by 1998 and 130 percent by the year 2004—which once again raises questions about government credibility and the possible misuse of power.

The Digital Telephony law had been unsuccessfully proposed in 1991, 1992, and 1993. It was beaten back by a coalition of civil liberties organizations such as the ACLU, the Electronic Frontier Foundation, and Computer Professionals for Social Responsibility, and over twenty communications companies such as AT&T, Lotus, Microsoft, and IBM. One reason was concern for privacy; another was opposition from the telephone industry, which objected to a set of provisions in the proposal that would have had the Federal Communications Commission draw up rules in secret and another that would have financed the system by having industry pass on the considerable cost to consumers through substantial rate increases. A third reason, however, was doubt about the necessity for the law. In May 1992 the General Services Administration said that equipment for wiretapping digital communications lines already existed and that permitting government agents to tap lines from remote sites would also make it easier for "criminals, terrorists, foreign intelligence, and computer hacks" to penetrate the nation's telephone network.

CALEA was reintroduced in 1994 and passed by Congress. Industry still strongly opposed the measure, but a provision was added to the law providing telecommunications companies with $500 million to make the necessary technological changes to old equipment. This provision did not completely satisfy the companies, which estimated that the cost of redesigning their networks to facilitate wiretapping would cost more than $2 billion. The legislative process has two steps: first, governmental action is authorized and then money for it is included in an appropriations bill. Concerned with the extent of wiretapping and with its costs during a time of budgetary contraction, the House of Representatives refused in 1995 to include language in the omnibus budget bill to fund CALEA.

A year after passage of the Digital Telephony law, the FBI announced plans to require telephone companies to build into their infrastructure the capacity to wiretap simultaneously one out of every 1,000 telephone lines throughout the country and one out of every 100 phone calls in major U.S. cities that it considered high crime areas. This would have been more than a thousandfold increase over previous levels in the number of phones that could be wiretapped. Public outrage defeated the proposal.

The country was shocked and appalled when, on April 19, 1995, a federal building in Oklahoma City was bombed with extensive loss of life, including very young children. Among the variety of laws promptly proposed by President Clinton to combat terrorism was amendment of the Fair Credit Reporting Act so that the FBI could obtain credit records for counterintelligence and counterterrorism. There was no requirement that a person whose records were to be obtained had to be a suspect in a specific crime. Clinton urged that the FBI be permitted to use pen registers, which record numbers dialed on a telephone, and "trap and trace" devices, which show the telephone number from which a call originates. He asked for congressional authorization that would enable the FBI to investigate a person without evidence of criminal conduct, obtain records of local telephone calls without first getting a court order, and obtain warrants for roving wiretaps. In addition, hotels, motels, and "common carriers" such as airlines and bus companies would be required to provide records to the FBI for counterterrorism and surveillance purposes. Clinton also wanted Congress to fund the Digital Telephony law, permit participation of the military in domestic law enforcement in some cases, and amend the 1986 Electronic Communications Privacy Act to permit use of illegally seized electronic evidence in court unless law enforcement agents could be shown to have acted in "bad faith." His proposal to permit the president unilaterally to designate foreign groups as "terrorist organizations," which would target them for massive investigation, was dropped because of strenuous objections by civil liberties groups and replaced with one that allowed courts to review such designations.

One week after the Oklahoma City bombing, FBI Director Louis J. Freeh and Deputy Attorney General Jamie S. Gorelick told

Congress that the Justice Department would loosen its standards for investigating suspicious organizations, allowing it to conduct broad inquiries into "domestic terrorism" groups. The announcement brought immediate reactions from civil liberties organizations as well as from Representative Sheila Jackson Lee who, along with a number of other lawmakers, was concerned that the FBI might abuse its authority to monitor domestic organizations as it had in the 1960s. Lee, remembering COINTELPRO, asked Freeh what lessons the FBI had learned from it. According to news reports Freeh "went blank" and was able only to mutter, after pausing briefly, "I don't think I could give you either a short or informed answer to that . . . . I would really have to do some research to give you an intelligent answer."

Some of the additional powers to wiretap were included in the Counter-Terrorism Act of 1996 enacted exactly a year after the Oklahoma City bombing. Proponents said the statute would give law enforcement agents a much-needed arsenal in the era of terrorism. National security expert Gregory T. Nojeim challenged this assertion, however, pointing to the statistics showing that law enforcement personnel virtually never sought to use electronic surveillance while investigating crimes such as arson, bombings, or firearms violations that are commonly associated with terrorism. Law enforcement officials had found wiretapping to be an ineffective technique for preventing such crimes.

The month of July 1996 saw two tragic alleged acts of terrorism in the United States: the explosion of a TWA airplane, initially assumed to be the work of a bomber, after it took off from New York's Kennedy airport, and the bombing of a park within the 1996 Olympics compound in Atlanta, Georgia. The president and Congress immediately began reconsidering the antiterrorism measures proposed in 1995 but left unenacted by Congress, such as legalizing roving wiretaps. On August 1 Representative Bob Barr, a former federal prosecutor, asserted at a news conference that the administration already had the power necessary to combat terrorism. Barr called upon the government to "stop looking for scapegoats and truly commit itself to fighting terrorism." The following day the House of Representatives passed an antiterrorism bill without the roving wiretap provision. What interested privacy experts at least as much was the inclusion in the bill of privacy *protections:* doubling of the punishment, to ten years, for the unlawful disclosure of information obtained from a wiretap; changing violation of the Privacy Act from a misdemeanor to a felony; and increasing the minimum penalty for civil violations of the Privacy Act from $1,000 to $5,000.

A year later FBI Director Freeh concluded that the TWA crash was not the work of terrorists but the result of mechanical malfunction.

Two final stories of government information gathering and misuse of information in the 1990s, both with privacy implications, should be mentioned here. The first is the scandal that came to be known as "Filegate."

The Clinton White House acknowledged in 1996 that during four months in 1993 it collected FBI background reports on more than 300 people, among them prominent Republicans such as former Secretary of State James A. Baker III; former White House Counsel A. B. Culvahouse; and Tony Blankley, then House Speaker Newt Gingrich's press secretary. The White House claimed that a low-level bureaucrat had realized that the security files kept on White House employees were missing for some permanent employees—those in nonpartisan positions who keep their jobs no matter who is president. The bureaucrat asked the FBI for the relevant files. Those requested came from a list of White House employees so outdated that it included Republicans no longer working in the White House. The bureaucrat, who was later identified as a civilian investigator for the Army, left the White House a few months after beginning the update. The person who replaced him realized the error and stopped the requests. Between 330 and 340 files were obtained, the White House admitted at first; the number was then changed to about 407. Later still the number was raised to about 907.

Whatever the inconsistencies in the White House explanation, two facts were incontrovertible: the White House had requested FBI files for which it had no legitimate use, and the FBI had simply turned them over. FBI officials admitted that the bureau's safeguards were inadequate. The Clinton administration called the episode an innocent blunder; Republicans charged that the White House was replicating the tactics of President Richard Nixon in creating an "enemies list." The scandal died down when the White House said it was putting the entire matter in the hands of an independent special counsel. What did not die down were the reminders that the government is as capable as any other institution of seeking private information improperly, that the government has a great deal of information about Americans on file, and that the privacy-violative "sharing" of such information is not uncommon. The military's reliance on supposedly confidential Census Bureau information to round up Japanese Americans charged with no crime other than that of being Japanese American during World War II will be remembered as another example of government misuse of data.

The last story about government surveillance has to do with the "clipper chip" proposal announced by the White House's National Security Agency in 1993 and developed jointly by the agency and the FBI.

The FBI first suggested the clipper chip in 1991. Claiming that sophisticated code-producing technology had made it possible to encode computer and telephone messages so that they could not be deciphered by the most powerful code-breaking computers, the FBI suggested that all communications and computer companies doing business with the federal government be required to put a special government-designed computer chip into their telephones and computer hardware and software that would permit breaking of any code. The "key" to any code would thereby be put into the hands of the government. It was expected that if manufacturers had to include the chip in products built for the government, cost considerations would lead them to put it into all such products, so that eventually the only encryption system available in U.S.-made machines would be accessible by the government. Objections about possible government misuse of information led the Clinton administration to alter the proposal in April 1993, suggesting that two separate keys would each be held by the Treasury Department and the National Institute of Standards and Technology. In 1994 the administration announced it was adopting the technology.

Business and civil liberties groups objected. No one doubted that encryption could be used by criminals. The concern was that the power given to the government would not be sufficiently limited, as it would allow access to *all* computers and telephones.

Communications companies feared that domestic customers would not trust an encryption program built by the government and that foreign customers would refuse to buy equipment containing decoding technology devised by the U.S. government. Civil libertarians argued that the goal of combating crime would not be reached: criminals sophisticated enough to encode their messages would not use encryption to which government held the keys. They also pointed out that allowing the government access to all encrypted messages was analogous to giving the government access to all mail on the theory that criminals sometimes use the postal system. Computer experts said that before long some hacker surely would crack the code, making it worthless. They were additionally concerned that the National Security Agency might build a secret "trap door" into the chip, allowing access by government agencies that did not have the official keys.

A national debate followed. One point of view, presented by FBI Director Freeh to the House Subcommittee on Crime, was that "Powerful encryption is becoming commonplace. The drug cartels are buying sophisticated communications equipment. Unless the issue of encryption is resolved soon, criminal conversations over the telephone and other communications devices will become indecipherable by law enforcement." The FBI's chief of investigative technology added that "we need these tools to do our job."

A leading cryptographer at Sun Microsystems, on the other hand, objected that the clipper chip was like "the little keyhole in the back of the combination locks used on the lockers of schoolchildren," which keeps out other students but permits the locks to be opened by the teacher who holds the key. Yankelovich Partners conducted a survey for *Time* magazine and CNN, finding that 80 percent of the public knowledgeable about the clipper chip opposed it. In June 1993, the National Institute of Standards and Technology's advisory panel on privacy issues held two days of hearings and concluded that the proposal led to "serious concerns" because the government had not made a convincing case about law enforcement's need for the chip and because the plan would damage the American software industry's exports. Columnist William Safire urged readers all over the country to consider the consequences of enabling the government to tap phones and computers when it also had access to credit card data, psychological and student test scores, tax returns, welfare records, and CIA dossiers. The White House finally announced that it would review its policy and limit its action to buying the roughly 10,000 clipper-equipped telephones already on order.

During the following year the White House made several proposals (labeled "Clipper 2," "Clipper 3," "Clipper 4," and so on by privacy advocates) to require that encryption users leave a decoding key to their encryption program with a government agent, a government-certified agent, or an agent who would turn the key over to the government without informing the person or business who had provided the key. Governmental control of encryption became a campaign issue in 1996. In 1997 newly reelected President Clinton reintroduced his proposal while continuing to engage in negotiations aimed at satisfying the communications industry. The media then reported that government threats to deny export licenses to manufacturers of digital cell telephones had led the companies to weaken the encryption program in the phones so that electronic eavesdropping by government would be easier. This accommodation in turn made calls vulnerable to interception by anyone. Next came news of a successful effort by hackers to crack the weaker program, which rendered even cellular calls on digital phones open to interception.

Ironically, the FBI's focus on restricting strong encryption as providing too much privacy protection had become the biggest threat to law enforcement and an aid to terrorism. The Committee on National Cryptography Policy of the National Research Council (NRC) noted in 1997 that all of the nation's computer-driven infrastructure—dams, power grids, medical facilities, telecommunications and financial networks, governmental records—were at greater risk because of the administration's effort to weaken encryption. The NRC committee concluded,

> If cryptography can protect the trade secrets and proprietary
> information of businesses and thereby reduce economic espi-
> onage (which it can), it also supports in a most important man-
> ner the job of law enforcement. If cryptography can help protect
> nationally critical information systems and networks against
> unauthorized penetration (which it can), it also supports the
> national security of the United States.

As of late 1997, negotiations between the White House and the computer industry were continuing.

In 1996 Philip Zimmerman testified before Congress. He had become concerned about communications privacy when the digital telephony sense-of-the-Congress resolution was introduced in 1991. Before the resolution was defeated he wrote a computer software program he called "Pretty Good Privacy" (PGP), which enabled computer users to encrypt their messages so as to avoid government decoding. "I did it because I wanted cryptography to be made available to the American public before it became illegal to use it," Zimmerman said. "I wrote PGP from information in the open literature, putting it into a convenient package that everyone can use in a desktop or palmtop computer. Then I gave it away for free, for the good of democracy." As Zimmerman noted in his testimony, by 1996 organizations all over the world that were concerned about communications privacy were using the program. "Amnesty International uses it. The human rights group in the American Association for the Advancement of Science uses it. It is used to protect witnesses who report human rights abuses in the Balkans, in Burma, in Guatemala, in Tibet," and by human rights groups in Eastern Europe. "Some Americans don't understand why I should be this concerned about the power of government," Zimmerman continued. "But talking to people in Eastern Europe, you don't have to explain it to them. They already get it—and they don't understand why we don't."

Chapter Eight

PRIVACY IN THE WORKPLACE

I might have been a gold-fish in a glass bowl for all the privacy I got.

—H. H. Munro ("Saki"), *Reginald I*

Michael Smyth and his supervisor at the Pillsbury Company were having a laugh at their boss's expense, sitting in their respective offices and exchanging derogatory E-mail messages. They expected no trouble. In order to safeguard one's E-mail account, after all, one has a private password, and in addition, Pillsbury had promised its employees that it would not violate the confidentiality and privacy of E-mail communications and that E-mail never would be used by the company as grounds for termination. But Pillsbury was monitoring E-mail and, not much liking what Smyth had to say, fired him. In 1996 a federal court ruled that the company had the right to do so (*Smyth* v. *Pillsbury*).

The workplace situation couldn't have been more different from the one that existed when the Bill of Rights was ratified. Imagine a typical workplace in, say, 1796 rather than 1997. An American farmer, his wife, their children, and a hired hand are working side by side in the fields. Much of their lives are spent together, and each tends to know a substantial amount about the others. There is no differential in privacy between employer and employee.

Now leap forward to the 1990s. The workplace is far likelier to be an office or an urban store than a farm. It may even resemble the set of the 1994 film *Disclosure,* which took place in a Seattle high-tech computer firm. The work space was made up of glass compartments. People with lower status shared a room, those with higher status had individually partitioned spaces, but all except the very top executives were visible to anyone walking by. A flunky with a cellular telephone reported to the company's president on the easily seen movements of the hero. The difference in privacy between employer and almost all employees could not have been greater.

Privacy in the workplace becomes a problem when a business enterprise is large enough for separation of employees and employers, with the space occupied by employees open to employers but the space occupied by the employers one that is considered "private." So it is not surprising that workplace privacy became a major concern as the United States industrialized, that the situation worsened with the introduction to the office and factory of "time-management" techniques and "sociological engineering" designed to increase the pace of work, and that the problem became greater still as post–World War II technology permitted invasions of privacy that went beyond visible behavior.

Centralization and a contracting economy also have affected workplace privacy. When businesses were small enough so that workers had the option of leaving one firm for another, an overly intrusive employer could be avoided. As technology has enabled first machines and then computers to replace human beings on the job, however; as the number of businesses has decreased; and as job security has become relatively rare in the late-twentieth century economy, the ability to leave a job because of violation of one's privacy rights has become a luxury affordable by very few.

Post–World War II corporations arguably have become the largest and most powerful institutions in the nation. General Motors, for example, has nearly 1 million employees. Its economic resources not only exceed those of any city or state in the United States, they are larger than those of many countries. Affiliated Publications, the smallest of the companies listed in the Fortune 500, has an annual income of more than $500 million. In other words, corporations have far more control over their employees' lives today than the U. S. government had over anyone at the time the Bill of Rights was written. We have already seen the substantial impact that genetic testing and use of the "records of one's life" have had on potential and actual employees of the 1980s and 1990s. In the 1990s, employer attempts to identify habits such as smoking during employees' hours away from the job have raised the additional question of the extent to which employers can extend their knowledge of their workers' lives into the workers' behavior off the job.

Employers argue that precisely because the workplace has become so big, it is necessary to resort to new privacy-invasive techniques to monitor employee performance. And employers, too, are affected by a contracting economy. They want to know which employees are likely to drive up their health insurance plan costs, which engage in behavior likely to interfere with their job performance, which are slacking off. It's not only employers who will benefit from this knowledge, they argue; savings can be passed on to consumers. What, if any, legal protection has been provided for workers in the private sector? Does the historical record suggest that there is a way to resolve what seem to be the conflicting rights of the workers and the needs of the employers?

FROM "THE GOOD OLD DAYS" TO THE 1980s

The belief of employers that the economic consequences of employee performance give businesses a right to monitor employees' off-the-job lives is not as new as some of the current discussion would lead one to believe. The bustling textile mills of New England in the 1830s, for example, required their largely unmarried young women workers to live in company-owned boardinghouses unless their families resided in the town. One such mill included the following among its regulations:

> The tenants of the Boarding Houses . . . will be considered answerable for any improper conduct in their houses, and are not to permit their boarders to have company at unseasonable hours.
> The doors must be closed at ten o'clock in the evening . . . .
> The keepers of the Boarding Houses must . . . . report the names of such as are guilty of any improper conduct, or are not in the regular habit of attending public worship.

Similarly, the Lawrence Company required boardinghouse keepers to report "all cases of intemperance, or of dissolute manners" to the company. All of the companies expected their workers to attend church, the Suffolk Company regulations stating explicitly that "regular attendance at public worship on the Sabbath is necessary for the preservation of good order." The women boarders—and men as well, for many of the men drawn to the factories came from distant localities and could find no other lodging—were forbidden alcoholic beverages and were expected to provide the companies with the names of their visitors when requested to do so. Anyone violating these rules would be fired and blacklisted by other mills in the area. In a foretaste of the late-twentieth century rationale for controlling employees' lives off the jobs, mill owners organized their workers' lives so as to ensure compliant, well-rested operatives who would be able to carry out their jobs in a manner that their employers considered responsible.

Off-the-job monitoring of employees was confined neither to mills nor to New England. A carriage shop in New York City in 1878 posted the following rules:

> Working hours shall be 7:00 A.M. to 8:00 P.M. every evening but the Sabbath. On the Sabbath, everyone is expected to be in the Lord's House.
> It is expected that each employee shall participate in the activities of the church . . .
> All employees are expected to be in bed by 10:00 P.M. Except: Each male employee may be given one evening a week for courting purposes and two evenings a week in the Lord's House.
> It is the bounden duty of each employee to put away at least 10% of his wages for his declining years, so that he will not become a burden upon the charity of his betters.

The attitude of the employers clearly was that they not only had economic interests to protect but that the status of employer carried with it a kind of noblesse oblige—the responsibility of the "better" classes to safeguard the morals of the "lower." This can be seen in Allan Nevins's description of the "Sociological department" Henry Ford established at the Ford Motor Company in 1914. The department employed fifty investigators to visit the homes of employees, bringing back information about each employee's marital status, dependents, nationality, and religion. Investigators were expected to find out in addition whether employees owned their homes, whether they were in debt, how much they had in savings and where the savings were kept, whether they had life insurance, and what they did for recreation. In the 1920s about a third of all employees worked for employers who agreed with *Forbes* magazine that paid vacations for workers brought economic benefits to the companies. Some of the employers involved sought to protect their "investment" by prohibiting employees from outside work during vacations and by building camps where company employees and their families were expected to spend their vacation time.

The interest in workers' lives away from the workplace decreased in the 1930s and 1940s as businesses grew even bigger, unions earned the legal right to bargain collectively, and the Second World War left employers little time or motivation to pay attention to anything other than greater productivity. The postwar period brought increased social conformity, however, as well as a managerial class whose members understood that their lifestyle was as important to their success as their job performance. IBM became notorious for its dress code, which was not formally ordained but which resulted in all its executives striding into their offices dressed in white shirts, strikingly similar discreet ties, and innocuously gray flannel suits. As William H. Whyte, Jr. showed in his widely cited work, *The Organization Man* (1956), there was no formal inquiry into executives' lifestyles, but those involved understood who and how they were expected to entertain, which country clubs they should belong to, what kind of car they were expected to drive. Certainly one can argue that their off-the-job privacy was invaded, with their behavior at home and play becoming a key to on-the-job success.

One aspect of the social revolution of the 1960s, when the civil rights movement was in its heyday and young people were questioning social mores, was the entry of the sixties generation into the workplace. They took with them their disdain for conformity and their penchant for dissent. The workplace became a more variegated environment, not only in clothing but in people. Women moved into job categories previously closed to them, as did African Americans and other people of color. Employees who thought that their privacy was invaded increasingly turned to the courts, as they had in the civil rights movement, the women's liberation movement, and the students' rights movement. In 1971 the Supreme Court held that under the Civil Rights Act of 1964, any tests for jobs had to be job-related (*Griggs* v. *Duke Power Company*). Given the mores of the younger generation, the new diversity of workers and the holdings of the courts, workplace privacy seemed to be in good hands. It wasn't.

One reason was that in the 1970s employers increasingly began to administer health care and insurance plans. Consequently, they wanted any piece of information about employees, no matter how personal, that they thought might conceivably affect costs. In the mid-1990s, David Linowes, the chair of the federal Privacy Protection Commission under Presidents Ford and Carter and the author of *Privacy in America: Is Your Private Life in the Public Eye?*, conducted a survey of Fortune 500 companies and found that half of them had used medical records to make hiring decisions. The reason, Linowes wrote in 1995, was the employers' fear of the rising costs of health care. Linowes expected a follow-up survey to reveal that even more companies were engaging in the practice.

Another reason for privacy's being under threat was the growing societal fear of drugs.

Although many members of the sixties generation no doubt eschewed drugs, the popular stereotype was of hippies smoking marijuana and dropping acid. It became a source of some societal concern and, for many older Americans, of scorn. But while it may have been regarded as a moral failing, it was not viewed in the 1960s and 1970s as a phenomenon that threatened the American way of life. That relative lack of concern changed with what seemed to be a national epidemic of drug-related crime in the 1980s.

Whether crime actually increased, and how much of it was drug-related, remains a matter of contention. Criminologists disagree about whether it was crime or reporting about crime that became more common. Philosopher Michael Foucault may be correct in arguing that widespread dissent, of the kind that occurred in the 1960s and lasted into the early 1970s, leads political leaders to feel an increased need for the "disciplining" of society and, presumably, for the winnowing out of dissident lifestyles. Whatever the explanation, surveys show that media coverage of drug-related crime skyrocketed in the mid-1980s. In 1986 President Ronald Reagan and his wife Nancy went on television to declare a national crusade against drug use and to call for drug testing of millions of workers. "Drugs are menacing our society," Reagan told television viewers on September 14, 1986, and the following day Reagan signed an executive order requiring mandatory random urine testing of

1,200,000 federal employees. Four years earlier Nancy Reagan had embarked on her "Just Say No" campaign as an answer to the perceived drug crisis. By 1986, the Reagans, and employers around the country, had decided that workers who declined to "just say no" were in some undefined way adding to the crime statistics and costing their employers profits through faulty performance on the job. Given both the premise that crime was a matter of individual will without systemic causes, so that deterrence was a solution, and the assumption that drug use affected job performance, it seemed logical to test workers not only for drug use in the workplace but, eventually, outside of it as well.

Ironically, a major reason for employers' turning to drug testing was the legal prohibition on the use of polygraph ("lie detector") tests. The tests' limitations should be kept in mind when considering the current drug testing debate.

In every year of the 1980s, more than two million private sector employees or prospective employees were asked to take a "lie detector" test. The American Civil Liberties Union (ACLU) estimated that as a result approximately 300,000 workers annually were branded liars and fired, disciplined, or not hired. Employers interviewing prospective employees wanted to know if they were having money problems that might lead to dishonesty or lived lifestyles that might make them unacceptable employees. Businesses that were already experiencing thefts felt justified in testing current employees. But as in many other "necessary" invasions of privacy, polygraphs were shown to be extraordinarily fallible mechanisms for ascertaining the truth. Polygraphs measure changes in blood pressure, breath rate, and perspiration rate, all supposedly indicators of lying. The changes, however, can be caused by a range of emotions as well as such medical conditions as colds, headaches, neurological and muscular problems. Polygraphs were and are so unreliable that, as an American Medical Association expert testified during public hearings before Congress, "the [lie detector] cannot detect lies much better than a coin toss." It can nonetheless be extremely violative of privacy. One of the reasons Congress became concerned was because many tests included questions such as "When was the last time you unintentionally exposed yourself after drinking?" and "Who was the last child that got you sexy?" What seemed to be a reasonable precaution for employers had turned into something else. Congress therefore passed the Employee Polygraph Protection Act of 1988, prohibiting the use of polygraphs for most preemployment and all random on-the-job testing. There are some exceptions, such as testing of government employees, contractors in national security-related activities, and certain jobs in pharmaceutical companies. But the act eliminated at least 80 percent of the testing previously done in the private sector.

The act said nothing, however, about written tests, and nothing about drug testing. Nor did it mention credit checks. All three immediately became substitutes for polygraphs, and at least as threatening to privacy.

Perhaps the problems with credit checks are best summarized first, as we have already discussed their use in Chapter Four. As soon as the Employee Polygraph Protection Act was enacted, the nation's three largest credit-reporting agencies—Equifax, TransUnion, and TRW (Experian)—began offering their information to employers. Equifax, first into the market, sold 350,000 reports to 15,000 employers in 1989. In the first quarter of 1990, demand for its reports was up 71 percent from the first quarter of the preceding year. At an average of $5 each, the reports were a cheap tool, and were already computerized. Applicants for jobs, or employees whose employers requested their records, usually had no idea that their credit ratings were being used. Employers have no obligation to inform applicants about checks unless, according to the Fair Credit Reporting Act, a negative decision is made "either wholly or partly because of information contained" in a credit record. It is obviously difficult to know to what extent companies are complying with that requirement, but a former security manager for TRW's credit data business was quoted by the *Wall Street Journal* in 1990 as commenting, "People are being denied employment because of what's in their credit report, and are never told that's the reason." An applicant who doesn't know about the credit check of course has no opportunity to counter any incorrect information it may produce. As mentioned in Chapter Four, it has been estimated that forty percent of the major credit reporting companies' files contain errors. Credit checks also provide answers to personal questions that employers are forbidden by equal employment laws from asking of applicants, such as those concerning marital status, pregnancies, religion, and age.

No one has been able to cite any studies demonstrating that the information available in credit checks has any connection to the trait that employers say they're looking for: employee honesty. Someone who has run up a big Visa bill, for example, is not necessarily going to be a thief. The vice president of Personnel Decisions, Inc., a Minneapolis testing firm, has estimated that prehire credit checks result in the "flagging" of no more than 10 percent of all people who are likely to act irresponsibly on the job—and even that number is simply a guess. The president of Development Dimensions International, Inc., another personnel testing firm, says that credit checks prove little and demonstrate only that company hiring departments are "looking for [an illusory] quick fix."

Companies are seeking something that certainly is desirable but seems not to exist: a foolproof method for ascertaining who will be a model employee. Such an employee is responsible, honest, hardworking, healthy, and with a long-enough life span to justify the cost of on-the-job training. So companies' application forms contain a plethora of privacy-invasive questions that have little relationship to the skills, abilities, and qualities needed for the job: spouse's occupation, how one's education was funded, year and make of one's automobile, the number of one's children. Other questions routinely found on application forms, such as those about social security numbers and who should be notified in an emergency, are irrelevant until and unless the person is hired. One of the few major companies to realize this irrelevance was IBM, which pared down its application forms in the mid-1970s so that they contained only a few basic questions about education, previous employment, and criminal convictions (rather than instances of arrests that resulted in no charges being brought or charges being dismissed). IBM found no difference in the caliber of the people it hired. The majority of large companies have not followed its example, however, and still require applicants or employees or both to take written personality tests that include questions about their sex lives, bathroom habits, and feelings about family members. Most states place no limitations on the kinds of questions prospective employers can ask, with the exception of inquiries about arrests that did not result in convictions.

It is worth noting that IBM also has adopted a policy that any information collected about employees must be relevant to their job performance. Access to such information is restricted to those who have a need for it. Obviously, IBM believes this policy has not hurt the company.

The third substitute for polygraphs of applicants and current employees has been drug testing. Within a few years after President

Reagan announced his antidrug crusade, more than half of the nation's largest companies, employing twenty percent of the work force, were testing employees for drug use. By the early 1990s, Roche Biomedical Labs and SmithKline Beecham, two of the country's largest drug-testing companies, estimated that fifteen million Americans, thirteen percent of the entire workforce, were being required by their employers to supply urine samples every year.

Mandatory random drug testing is found most consistently in jobs, private or public, that affect public safety: pilots, workers at nuclear power plants, railroad engineers, truck drivers. President Reagan's 1986 order had mandated testing of federal workers in "sensitive positions" and of applicants for such jobs. The Department of Transportation began random screening of its over 25,000 workers; the Federal Rail Administration (FRA) instituted screening of applicants and of workers involved in accidents. The nation was therefore shocked in 1987, when sixteen people were killed in a railroad accident involving an engineer and another employee who had smoked marijuana on the job. The incident appeared to validate concern about drug use and the utility of drug testing.

In 1989 the Supreme Court upheld urinalysis for two groups of federal employees, with the implication that it would do so for others as well. In *Skinner* v. *Railway Labor Executives' Association* the Court considered FRA rules that mandated blood and urine tests of rail personnel who had been involved in serious accidents and that authorized (but did not require) testing of individual workers on the basis of reasonable suspicion or after a violation of the FRA safety regulations. Whole train crews were tested after accidents or rules violations, even when many crew members clearly were in no way involved in the accident or violation. The Railway Labor Executives' Association challenged testing of employees in the absence of individual suspicion of drug use, as well as the intrusive nature of the test.

Justice Anthony Kennedy held for the Court that, since FRA studies showed that drugs and alcohol were contributing factors in accidents in the 1970s and early 1980s, it was legitimate to conclude that a "special need" for safety on the nation's railroads outweighed what he called the "minimal" privacy interests involved. By going to work for the railroad industry, its employees had implicitly agreed that they had limited "expectations of privacy." Kennedy denied that drug tests were invasive of the body.

Justice Thurgood Marshall noted in his dissent that the FRA Field Manual called for visual monitoring of the test, to which he objected strenuously, and also pointed out that the regulations gave access to the samples to non-FRA personnel, including law enforcement officials. He warned against "particularly draconian weapon[s]" that violated the Fourth Amendment:

> Precisely because the need for action against the drug scourge is manifest, the need for vigilance against unconstitutional excess is great. History teaches that grave threats to liberty often come in times of urgency, when constitutional rights seem too extravagant to endure.

Justice Kennedy wrote for the Court again in *National Treasury Employees Union* v. *von Raab* (1989). The Customs Service had decided in May 1986, the month in which President Reagan authorized mandatory random urine testing for large numbers of federal employees, that anyone seeking a promotion in the Customs Service or a transfer to a position involving illegal drug trafficking, firearms, or classified material would have to submit to urinalysis. The person being tested was permitted to go behind a partition or into a bathroom stall, but an official was stationed nearby to listen for the sounds of urination. The district court that tried the case called such programs "dragnet searches" repugnant to the Constitution. Justice Kennedy differed, upholding the tests when they were used for drug- or firearms-related positions. Calling the Customs Service "our Nation's first line of defense against one of the greatest problems affecting the health and welfare of our population," he found the public interest in testing "compelling."

Justices Marshall and Brennan said in dissent that the tests were unconstitutional because they were based on no individualized suspicion, warrant, or probable cause. It was more surprising, however, to find a dissent written by Justice Antonin Scalia, who does not believe in a constitutional right to privacy. "It is obvious," Scalia stated, that urinalysis "is a type of search particularly destructive of privacy and offensive to personal dignity." Although his typification of urine testing seemed to render it categorically questionable, the reason for his dissent was that in this case it constituted "a kind of immolation of privacy and human dignity in symbolic opposition to drug use"—"symbolic" because there was no history of drug-related accidents in the Customs Service. The Court's own opinion quoted the Customs Service commissioner as stating that "Customs is largely drug-free." That admission, coupled with the May 1986 date on which the program was instituted, seems evidence that the program had more to do with the general national concern about drugs than with any direct need for testing by the Customs Service.

In the remainder of 1989, following the two Supreme Court cases, lower federal courts upheld random testing of motor vehicle operators and hazardous materials inspectors; Boston police officers who carried guns or worked in drug interdiction; sheriff's deputies who worked with prisoners, armed federal security personnel, vehicle drivers, and those with top secret clearance (but not data processors); and civilian army employees in aviation and law enforcement, but not in "chemical and nuclear surety positions" when that description includes secretaries and animal caretakers. Random testing was struck down in cases involving mandatory testing of all Federal Bureau of Prisons employees and of all General Services Administration and executive office employees, and all Justice Department employees involved in criminal prosecutions— although the courts upheld its application to Justice Department employees with top secret security clearances and drug enforcement responsibilities. Since 1989, state and federal courts have struck down random testing for police officers, fire fighters, teachers, civilian army employees, prison guards, and various federal employees, and for state employees seeking promotion. Some decisions drew on privacy provisions in state constitutions. Others invoked the federal right to privacy, with one federal judge commenting that random testing constituted "a wholesale deprivation of the most fundamental privacy rights of thousands upon thousands of loyal, law-abiding citizens." Another called urinalysis degrading and as invasive as a body cavity search.

The only case in which the U.S. Supreme Court struck down a federal drug-testing program was decided in 1997 (*Chandler* v. *Miller*). An eight-judge panel overturned a Georgia statute that required political candidates to take urine tests as a condition for appearing on the ballot. Justice Ginsburg wrote for the Court that the test addressed a problem that was only "hypothetical" and that it was ineffective, as candidates could choose the day on which they were to be tested. The test "diminishes privacy for a symbol's sake," she continued, and was a violation of the Fourth Amendment's search and seizure clause.

While the case law is anything but clear, the rule of thumb appears to be that random testing is most likely to be upheld when required of employees who are directly involved with public safety or the handling of drugs. Such testing has been severely restricted in the private workplace by the legislatures of only seven states which, in addition either to prohibiting random testing or permitting it only of employees in "safety sensitive positions," require confirmatory testing, use of certified laboratories, and confidentiality of test results. In addition, random drug testing undertaken in one of the ten states with a privacy clause in its constitution (Alaska, Arizona, California, Florida, Hawaii, Illinois, Louisiana, Montana, South Carolina, Washington) usually has been struck down. Some states without such constitutional clauses have enacted statutes prohibiting testing without probable cause.

Employers would seem to have good reason to require the tests. Testing programs are so successful that Florida has lowered the workers' compensation payments of companies utilizing them by five percent. Executives of nearly every major American company and drug experts claim that testing has reduced drug use on the job as well as resulted in fewer accidents, lower absenteeism, and less employee turnover, and that it has contributed to an overall decline in casual drug use in the United States.

The study that employers cite most frequently is one done through the Employee Assistance Program at the Firestone Tire and Rubber Company. It found that drug users are 3.6 times more likely to be involved in on-the-job accidents, 2.5 times more likely to miss work for at least eight days, and five times more likely to file workers' compensation claims. They receive three times the health benefits of non-users and work at sixty-seven percent of the potential displayed by others. Alcohol is of course a drug, and studies by the Research Triangle Institute and the Employee Assistance Society of North America have estimated that alcohol abuse costs anywhere between $39.1 billion and $71.5 billion a year in lost productivity and employment. It seems indisputable that drug testing, *when* it is used in combination with education and rehabilitation, has reduced the use of drugs—at least around the time the employees are being tested.

Opponents of drug testing find it troubling that no outside researchers have ever been allowed to see the original data. Even more importantly, the subjects of the study were employees whose job performance had been substantially impaired by alcohol use and who had volunteered for or been ordered to enter Firestone's Employee Assistance Program. The widely relied upon statistics, in other words, are about self-acknowledged alcoholics—not average workers.

As Justice Kennedy noted in *Skinner,* the Federal Rail Administration found drugs and alcohol to have contributed to accidents in the 1970s and 1980s. Justice Kennedy ignored the FRA's subsequent eleven-month drug-testing program in 1989 that involved screening of both job applicants and workers involved in accidents. The study failed to demonstrate a link between drug use and accidents and led the FRA to report that its "data are not conclusive of alcohol/drug role in industrial accidents" and that levels of drug use in the railroad industry were "below many previous estimates." In 1996, additional doubt was thrown upon the assumption that drugs bore primary responsibility for railroad accidents. Following the fatal crash of two New Jersey Transit trains, the *New York Times* reviewed disciplinary records of the New Jersey Transit system, the Metro-North Commuter Railroad and the Long Island Rail Road, and found that a handful of engineers accounted for half the violations of train-operating rules. The companies, however, almost never dismissed or demoted engineers found to break rules, and thereby contributed to the safety problem. The *Times* also reported that ignoring engineers' errors was "not unusual" in the industry and that the three lines it studied were more vigilant in their monitoring and punishment practices than federal law required. The engineer thought responsible for the crash in question, who was killed in the accident, had one of the worst safety records among engineers at the three railroads. Federal investigators hypothesized that he had caused the crash by running a red light. He had done so twice before—but the company had taken no action.

The November 1990 issue of the *Journal of the American Medical Association* questioned the relevance of a study of 2,537 post office job applicants who were given drug tests and then monitored on the job for over 400 days. Of workers who tested negative for drug use, 19.2 percent were involved in accidents, as were 26.3 percent of workers who tested positive for marijuana use and 27.3 percent of those who tested positive for cocaine use. The authors concluded that their findings "suggest that many of the claims cited to justify preemployment drug screening have been exaggerated."

Unfortunately, the study made the correlation between illicit drugs and accidents even more questionable by failing to control for the use of a more widely imbibed drug: alcohol. It is possible that some of the marijuana and cocaine users also used alcohol, and that the alcohol affected their performance; it is equally possible that some of those who did not use marijuana and cocaine were using alcohol.

Drug testing has become a fact of life for many American employees. Approximately one half of all American employers now require urine tests of at least some employees. Some of this testing is done to monitor employees' habits off the job. Employers deny that they are tacitly reverting to the tradition of considering it part of their social responsibility to monitor their employees' morals but claim that as drugs remain in the user's system, the use of illicit drugs at home is relevant to job performance.

Urinalysis, however, does not necessarily provide evidence of present intoxication or impairment, nor does it indicate when a drug was used. A "positive" result suggests that the subject has taken a drug at some time in the recent past. Because urine tests can detect only the "metabolites," or inactive leftover traces of previously ingested substances, an employee who smoked marijuana on Saturday night might test positive the following Wednesday, when the drug no longer has any effect on job performance. Ironically, if someone has snorted cocaine on the way to work and is tested upon arrival, the test result will be negative, because the cocaine will not yet have been metabolized and therefore will not show up in the worker's urine.

So far we have assumed that the drug test is reliable. In fact, however, the enzyme immunoassay technique test used by most companies yields false positive results at least ten percent and possibly as much as thirty percent of the time. At a meeting in the 1990s, 120 forensic scientists, including some who worked for manufacturers of drug tests, were asked, "Is there anybody who would submit urine for drug testing if his career, reputation, freedom, or livelihood depended on it?" Not a single hand was raised. Experts also know that the tests can be "beaten" if people manage to submit a sample of someone else's urine or take various substances that diminish the percentage of drugs in the system.

The more accurate gas chromatography/mass spectrometer test, which in theory can be accurate 100 percent of the time, is expensive and therefore less frequently used. (The federal government uses it as a follow-up test for workers who test positive on the enzyme immunoassay technique test.) But even this test is, in practice, only *more* accurate, not entirely accurate, because of its tendency to confuse similar chemical compounds. A person who has taken Vicks Formula 44-M or codeine may test positive for heroin use. Advil can cause a positive result for marijuana use; Nyquil, for amphetamines. Mistaken positive results also may be caused by Dristan, Midol, by pigments in the blood of dark-skinned people, or by the passive inhalation of someone else's marijuana smoke—or, in what is perhaps the most famous example of the tests' failings, after someone has eaten a poppy seed bagel. According to a report by the government's National Institute of Drug Abuse in the 1990s, the combination of the two tests' inaccuracies and human error led to twenty percent of the laboratories it surveyed mistakenly "finding" the presence of illegal drugs in drug-free urine samples. The only rational conclusion appears to be that the results of urinalysis may prove nothing whatsoever about work performance.

Further, if one goes back to the constantly recurring dilemma of attempting to balance a legitimate social concern against privacy rights, and refers to the standards not only of accuracy but of the least intrusive and humiliating way of acquiring information, urinalysis becomes problematic. The only way to make certain that employees are not cheating on urine tests by substituting a specimen produced at another time is by having a witness present. Susan Register, formerly an employee at a Georgia Power nuclear plant, described her testing experience in the course of a lawsuit. "The first day I went," she reported, "they told me I [had not been able to] give enough urine. The second day, the nurse made me stand in the middle of the bathroom with one hand in the air, with my pants around my ankles, and a bottle between my legs . . . . She screamed at me that I had not followed procedure, and I was going to have to do it again. Well, needless to say, I did not do it again, and I will never, if it means that I will never have a job again, I will never eat, I will never do that again." A judge hearing a case brought by an employee of another company commented that such safeguards made for "an experience which even if courteously supervised can be humiliating and degrading."

In addition to the obvious privacy invasion involved in urinalysis, the test also lacks specificity. It does not show only use of illegal drugs; it also indicates the presence of drugs that frequently are used to treat heart conditions, depression, epilepsy, or diabetes, and it may reveal an employee's pregnancy. These are details of the worker's life that have no necessary connection to work performance but may lead an employer or prospective employer fearful of health-related costs to refuse to hire or to fire someone. One can argue that employers should know the risks they are running. They are understandably concerned about the escalating costs of employee health insurance, and are attempting to deal with the problem by firing or refusing to hire people whose lifestyles appear to place them at risk of illness or injury. That logic leads to allowing employers the right not only to require regular urinalysis of all employees but to the kind of genetic testing discussed earlier and to inquiries into the employees' off-the-job activities.

If private activities affect work performance, it does not seem irrational for companies to mandate tests or demands for information about weight, diet, exercise, sleeping patterns, and of course drinking habits. One employer uses a serum cholesterol test for prospective employees, the employer claiming that the correlation between cholesterol and heart attacks legitimizes such tests. According to this logic, people who ski or scuba dive may be higher risk employees than people whose only athletic activity is riding a bicycle, so employers should be able to eliminate them from the workplace— but bicyclists, too, can have accidents, and sunbathing has been shown to cause cancer.

The federal Privacy Commission noted in 1974 that "almost any personal information may be related to an individual's health." And some companies feel free to request "almost any personal information" and set their policies accordingly. A Pennsylvania company, for example, prohibits its managers from riding motorcycles. Employees of an Oregon company who refuse to participate in the company's exercise program are "punished" by being barred from company picnics. Many companies insist that their employees tell them whether they smoke off the job. A pattern across the nation suggests that overweight people and those who smoke have become particular targets of concern. Perhaps the most extreme example is that of the Motorola cellular telephone plants in Illinois, where employees are banned from smoking in their cars in the parking lots. As employers such as Motorola point out, health care personnel agree that obesity can affect one's health and there no longer seems to be any disagreement in the United States that smoking causes numerous serious diseases. At the same time, the right of privacy leads to the question of where a line should be drawn and whether the law should be that physical conditions, the potential of physical illness, and one's personal life are not the employer's business. Should companies be permitted to inquire into all of the activities of employees and base employment decisions on the answers? Is there any lifestyle that does not entail some health risk?

Society's answer is mixed. Fourteen states have enacted laws limiting employers' powers to prohibit legal off-the-job activities as a condition of employment. As of the mid-1990s, almost half the states had laws restricting or eliminating employment discrimination based on lifestyle choices that do not affect job performance. This number was up from five states a few years earlier, suggesting that public concern about employee privacy in the home had grown. The National Consumers League's National Opinion Poll on Workplace Privacy in 1992 showed that eighty-four percent of Americans believed that an employer did not have the right to refuse to hire an overweight person—perhaps in part because so many Americans consider themselves overweight. Ninety-three percent felt that an employer should not be able to base employment decisions on whether an employee smoked after work, and ninety-six percent said it was inappropriate to make such decisions dependent upon a person's use of a motorcycle.

One answer to the employer-need–employee-privacy dilemma may lie in the policies followed by Drexelbrook Control, Inc. Drexelbrook manufactures electronic control systems for toxic chemical tanks and says that "a single product failure could cause loss of life and serious environmental damage." It nonetheless has never conducted a drug test on employees or applicants. All prospective employees are interviewed extensively and their references are carefully checked. Drexelbrook supervisors are required to take a 39-week management course that includes instruction in setting performance standards and measuring results by means other than drug testing. The absence of such tests has hurt neither profits nor performance: Drexelbrook's lifetime growth rate is 20 percent a year. It has never had a layoff or a year without a profit. Although it has installed more than twenty-five thousand systems around the world for the most dangerous industrial chemicals, it has never been involved in an accident. The record would appear to speak for itself.

Similarly, NASA has used computer-assisted flight simulation performance observations of astronauts and test pilots for years. The tests, which measure hand-eye coordination and response time, are entirely performance-related and in no way invasive of privacy. There are other video "games" that also measure alertness, responsiveness, and capacity, thereby achieving precisely the result that society understandably wants from workers whose performance has the potential of endangering people. The tests could be used as they stand or they could be adapted for railroad and commercial airline workers, police officers, fire fighters, and others upon whom the public depends for its safety.

PRIVACY FOR SOME

The majority of the country's sixty million workers fall under the "employment at will" doctrine, which dates back to the antilabor laws of the nineteenth century and gives employers an unfettered right to fire workers for any reason or for none at all. There are a few exceptions to the "employment at will" doctrine. One consists of the federal and state laws that prohibit discrimination on the basis of race, religion, sex, national origin, age, and disability. However, as these laws require only that employees be treated equally, employers are free to be as intrusive as they choose as long as they are equally intrusive of all employees. Another exception lies in the few statutes that provide some protection to whistle-blowers against employer retaliation and, as mentioned above, against polygraph testing of employees.

There are three categories of workers who have additional protections. These are, first of all, government employees, who, like all Americans, are protected by the Fifth and Fourteenth Amendments from being deprived of their "life, liberty or property" without due process of law. Courts have interpreted these amendments to mean that government workers have a property interest in their jobs and that the due process requirement restricts their being dismissed arbitrarily for reasons unrelated to job performance. Similarly, many private sector collective bargaining agreements stipulate that unionized employees can be fired only for just cause after a due process hearing. Less than 20 percent of American workers, however, belong to unions. Finally, the small number of employees who make up the ranks of such categories as senior executives, academics, performers, and athletes work under contracts that protect them from arbitrary dismissal. These laws and agreements nonetheless leave the great bulk of American workers at risk of privacy violations in the workplace.

Oddly enough, the federal government may inadvertently have contributed to privacy violations in the private sector. Although employers as a whole undoubtedly have succumbed to the temptation to collect and retain far more information about their employees than is demonstrably work-related, some of them may have been responding in good faith to governmental regulations of the workplace designed to aid employees. The Equal Employment Opportunity Act, the Occupational Safety and Health Act (OSHA), the Fair Credit Reporting Act, and the Employee Retirement Income Security Act, for example, were enacted to prevent discrimination, protect the health of employees, minimize misuse of credit information, and safeguard employee pensions. But in order to demonstrate compliance with the regulations promulgated by government agencies charged with implementing the laws, employers have generated records that contain privacy-intrusive information; for example, information about employees' race, gender, age, physical disabilities, and health. OSHA requires employers whose workplaces may pose specific health hazards to offer employees medical examinations. The results, which must be furnished to the employee's physician at the employee's request, also can be made available to a prospective employer with the employee's permission—and of course it is difficult for people seeking jobs to deny prospective employers access to their health records. The prospect of such records following an employee from job to job has led some employees to refuse to undergo employer-sponsored health examinations for fear that their records will then reflect exposure to health hazards and make other employers reluctant to hire them. Some states mandate similar record-keeping. Clearly, legislators must make themselves aware of privacy concerns in enacting any such statutes in the future.

ELECTRONIC AND OTHER SURVEILLANCE IN THE WORKPLACE

Government and private employers are prohibited by federal law from intercepting employees' personal telephone communications. They are permitted to monitor employees calls "in the ordinary course of business," however, to check employee performance.

They are not required to provide any notice to employees that calls are being monitored. The law states that employers have a "reasonable" length of time to decide if a call is personal and to stop monitoring, but once again the definition of *reasonable* is a matter of contention. Some courts have interpreted it as meaning up to five minutes. The federal wiretapping law also permits electronic surveillance "where one of the parties to the communication has given prior consent." Some courts have interpreted this to mean that a company legally can tap its own telephones.

It is not necessary for companies to incur the costs of hiring people to listen to employees' calls in order to monitor them. An inexpensive device called a station message detail recorder can be attached to a telephone system in order to record and organize information about which numbers each employee calls, how frequently, and for how long. The device of course does not differentiate among calls so that employee conversations with family members, physicians, and psychiatrists may all be recorded for up to five minutes.

Computers, too, can be used for electronic surveillance. We are all aware that computers have become common in the workplace, but it is probable that few Americans realize that at least 50 million workers, including data entry clerks, salespeople ringing up purchases, word processors, journalists, and engineers now use computers in the course of their jobs. Employees' computers are plugged into their companies' mainframes, enabling employers to monitor job performance and general employee behavior by checking the computers. A journalist who has typed information about confidential sources into a computer may not know that the information is being monitored while the journalist is accessing it in order to write a story. The supposedly confidential records kept by psychologists and lawyers working in large firms are subject to similar checks. Both situations raise issues of employee privacy as well as that of their patients and clients.

Some employers, wanting to measure employee efficiency, have programmed employees' computers to provide minute-by-minute accounts about the employees' activities. The programs can report who is using a computer, the tasks being performed, the length of time spent on each task, the number of minutes that have elapsed between tasks, and how often, when, and for how long the computer is not in use—how long the employee may be away from the computer, for example, while on a coffee or bathroom break. At least 5 million employees already are subject to such monitoring. Many of them know nothing about it. Others know all too well, as some companies post daily records on bulletin boards, giving everyone who cares to read it information about the length and frequency of employees' bathroom breaks.

Employers can monitor not only employee computer files but their E-mail and their voice mail as well. (The exception, of course, is where the employer is the government, in which case employee privacy is protected by the Fourth and Fifth Amendments and by the Electronic Communications Privacy Act of 1986, which prohibits interception by government employers unless they have a warrant.) The computer magazine *Macworld* found that about twenty-five percent of the businesses it contacted admitted eavesdropping on employee computer files, E-mail, and voice mail. A mid-1990s study by the Society for Human Resource Management reported that only thirty-four percent of companies that used E-mail had written privacy policies. One computer expert asked the chief executive officer of a Silicon Valley, California, computer company whether he used E-mail. "Hell no," came the reply. "Half the nerds in my company can hack E-mail. E-mail is a party line!" Unbeknownst to most workers, some voice mail systems and most E-mail systems have backup tapes that automatically store messages electronically for anywhere from weeks to years, even if their recipients delete them. Backup tapes became alarming for "Jim," a young man who worked for a junior college, when one of his colleagues hinted that the colleague knew about messages left on Jim's voice mail. The messages indicated that Jim was gay, leading him to wonder how possibly homophobic employers would react to the information when they made personnel decisions about him in the future.

The Electronic Communications Privacy Act of 1986 prohibits interception of communications by unauthorized individuals. An exception is made, however, for situations where the provider of the service being utilized for communications can monitor it. State courts have held that E-mail is not personal when it's written on a company machine, and in fact it can be subpoenaed in lawsuits. In January 1996, in the first federal court decision on the issue, a district court in Pennsylvania ruled that there is no expectation of privacy in workplace E-mail even if an employer has promised not to intercept such mail. Judge Charles R. Weiner wrote, in upholding the firing of the Michael Smyth whose story is recounted at the beginning of this chapter, that "Once plaintiff communicated the alleged unprofessional comments to a second person over an E-mail system which was apparently utilized by the entire company, any reasonable expectation of privacy was lost . . . . [W]e find no privacy interests in such communications."

Hidden cameras also can be used to monitor employees. In one instance, administrators of a Silver Springs, Maryland, hospital mistakenly believed that nurses were stealing drugs. The camera they installed in the nurses' locker room was monitored by male security guards—something that the outraged nurses discovered accidentally. A Baltimore firm similarly concerned about thefts installed a hidden camera pointed at the toilet in the women's rest room.

The question implicitly raised by the use of electronic and high-technology monitoring devices is similar to one discussed in Chapter Six. Do workers have a legitimate expectation of privacy in the workplace? If they do, is it limited? Most people would agree that an employee has a reasonable expectation of privacy in a bathroom or locker room, but is the expectation legitimate in a situation such as the one above—where employees are suspected of theft and may be using bathrooms or locker rooms to camouflage stolen goods? Would the privacy invasion of the locker room have been acceptable if female security agents had monitored the camera? What if an employer did not suspect theft but simply wanted to know if employees were away from their jobs longer than they had to be, using the bathrooms for what the employer considered to be excessive socializing on company time? Again, would it make a difference if the place being monitored was a locker room rather than a bathroom, or an employee lounge rather than a locker room? The answers to such questions entail a difficult balancing of interests—a balancing so difficult that as of 1997 Connecticut was the only state with a law prohibiting electronic surveillance of "any area designed for the health and comfort of employees or for safeguarding of their possessions."

If electronic monitoring raises thorny issues, so does the phenomenon of subjecting employees to physical searches. Tennessee's largest convention center, the Opryland Hotel, randomly searches the handbags of women employees in an attempt to deter theft. Other companies utilize dogs to sniff-search employees; yet others regularly search employees' lockers, desks, and the cars they park in the company parking lot. Some employers use undercover agents to report on employees' activities. For many Americans, workplace surveillance has become the norm.

CONCLUSION

Colonial Americans were subjected to "general warrants" that allowed British soldiers to search everyone in order to expose the few who might be guilty of offenses against the crown. That memory was fresh when the Fourth Amendment was written to prohibit the government from undertaking "unreasonable" searches and seizures, that is, searches and seizures of people about whom there was no good reason for suspicion. One might argue about whether searching and seizing large numbers of people in order to find a few lawbreakers is cost effective. It is harder to deny that the relatively inexpensive general searches that companies carry out in today's workplace—of people's computers, telephone calls, voice mail, physical belongings, bodily fluids—present an easy and cheap way of monitoring. There are still questions, however, about what actually is being monitored—the inaccuracy of urine tests is a case in point—and whether the price paid in privacy is worth it for the society or provides information that is truly useful to the employers. Employers' impact on employees' lives can be quite as great today as was the impact of the eighteenth-century government on the lives of citizens, so the argument for privacy against employers is similar to the earlier argument for privacy against the government.

We have already seen that privacy is not an absolute. Profit-minded employers have a legitimate interest in seeing that their businesses provide the best possible service to customers at the lowest possible cost to themselves, that their employees are honest and are fulfilling their obligation to work during the hours for which they are being paid, and that expenses incurred in job training will be warranted by employees being physically able to remain on the job long enough to have paid back the employers' investment.

The profit motive, however, is no more an absolute than is privacy. If it were, there would be no laws regulating minimum wages, maximum hours, sanitary conditions, the right to unionize, and so on. In other words, society has made the decision that employers should be able to make a profit but that it cannot be achieved entirely at the price of the employees' well-being.

So far, society has agreed that the employee's well-being includes such things as his or her right to be paid what the government considers an adequate wage, to be guarded from health hazards, and to be left sufficient time for leisure. But even those answers are not permanent. The country's political agenda continues to reflect disagreement about what constitutes an adequate wage; there is a constantly changing consensus about the meaning of healthful conditions in the workplace; discussion continues about whether there should be a lower minimum wage for workers such as teenagers. Answers to how we balance competing interests are rarely permanent.

Similarly, the question of how to balance workers' privacy and employers' needs is one that will be decided on the basis of compromise between the two competing demands and will have different solutions at different historical moments. Some of the answers may come not from the federal government but from the states, which traditionally have experimented with legislation that other states and the federal government can adopt later. At the moment, for example, even though most states permit employers to turn away prospective workers without an explanation, New Jersey prohibits employment discrimination based on an "atypical hereditary cellular or blood trait," including the traits for sickle-cell anemia, hemoglobin C, thalassemia, Tay-Sachs disease, and cystic fibrosis. Ohio does not permit health insurers to discriminate on the basis of genetic tests but does allow the use of other medical information, which will of course affect employment decisions. It would not be difficult to pass a statute that brings the people's desire to be free of unreasonable searches and seizures into the workplace. Such a statute might embody provisions along these lines:

1) all surveillance, whether physical or electronic, must be undertaken only for the purpose of gathering information that is demonstrably related to job performance;
2) if general electronic monitoring of job performance is used—for example, occasional checks of telephone calls to ensure that customers are receiving proper service—it must be accompanied by a signal informing the employee that such monitoring is taking place;
3) an employee may be searched for evidence of misconduct only where there is a reasonable, articulable suspicion of specific wrongdoing;

4) any job-performance-related searches of employees must be carried out in the least intrusive manner possible. All other searches are forbidden. Electronic surveillance done without notice, because of reasonable suspicion of specific wrongdoing by an employee, is permissible only if notice would defeat the purpose of the surveillance. (An example would be monitors in the changing room if a specific employee was suspected of drug dealing there.)

The suggested criteria are similar to those written into the Employee Polygraph Protection Act. In the few situations where polygraphs are allowed by the act, they can be undertaken only if an employer is investigating a specific loss or injury to the business, the employee tested is under suspicion and had access to the property in question, and the employer states in writing the basis for a reasonable suspicion that the employee is guilty. Any employee tested must be given written advance notice of the test and of the right to be counseled by a lawyer or an employee representative, as well as a list of the questions to be asked. Employees who believe their rights under the act have been violated can appeal to the secretary of labor, who in turn can ask a court for an injunction against the practice, back pay if the employee has been fired, and a fine of up to $10,000. Employees also can bring private civil actions against employers. In other words, the act not only strikes a balance between employer needs and employee rights but also provides an enforcement mechanism. The balance in other situations such as electronic surveillance would differ in details, but the polygraph example indicates that finding such a balance is indeed possible.

These are merely some possible solutions among many others. Whether because the rate of unionization is so low in the United States, because we have no workers' political party, or because some other countries have a more cohesive lobby for privacy, the United States is well behind other industrialized countries when it comes to protection for workers' privacy. The Organization for Economic Cooperation and Development, an international organization that promotes economic and social welfare, adopted privacy guidelines in 1980. By 1983, 182 major multinational corporations and trade associations in the United States had done so. They have not been incorporated into American law, however. David Flaherty, the privacy commissioner for British Columbia, told a congressional subcommittee that the absence of an official American presence at international data protection events is embarrassing:

> There is nobody in the United States for the French data protection agency or the Canadian data protection agency or the German data protection agency to talk to. It is a considerable embarrassment to me as a student of American affairs to sit at these international meetings of data protection officials, which happen once a year, and there is an empty chair where the United States should be . . . . [T]here is simply nobody carrying the can for the United States, and it is regrettable.

Flaherty was referring to the meetings that discuss private sector compliance with privacy guidelines and data protection issues. Perhaps it is time for the American government to give its workers at least as much legal privacy protection as they would receive elsewhere.

Chapter Nine

IS PRIVACY DEAD?

Private thoughts are more complicated and confused than public announcements, thus usually more true.

—Roger Rosenblatt

In 1996 a frightened woman called the Privacy Clearinghouse to ask whether she had just put herself in jeopardy of being labeled politically suspect by sending an E-mail message to the White House, criticizing some of President Clinton's policies. Many governmental officials now have E-mail addresses for their constituents' use. This is clearly time- and money-saving for officials and voters, as the letters cost the constituents little to send and an official's staff can quickly sort them by subject matter and opinion. But the combination of telephone and computer that has given us E-mail could be utilized to identify political dissidents whose views and actions are completely legal but considered unfriendly by government officials.

This is the kind of new privacy issue that bothers Americans, along with other privacy issues that have long been with us. In early November 1995, the "Equifax-Harris Mid-Decade Consumer Privacy Survey" reported that 82 percent of Americans were very concerned or somewhat concerned about privacy and that 80 percent of Americans believed they had lost all control over personal information.

The Yankelovich poll taken at about the same time came up with a slightly different figure, finding that 90 percent of Americans favored legislation to protect them from businesses that invade their privacy. Whatever the exact numbers, the overwhelming majority of Americans in the 1990s realized that lack of privacy had become a problem and that dangers to privacy were continuing to grow.

Threats to privacy certainly existed in the United States before World War II. In the seventeenth century, many of the colonies had laws against "drunckenes in private howses," complete with penalties for homeowners who permitted visitors to become drunk. Massachusetts established the governmental office of tythingman in 1675. A tythingman's duties consisted of monitoring the behavior of ten families. The county of Hampshire added that tythingmen were "faithfully to act in their Inspection of their Neighbors, so as that sin and disorder may be prevented and Suppressed." The history of Americans first accepting and then battling against privacy invasions may be seen in the actions of the citizens of Boston, who appointed tythingmen annually for some years but by the 1730s apparently had enough and refused to name anyone to the post.

The addition of Amendments I, III, IV, V, and IX to the Constitution demonstrated an awareness that governments could threaten the privacy and integrity of each person and of his or her religious practices, speech, association, home, and personal possessions. Samuel D. Warren and Louis D. Brandeis's 1890 article on "The Right to Privacy" was addressed to violations of privacy by a nongovernmental institution, the press. Brandeis's eloquent defense of the right to privacy even when an invasion incurred in the name of law enforcement was written in 1928 (*Olmstead* v. *United States*). By the late 1930s the federal bureaucracy had become big enough to constitute a privacy threat.

By comparison to the dangers of the 1990s, however, those earlier threats were minimal. There was no computerization, genetic testing, mass use of social security numbers, electronic data banks, credit reporting agencies, Caller ID, transportation surveillance systems, or any of the other potentially privacy-threatening mechanisms that are the boon and bane of technology. If protection of privacy is more of a problem in today's United States than ever before, worse news is in sight: there is every reason to assume that the problem will become greater.

Some of the privacy questions that have been given increasing attention in recent years, however, do not stem from the growth of technology but from changing values. An example is the asserted public right to know about the health and morals of political figures. When Senator Paul E. Tsongas was campaigning for the Democratic Party nomination for president in 1992, for example, reporters discovered that he had been treated for non-Hodgkin's lymphoma. The disease causes a slow-growing, potentially lethal cancer of the lymph system. Tsongas assured journalists that he had triumphed over the disease, and his doctors declared him to be "cancer free." Tsongas did not win the nomination, but after the 1992 election a cancerous lump was found in his abdomen. He was in the hospital battling lymphoma again in January 1993 and May 1996. He died in January 1997 from complications caused by his cancer therapy and clearly would not have been able to perform his presidential duties throughout his term if he had won. Presidents Dwight Eisenhower and John F. Kennedy suffered from various and not completely disclosed ailments while they served in the White House. The privacy issue, of course, is whether the public has a right to such information and the right to decide for itself whether illness or other physical incapacity will impair a candidate's or an official's ability to function fully. Similarly, the electorate might consider a candidate's or official's extramarital sex life to be an indication of the kind of faulty moral judgment that should keep him or her from gaining or staying in office. Is this an instance where the public has a "right to know," or is it private information?

Other current privacy questions are given a new twist by technology. One concerns professional confidentiality: the privacy of communication between clergy and penitents, attorneys and clients, and doctors and patients. In 1996 Oregon prison authorities surreptitiously taped a conversation between a priest and a murder suspect. The information became public only because the district attorney was considering using the tape in the trial. It is a crime in Oregon to tape lawyer-client communications but the law does not protect those of clergy and penitent. The outcry that followed led the prosecutor to give up the tape but did not solve the professional confidentiality problem, which still exists in Oregon and most other states.

A tape recorder seems almost technologically primitive when compared with a computer. Almost all privacy problems are exacerbated by the existence of the computer, which is now such a crucial key to information exchange that much of this volume is actually about the problem of privacy in the computer age. In many instances computerized information has simply made basic privacy questions about the compilation and use of personal information more dramatic, but there are also problems specific to the computer.

One is the way in which an individual's acquisition of information can be "tracked." An Internet user who clicks to computerized news groups unknowingly creates a hidden file on his or her machine that records which groups the user has subscribed to and which articles the user has read within each group. The original purpose of the file supposedly was to prevent the news reading program from offering the user articles he or she had already read. Then, in the mid-1990s, computer privacy experts discovered that there was a periodic electronic version of television's viewer habit-tracking "Nielsen report," which scans the Internet and reports how many people read each group's news. The implication was that individuals' reading habits were available to the keepers of the "report." Experts next realized that each time a person went to a particular Web site, the site kept a record of the computer address of the visitor. Web site owners who wanted to exchange this information could easily do so. In addition, some Web sites were designed to interact with a user's computer to find out which kind of browsing software was being used, the name of the user's Internet access service, the part of the country in which the machine was located (indicated by the user's "address"), which Web pages the user had visited, and how frequently the visits had been paid.

As the London *Financial Times* discovered, Netscape, the leading software used on the World Wide Web, enables companies to track the Web sites that an individual visits, merge the information with records of other Internet use such as ordering merchandise through the Net with a credit card number, and compile a comprehensive record of the individual's behavior. The information is kept on the customer's computer in what is known as "persistent client-state hypertext transfer protocol cookies," accessible by Netscape.

Netscape is not the only program that quietly keeps track of individuals' computer habits. In 1995, Microsoft introduced a new version of the software program called Windows. A purchaser of Windows 95 was asked by a computerized form that appeared on the screen when the program was first run to fill in various bits of registration information. What Microsoft did not initially announce, however, was that by plugging into the registration system the computer user activated a program that monitored each machine and kept a list of what software was being run on it. According to *Information Week* magazine, Microsoft's Network Services, launched later that year, also was programmed to transmit to Microsoft the entire "directory structure" of a user's software. That means the company has a list of all the programs used on a given machine and, potentially, the ability to compile a list of all the files created by the user.

Whenever someone enters *any* Web site, the site's "host server" automatically collects and stores information about the person in its files. The server can be programmed to send a unique identification number directly to the user's hard drive, putting it into a file called "cookies.txt." When the user subsequently clicks throughout the site, the server collects the ID number from the "cookies.txt" file and matches it with the data already in the log file database. Once a computer is so tagged, every time the user returns to the site, the server makes a record of every place the user goes within that site. The New England Internet Company's Pekoe Track goes further, gathering detailed information not only about what a user is looking for within a Web site, but also what the user seeks after he or she leaves the site. The Magellan Internet Guide, a major Web search service, has a feature called "Search Voyeur" that allows anyone to "spy" on other people's searches. The mechanism enables a user to see the text of twenty current randomly selected searches by other users. Magellan differs from other services only in letting other users see the information rather than keeping it for potential sale.

Today, more and more transactions can be performed over the Internet: buying an airplane ticket, making a hotel reservation, checking one's bank account, paying one's bills. Given the proper software and an individual's propensity to utilize services available through the Internet, a company can put together a summary of the person's finances, transactions, assets, and movements. Technology has run ahead of the law, as is so frequently the case, and these practices remain to be regulated by the government.

Does all this mean that privacy is dead? Has the development of new technologies, coupled with the compilation of huge amounts of quickly accessible information, made privacy obsolete?

The answer is that privacy has become an endangered species but that it is not quite extinct. Whether it still has a future is very much a matter of what Americans demand of their lawmakers.

Groups like the American Civil Liberties Union, the Electronic Frontier Foundation, the Electronic Privacy Information Center, Computer Professionals for Social Responsibility, the United States Privacy Council, the Privacy Rights Clearinghouse, and publications such as *Privacy Journal, Computer Privacy Journal, Privacy Times, PRIVACY Forum,* and *Full Disclosure* are responsible for much of the privacy that still exists in the United States. These are the institutions that monitor encroachments on privacy, lobby against them, and maintain a network to alert the public about new developments. They alone cannot safeguard privacy, however, for as public interest groups their power is only as great as the number of concerned citizens they reach and the resources those citizen-voter-consumers can muster. Together, these and a variety of other groups and experts have worked out potential guidelines for different aspects of privacy that could go far towards redressing the current situation. The guidelines, all traceable in one way or another to the report of the Privacy Commission in 1977, are,

1) no personal information shall be collected without the explicit permission of the person involved;
2) no personal information shall be collected without explicit identification of the *reason* for its collection. If the purpose behind its collection ceases to exist, the information shall be destroyed;
3) no personal information gathered by one institution or organization shall be *shared* with other institutions or organizations or used for a purpose other than that for which it was collected, unless the consent of the individual has been obtained;
4) when information gathered by one institution or organization is shared, with the consent of the individual, the individual shall be *notified;*
5) all individuals shall have access to information collected about them and shall have the right to *amend* the information if they can demonstrate that it is incorrect;
6) personal information collected by an institution or organization shall be protected by *security* safeguards;
7) the law shall permit individuals to *safeguard* personal information through such technologies as encryption;

8) in the absence of a showing of *compelling need,* governmental and other institutions shall not interfere with the privacy of the person or with information about the person;

9) adequate *enforcement mechanisms* shall be created to ensure all the above.

The guidelines are simply that; they are not meant as codes. One would want to spell out, for example, how and how much individuals must be told about information gathered about them, depending in part on the kind of information: medical, genetic, credit, and so on. Creation of enforcement mechanisms may mean not only laws but ombudspersons or privacy commissions. Appropriate penalties for noncompliance would have to be determined. Exceptions might have to be made and differing procedures might have to be designed for information gathered, e.g., by law enforcement officials. A health maintenance organization would have to adopt one code of restrictions on access to information, while that utilized by another type of employer or a government agency or a credit bureau would look somewhat different.

The general approach, however, is quite simple. One starts with the idea that every person is entitled to privacy: the right to be let alone and the right to control information about oneself. The burden of proof falls on any attempt to interfere with that right.

Privacy and community are complementary. Both are necessary for a fulfilled human life and for the kind of political system known as democracy. The community provides the individual not only with physical safety but, more importantly in this context, the opportunity to interact with others, to hear others' ideas and try out one's own, to enjoy activities with others, to forge the human relationships that are necessary to a rich life and that help the individual to develop.

Privacy is equally necessary. As Justice O'Connor said in *Planned Parenthood* v. *Casey,* "At the heart of liberty is the right to define one's own concept of existence, of the meaning of the universe, and of the mystery of human life. Beliefs about these matters could not define the attributes of personhood were they formed under compulsion of the state." Human beings need a community in which to develop, but human development cannot take place in the absence of privacy. Community without privacy implies not individual growth but social control and conformity. Privacy deprives the community of its major and easiest method of social control: public exposure as a means of controlling individual behavior. But a society that must rely upon exposure rather than persuasion for social control is neither democratic nor best suited to create the strong individuals that enable a society to thrive. Any community would be poorer without individuals as developed and fulfilled as they can be; no true democracy can exist unless part of that development is political and results in citizen participation. But the political development of the individual, as with all other aspects of individual growth, requires privacy.

The tension between privacy and community exists in part because the community perceives a need to enforce social behavior and exercise social control. The reason may be a fear of those who challenge traditional beliefs by acting and speaking differently, or the presence of an external threat that is viewed as containable only if the society is completely united. There may be some cases where society's needs do have to take precedence over privacy, as in the privacy invasions of court-ordered searches and seizures. As we have seen, however, the argument for deprivation of privacy usually relies on the false assumption that community welfare inevitably will be best served by limits on privacy. And that, as the debates over computer encryption or warrantless wiretapping indicate, is rarely true of a society that derives its strength from the participation of mature individuals.

Supreme Court Justice Stephen Breyer said during his confirmation hearings in 1994 that the Constitution is "a document guaranteeing people rights that will enable them to lead lives of dignity." That is the goal: to forge a community in which individuals can lead lives of dignity. To that end, privacy is essential.

Since the Second World War, as the United States has experienced a history of political, economic, social, and technological change, there has been a constant reinterpretation of privacy and of the ways in which privacy and community can mesh. The balance between the two will never be fixed as long as change continues. The only certainty is that the parameters of privacy will be a matter of constant discussion. Even though the dialogue inevitably will be loud and contentious at times, its existence is the best indication that Americans understand how crucial privacy is to the welfare of both the individual citizen and the community at large.

BIBLIOGRAPHIC ESSAY

Now that privacy has become part of the American political agenda, there are so many excellent books, articles, and government reports about it that a complete bibliography would take up at least a volume in itself. Those mentioned here are a very limited selection of the works most likely to be useful to students. They frequently contain material on a variety of privacy subjects, not only the topic they are listed under. Students should not shy away from government documents in the field, as they usually are well written and readable. They are published by the Government Printing Office in Washington, D.C., unless another publisher is indicated.

It seems appropriate that a great deal of information about privacy in the computer age can be found on the Internet. The American Civil Liberties Union (www.aclu.org), Computer Professionals for Social Responsibility (CPSR) (www.cpsr.org), Electronic Frontier Foundation (www.eff.org), Electronic Privacy Information Clearinghouse (EPIC) (www.epic.org), Internet Society (www.isoc.org), Privacy Rights Clearinghouse (www.manymedia.com/prc/), and U.S. Privacy Council (E-mail: privtime@access.digex.net) are among the organizations that publish regular bulletins on the Net and also have Web pages that archive back issues. The CPSR Internet Library (www.cpsr.org) maintains online archives for CPSR, EPIC, Privacy International (www.privacy.org/pi/) and others. Magazines, journals, and moderated lists such as *PRIVACY Forum* (www.vortex.com), *Privacy Journal* (by subscription), *Computer Privacy Journal, Computer Privacy Digest, Privacy Times* (by subscription), and *Full Disclosure* (http://ripco.com:8080/~glr/glr.html) are published on the Net. They too have Web pages. Also see the Data Surveillance and Information Privacy Web Page. Check the Internet under "privacy" and the particular topic of interest, as new organizations, Web sites, and other information sources appear and disappear.

GENERAL DISCUSSIONS

There are a number of classic works about privacy in the United States. Alan F. Westin, *Privacy and Freedom* (Atheneum, 1968) explores the concept of privacy as well as the threats to it, as does Arthur R. Miller, *The Assault on Privacy: Computers, Data Banks, and Dossiers* (University of Michigan, 1971). Westin has a good follow-up article, "Public's Privacy Concerns Still Rising," 1 *Privacy and American Business* (Sept./Oct. 1993). *Privacy, Law, and Public Policy,* by David M. O'Brien (Praeger Special Studies, 1979), looks at the way various governmental bodies have attempted to reconcile the sometimes competing interests of privacy and public policy. O'Brien also has published an excellent if now somewhat dated bibliography entitled *The Right of Privacy—Its Constitutional & Social Dimensions: A Comprehensive Bibliography* (Tarlton Law Library, School of Law, University of Texas, 1980). Most aspects of the privacy problem, as well as suggested solutions, are to be found in the Privacy Protection Study Commission's report, *Personal Privacy in an Information Society* (1977), also published as *Final Report of the Privacy Protection Study Commission,* Senate Committee on Governmental Affairs, 95th Cong., 1st Sess. (1977).

Barrington Moore's *Privacy: Studies in Social and Cultural History* (M. E. Sharpe, 1984) is an analysis of the concept of privacy held by a variety of societies around the globe. A good place to start exploring the conflict between privacy and society's right to information, along with the history, philosophy, and current problems of privacy is Richard F. Hixson, *Privacy in a Public Society: Human Rights in Conflict* (Oxford University Press, 1987). Catherine A. MacKinnon attacks the American concept in *Feminism Unmodified* (Harvard University Press, 1987), arguing that it subordinates women by viewing the two people in a marriage as one and that the one is the man. Also see Alida Brill, *Nobody's Business: Paradoxes of Privacy* (Addison-Wesley, 1990).

There is a good discussion of Brandeis and the early history of American privacy law in Dorothy J. Glancy, "The Invention of the Right to Privacy," 21 *Arizona Law Review* (1979). Other historical accounts include David J. Seipp, *The Right to Privacy in American History* (Harvard University, 1978), and Ken Gormley, "One Hundred Years of Privacy," *Wisconsin Law Review,* 1992. David Sadofsky, *The Question of Privacy in Public Policy: An Analysis of the Reagan-Bush Era* (Praeger, 1993), looks at the making of privacy policies during the 1980s and early 1990s. Robert Ellis Smith, *War Stories: Accounts of Persons Victimized by Invasions of Privacy* (Providence, RI: Privacy Journal, 1993), recounts instances of violations of privacy in the 1980s and 1990s. Albert H. Cantril and Susan David Cantril, *Live and Let Live: American Public Opinion About Privacy at Home and at Work* (New York: ACLU Foundation, 1994), samples recent American public opinion on the topic.

The state of privacy law is presented in very readable form by Evan Hendricks (editor of *Privacy Times*), Trudy Hayden, and Jack D. Novik in *Your Right to Privacy* (Southern Illinois University Press, 1990). Ellen Alderman and Caroline Kennedy, *The Right to Privacy* (Knopf, 1995), addresses current questions in privacy by telling the tales behind recent cases.

MEDICAL AND GENETIC PRIVACY

Information about the use of medical and genetic information and the need for privacy can be found in David T. Suzuki and Peter Knudtson, *Genetics: The Clash Between the New Genetics and Human Values* (Harvard University Press, 1989); Daniel J. Kevles and Leroy Hood, *The Code of Codes: Scientific and Social Issues in the Human Genome Project* (Harvard University Press, 1992); Dorothy Nelkin and Laurence Tancredi, *Dangerous Diagnostics: The Social Power of Biological Information* (Basic, 1989); Philip Elmer-Dewitt, "The Genetic Revolution," *Time,* Jan. 17, 1994; Charles Siebert, "The DNA We've Been Dealt," *New York Times Magazine,* Sept. 17, 1995; Paul R. Billings et al., "Discrimination as a Consequence of Genetic Testing," 50 *American Journal of Human Genetics,* 1992; Xandra O. Breakefield, "Behavioral Genetics in Transition," *Science,* June 17, 1994; Dennis Overbye, "Born to Raise Hell?" *Time,* Feb. 21, 1994; Jeffrey Fox, "Who's Reading Your Medical Records?" *Consumer Reports,* Oct. 1994, and Robert Gellman, "Fair Health Information Practices," 4 *Behavioral Healthcare Tomorrow,* 1995. Both Paul Schwartz ("The Protection of Privacy in Health Care Reform," 48 *Vanderbilt Law Review,* 1995) and Lawrence O. Gostin ("Health Information Privacy," 45 *Cornell Law Review,* 1995) urge that privacy concerns be balanced against the necessity to collect health data if medical personnel are to provide efficient and effective service.

On problems of interpretation and reliability of genetic tests, see Stanley Reiser, *Medicine and the Reign of Technology* (Cambridge University Press, 1978). The subject is also covered in a number of articles in *Science,* June 17, 1994: Constance Holden, "Alcoholism Research: A Cautionary Genetic Tale: The Sobering Story of D_2," p. 1696; Eliot Marshall, "Manic Depression: Highs and Lows on the Research Roller Coaster," p. 1693; and Charles C. Mann, "Behavioral Genetics in Transition," p. 1687. Ruth Hubbard and Elijah Wald, *Exploding the Gene Myth* (Beacon, 1993), is an accessible, popularized but informed discussion. Theresa Morelli's story is told in "geneWATCH: Theresa Morelli" in Council for Responsible Genetics, *geneWATCH,* March 1993.

Governmental bodies, including courts, are of course active players in the debate about medical privacy. Their successes and failures are discussed in Marvin R. Natowicz et al., "Genetic Discrimination and the Law," 50 *American Journal of Human Genetics,* 1992; Rochelle Cooper Dreyfuss and Dorothy Nelkin, "The Jurisprudence of Genetics," 45 *Vanderbilt Law Review,* 1992; and Robert M. Gellman, "Fragmented, Incomplete, and Discontinuous: The Failure of Federal Privacy Regulatory Proposals and Institutions," 6 *Software Law Journal,* April 1993. One of the most authoritative overviews by a governmental body is *Protecting Privacy in Computerized Medical Information,* published by the United States Office of Technology Assessment in 1993. Two reports by the Institute of Medicine, *The Computer-Based Patient Record* (1991) and *Health Data in the Information Age: Use, Disclosure, and Privacy* (1994; both Washington, D.C.: National Academy Press), argue that current laws offer too little protection against disclosure of confidential health records.

There have been a number of congressional hearings on the subject. Reports of some of them are contained in *Legislation to Protect the Privacy of Medical Records,* Hearings before the Senate Committee on Governmental Affairs, 96th Cong., 1st Sess. (1979); *Federal Privacy of Medical Information Act,* House Committee on Government Operations, 96th Cong., 2d Sess. (1980);

Data Protection, Computers, and Changing Information Practices,
Hearing before the Subcommittee on Government Information, Justice, and Agriculture, House Comm. on Government Operations,
101st Cong., 2d Sess. (1990); *Health Reform, Health Records, Computers and Confidentiality,* Hearing before the Information, Justice,
Transportation, and Agriculture Subcomm. of the House Committee on Government Operations, 103rd Cong., 1st Sess. (1993); *Fair
Health Information Practices Act of 1994,* Hearings before the
Information, Justice, Transportation, and Agriculture Subcomm. of
the House Committee on Government Operations, 103rd Cong., 2d
Sess. (1994); and House Committee on Government Operations,
Health Security Act, 103rd Cong., 2d Sess. (1994).

Executive branch agencies also have produced excellent studies
of the computerization of medical records. Among them are Department of Health, Education, and Welfare, Secretary's Advisory Committee on Automated Personal Data Systems, *Records, Computers,
and the Rights of Citizens* (1973); Alan F. Westin, *Computers,
Health Records, and Citizen's Rights* (U.S. Department of Commerce, 1976); Workgroup for Electronic Data Interchange, *Report to
Secretary of U.S. Department of Health and Human Services*
(1992); as well as the Privacy Protection Study Commission report of
1973 mentioned above.

For material on the way the issue has been addressed by other
countries, see Organization for Economic Cooperation and Development, *Guidelines on the Protection of Privacy and Transborder Flows of Personal Data* (1981); Council of Europe, *Convention
for the Protection of Individuals With Regard to Automatic Processing of Personal Data* (1981); Privacy Commissioner of Canada,
Genetic Testing and Privacy (1992); and Colin J. Bennett, *Regulating Privacy: Data Protection and Public Policy in Europe and
the United States* (Cornell University Press, 1992).

Diane B. Paul, *Controlling Human Heredity, 1865 to the Present* (Humanities Press, 1995), is a book about eugenics written for
students.

RECORDS OF ONE'S LIFE

A good place to start research on the use of records such as social
security numbers and credit card transactions is Anne Wells
Branscomb, *Who Owns Information? From Privacy to Public*

Access (BasicBooks, 1994). The book covers current access to personal information including telephone numbers, medical records, electronic messages, photographic images. Also see Jeffrey Rothfeder, "Taking a Byte Out of Privacy," *Bill of Rights Journal,* Winter 1992. Floyd Abrams, "The New Effort to Control Information," *New York Times Magazine,* Sept. 25, 1983, is a short article on the subject by a leading civil liberties lawyer. Another useful article is Richard F. Hixson, "Whose Life Is It, Anyway? Information as Property," in Brent D. Ruben, *Information and Behavior,* Vol. 1 (Transaction Books, 1985). Arthur R. Miller, *The Assault on Privacy: Computers, Data Banks, and Dossiers* (University of Michigan, 1971), Alan Westin, *Data Banks in a Free Society: Computers, Record-Keeping, and Privacy* (Quadrangle Books, 1972), the 1977 Privacy Protection Study Commission report, David Linowes (former chairperson of the federal Privacy Protection Commission), *Privacy in America: Is Your Private Life in the Public Eye?* (University of Illinois, 1989), and Steven L. Nock, *The Costs of Privacy: Surveillance and Reputation in America* (A. De Gruyter, 1993), are studies of almost all aspects of informational privacy. David M. O'Brien, *Privacy, Law, and Public Policy* (Praeger, 1979), suggests that informational privacy became a policy issue in the 1970s because of a lack of sufficient judicial safeguards. Methods of regulation are discussed in Colin J. Bennett, *Regulating Privacy: Data Protection and Public Policy in Europe and the United States* (Cornell University, 1992), and by Paul Sieghart, "Information Privacy and the Data Protection Bill," in *Data Protection: Perspectives on Information Privacy,* edited by Colin J. Bourn and John Benyon (University of Leicester, 1983). In addition, see Panel on Confidentiality and Data Access (U.S.), *Private Lives and Public Policies: Confidentiality and Accessibility of Government Statistics* (Washington, D.C.: National Academy Press, 1993).

H. Jeff Smith, *Managing Privacy: Information Technology and Corporate America* (University of North Carolina Press, 1996), is an insider's account of privacy violations in the business world, along with suggestions for reform. Joseph W. Easton examines the issues surrounding a national ID in *Card-carrying Americans: Privacy, Security, and the National ID Card Debate* (Rowman & Littlefield, 1986). More recent information is in Statement of Jeffrey Rothfeder, *Use of the Social Security Number as a National Identifier,* Hearing before the Subcommittee on Social Security of the House Committee on Ways and Means, 102d Cong., 1st Sess. (1991). Credit cards are the focus of Lewis Mandell, *The Credit Card Industry: A History* (Twayne, 1990).

The topic of intelligent transportation systems is generating an increasing amount of literature, much of it in newspapers such as the *New York Times* and the *Washington Post* (check their indexes as well as those of the newspapers in your area). Two useful studies are Philip E. Agre and Christine A. Harbs, "Social Choice About Privacy: Intelligent Vehicle-Highway Systems in the United States," 7 *Information Technology & People*, 1994, and Don Phillips, "Big Brother in the Back Seat?: The Advent of the 'Intelligent Highway' Spurs a Debate over Privacy," *Washington Post*, Feb. 23, 1995.

BODILY PRIVACY

Catherine G. Roraback, one of the original lawyers in the case that led to privacy's being declared a constitutional right, tells the story of the people and situation behind the case in nonlegalese ("Griswold v. Connecticut: A Brief Case History," 16 *Ohio Northern University Law Review*, 1989). The history of Griswold and the first major abortion rights case is also recounted in David J. Garrow's highly detailed *Liberty and Sexuality: The Right to Privacy and the Making of Roe v. Wade* (Macmillan, 1994). Marian Faux, *Roe v. Wade* (Mentor, 1988), is a shorter but comprehensive account. Stories about the handling of abortions by women, doctors, and unlicensed practitioners in the pre-*Roe* era are in Ellen Messer and Kathryn E. May, *Back Rooms: Voices from the Illegal Abortion Era* (St. Martin's, 1988), and Patricia G. Miller, *The Worst of Times* (Harper-Collins, 1993).

The politics surrounding the abortion issue and the right to privacy are covered in Kristin Luker, *Abortion & the Politics of Motherhood* (University of California, 1984), Roger Rosenblatt, *Life Itself: Abortion in the American Mind* (Random House, 1992), Barbara Craig and David O'Brien, *Abortion and American Politics* (Chatham House, 1993), and Karen O'Connor, *No Neutral Ground? Abortion Politics in an Age of Absolutes* (Westview Press, 1996). *Perspectives on the Politics of Abortion* is a collection of essays by abortion rights proponents, suggesting ways in which the issue might be resolved (Ted G. Jelen, ed.; Praeger, 1995). Joan C. Callahan, *Reproduction, Ethics, and the Law: Feminist Perspectives* (Indiana University

Press, 1996), discusses the historical practice and politics of abortion and concludes that the abortion issue may now be quieting down. Jenni Parrish, ed., *Abortion Law in the United States* (Garland Publishing, 1995), is an overview of current law.

Vincent J. Samar, *The Right to Privacy: Gays, Lesbians, and the Constitution* (Temple University, 1991), makes a strong argument for legal protection, as do Michael Nava and Robert Dawidoff, *Created Equal* (St. Martin's, 1994); Eric Marcus, *Making History: The Struggle for Gay and Lesbian Rights, 1945–1990* (HarperCollins, 1992), and Roger J. Magnuson, *Are Gay Rights Right?: Making Sense of the Controversy* (Multnomah, 1990). Anne Underwood and Bruce Shenitz report on the gay marriage controversy in "Do You, Tom, Take Harry . . . ?," *Newsweek,* Dec. 11, 1995.

Melvin I. Urofsky, *Letting Go: Death, Dying and the Law* (Scribner, 1993), analyzes approaches to suicide and assisted suicide in history, various religions, and American society and law, as does G. Steven Neeley, *The Constitutional Right to Suicide: A Legal and Philosophical Examination* (Peter Lang Publishing, 1996). Henry R. Glick, *The Right to Die: Policy Innovation and its Consequences* (Columbia University, 1994), is a comprehensive analysis of the issue with emphasis on policies in the different states; Darien A. McWhirter and Jon D. Bible look at the federal level in *Privacy as a Constitutional Right* (Quorum Books, 1992).

Timothy E. Quill, *Death and Dignity: Making Choices and Taking Charge* (W. W. Norton, 1993), is a pro-assisted-suicide book by the doctor who was a plaintiff in the New York State case. There are a number of anti-assisted-suicide volumes, including Daniel Callahan, *The Troubled Dream of Life: In Search of a Peaceful Death* (Simon & Schuster, 1993); Peter Singer, *Rethinking Life and Death* (St. Martin's Press, 1995), which argues against both legalized abortion and assisted suicide; and Herbert Hendin, *Suicide in America,* 2d ed. (Norton, 1995), in which a psychiatrist asserts that most people seeking assisted suicide are in a curable depression and that the average physician is unqualified to assess their mental state. The Dutch system is criticized as one that the United States should not follow in a second book by Hendin, *Seduced by Death: Doctors, Patients, and the Dutch Cure* (Norton, 1996).

Discussions of whether or not the Ninth Amendment should be interpreted to include a right of privacy are Marshall L. DeRosa, *The Ninth Amendment and the Politics of Creative Jurisprudence*

(Transaction, 1996); Mark N. Goodman, *The Ninth Amendment: History, Interpretation, and Meaning* (Exposition Press, 1981); Randy G. Barnett, *The Rights Retained by the People* (George Mason University Press, 1989); and Calvin R. Massey, *Silent Rights: The Ninth Amendment and the Constitution's Unenumerated Rights* (Temple University Press, 1995). David O'Brien looks at the role played by judges in altering the law in *Judicial Roulette: The Report of the Twentieth Century Fund Task Force on the Appointment of Federal Judges* (Twentieth Century Fund, 1988).

CRIMINAL JUSTICE

David H. Flaherty reports on the balance struck between privacy and the criminal law in *Privacy in Colonial New England* (University Press of Virginia, 1972). Donald A. Marchand, *The Politics of Privacy, Computers, and Criminal Justice Records: Controlling the Social Costs of Technological Change* (Information Resources, 1980), looks at more contemporary problems.

There is a substantial body of work on privacy concerns involving the use of DNA testing in the criminal justice system, including the question of reliability. See the articles by Nachama L. Wilker et al., "DNA Data Banking and the Public Interest," and Philip L. Bereano, "The Impact of DNA-based Identification Systems on Civil Liberties," in Paul R. Billings, ed., *DNA On Trial: Genetic Identification and Criminal Justice* (Cold Spring Harbor Laboratory Press, 1992); and J. C. Hoeffel, "The Dark Side of DNA Profiling: Unreliable Scientific Evidence Meets the Criminal Defendant," 42 *Stanford Law Review*, 1990. Also see R. Y. Nishimi, *Genetic Witness: Forensic Use of DNA Tests* (Office of Technology Assessment, 1990). Dorothy E. Roberts, "Punishing Drug Addicts Who Have Babies: Women of Color, Equality, and the Right of Privacy," 104 *Harvard Law Review*, 1991, is an account in laypersons' language about the prosecutions of African American mothers who take drugs during pregnancy, arguing that this is continued discrimination and suggesting the connection between privacy and racial equality. Two complementary articles are Lisa C. Ikemoto, "Furthering the Inquiry: Race, Class, and Culture in the Forced Medical Treatment of Pregnant Women," 59 *Tennessee Law Review* (1992), and Troy Duster, "Genetics, Race and Crime: Recurring Seduction to a False Precision," in Paul R.

Billings, ed., *DNA On Trial: Genetic Identification and Criminal Justice*, cited above.

GOVERNMENT SURVEILLANCE

You can find the Privacy Act of 1974, originally published by the federal government, at http://www.law.cornell.edu/uscode/5/552a.html. Congressional discussion about the act is in *Legislative History of the Privacy Act of 1974*, Senate Committee on Government Operations and House Committee on Government Operations, 1976. The politics surrounding its passage and that of other privacy-related statutes are surveyed in Priscilla Regan, *Legislating Privacy: Technology, Social Values, and Public Policy* (University of North Carolina Press, 1995). The follow-up to the 1974 act is Privacy Protection Study Commission, *Personal Privacy in an Information Age* (1977). Also see *Records, Computers, and the Rights of Citizens,* Report of the Secretary's Advisory Committee on Automated Personal Data Systems, U.S. Department of Health, Education and Welfare (1973); *Federal Tax Return Privacy,* Hearings before the Subcommittee on Administration of the Internal Revenue Code of the Committee on Finance, U.S. Senate, 94th Cong., 1st Sess., 1975; and Office of Technology Assessment, *Electronic Record Systems and Individual Privacy* (1986). Congress examined enforcement of the act in *Oversight of the Privacy Act of 1974,* Hearings before a Subcommittee of the House Committee on Government Operations, 98th Cong., 1st Sess., 1983.

David H. Flaherty makes the argument for more institutionalized protection in "The Need for an American Privacy Protection Commission," 1 *Government Information Quarterly* (1984). Robert M. Gellman, former chief counsel to the House of Representative's Subcommittee on Information, provides a history of governmental attempts and failure to create privacy protections in "Fragmented, Incomplete, and Discontinuous: The Failure of Federal Privacy Regulatory Proposals and Institutions," 6 *Software Law Journal,* 1993.

Congress's examination of governmental surveillance of civilians was in part the result of Christopher H. Pyle, "CONUS Intelligence: The Army Watches Civilian Politics," *Washington Monthly,* Jan. 1970. There is a more extensive account in Pyle, *Military Surveillance of Civilian Politics, 1967–1970* (Garland Publishing, 1986).

The definitive congressional study of that era is *Final Report of the Select Committee to Study Governmental Operations with Respect to Intelligence Activities* (Church Committee), U.S. Senate, 94th Cong., 2d Sess., Report No. 94-755 (Apr. 26, 1976), book 3.

The story of John Lennon's FBI file is in "I Read the News Today Oh Boy—John Lennon vs. the F.B.I.," *The New Republic,* May 2, 1983. I am grateful to Stephen G. Tompkins of *The Commercial Appeal* (Nashville, Tennessee) for providing me with two of his articles about government surveillance of Martin Luther King, Jr., the result of a 16-month investigation by the newspaper: "Army feared King, secretly watched him" and "In 1971, spy target was black America," both Mar. 21, 1993. Other accounts of government intelligence agencies and citizen privacy are *Records, Computers, and the Rights of Citizens,* Report of the Secretary's Advisory Committee on Automated Personal Data Systems, U.S. Department of Health, Education and Welfare (1973); Morton H. Halperin, Jerry J. Berman, Robert L. Borosage, and Christine M. Marwick, *The Lawless State: The Crimes of the U.S. Intelligence Agencies* (Penguin, 1976); and Christopher Andrew, *For the President's Eyes Only* (HarperCollins, 1995). Two different approaches to the Huston plan for spying on civilians during the Nixon era are taken in Richard M. Nixon, *RN: The Memoirs of Richard Nixon* (Touchstone, 1990), pp. 474-475, and Theodore H. White, *Breach of Faith* (Atheneum, 1975), pp. 1734-1778. David H. Flaherty, *Protecting Privacy in Surveillance Societies* (University of North Carolina, 1989), discusses both the United States and other Western countries.

WORKERS' PRIVACY

Philip E. Agre, "Surveillance and Capture: Two Models of Privacy," 10 *The Information Society,* 1994, contains a useful introduction to and helpful suggestions for research about current problems in workplace privacy. There is a good chapter on workplace privacy, written by the publisher of *Privacy Journal,* in Robert Ellis Smith, *Workrights* (Dutton, 1982).

Allan Nevins, *Ford: The Times, the Man, the Company* (Scribner, 1954), and Benita Eisler, ed., *The Lowell Offering: Writings by New England Mill Women* (Harper & Row, 1977), include first-rate discussions of workplace privacy during various periods of American history.

Privacy questions raised by employers' use of computers are surveyed in Charles Piller, "Bosses with X-Ray Eyes: Your Employer May Be Using Computers to Keep Tabs on You," and Charles Piller, "Privacy in Peril: How Computers Are Making Private Lives a Thing of the Past," both in *Macworld,* July 1993.

Among the numerous books about workplace drug testing and other aspects of worker privacy are Ira M. Shepard and Robert L. Duston, *Workplace Privacy: Employee Testing, Surveillance, Wrongful Discharge, and Other Areas of Vulnerability* (Rockville, Md., Bureau of National Affairs, 1987); John Gilliom, *Surveillance, Privacy, and the Law: Employee Drug Testing and the Politics of Social Control* (University of Michigan, 1994). The attitudes of Americans about workplace privacy are included in the study by Albert H. Cantril and Susan David Cantril, *Live and Let Live: American Public Opinion About Privacy at Home and at Work* (New York: ACLU Foundation, 1994), mentioned earlier. An approach from the employers' viewpoint is Jon D. Bible, *Privacy in the Workplace: A Guide for Human Resource Managers* (Quorum, 1990).

PRIVACY IN THE COMPUTER AGE

Many of the works listed in other sections include chapters or sections about this topic, as their titles suggest. Other books, articles and reports include David Lyon, *The Electronic Eye: the Rise of Surveillance Society* (University of Minnesota Press, 1994); David Lyon and Elia Zureik, eds., *Computers, Surveillance, and Privacy,* which brings together essays on the social implication of new surveillance technologies; John Shattuck, "In the Shadow of 1984: National Identification Systems, Computer Matching, and Privacy in the United States," 35 *Hastings Law Journal* (1984); the Winter 1992 edition of the National Emergency Civil Liberties Committee's *Bill of Rights Journal,* subtitled *Civil Liberties in the Age of Computers;* Office of Technology Assessment, *Issue Update on Information Security and Privacy in Network Environments* (Washington, D.C., 1995); and Jerry Berman and Daniel J. Weitzner, "Keys to Privacy in the Digital Information Age," 2 *Electronic Networking,* Winter

1992. Jeffrey Rothfeder has an excellent article on the subject, called "Invasions of Privacy," in the November 1995 issue of *PC World.*

Netlaw: Your Rights in the Online World by Lance Rose (Osborne/McGraw-Hill, 1995) is a thorough guidebook that addresses privacy as well as other issues. *Privacy-Enhancing Technologies: The Path to Anonymity* (Toronto: Information and Privacy Commission, 1995) is the Ontario, Canada, information and privacy commissioner's two-pamphlet report on current privacy invasive techniques and ways of making them less intrusive. Its extensive bibliography lists sources from a variety of countries.

INDEX